Silent Victims

The Plight of Arab & Muslim Americans in Post 9/11 America

By

Aladdin Elaasar

authorHOUSE

1663 LIBERTY DRIVE, SUITE 200
BLOOMINGTON, INDIANA 47403
(800) 839-8640
www.authorhouse.com

First published by AuthorHouse 05/18/04

ISBN: 1-4184-1055-1 (sc)

Library of Congress Control Number: 2004093480

Printed in the United States of America
Bloomington, Indiana

This book is printed on acid-free paper.

Dedication

This book is dedicated to the memory of the thousands of innocent people who lost their lives in the 9/11 terrorist attacks on America, and to those who aided rescue efforts, and those who extended a helping hand to the families of the victims, hundreds of them were Arab and Muslim Americans. It is also dedicated to the spirits of those innocent victims of ugly hate crimes; the result of homegrown violence, urban terrorism and a misguided sense of zeal.

"If one takes a one life,
it is as if one has taken the life of all humanity.

If one saves a single life,
it is as if he has saved the life of all humanity."

Qur'an 5:32.

"I have set before you life,
and I have set before you death. I have begged you to choose life
for the sake of your children."

Deuteronomy

Table of Contents

Testimonies from "We Are Not the Enemy: Hate Crimes Against Arabs, Muslims, and Those Perceived to be Arab or Muslim After September 11

"We don't care. You all look the same"

"I own a motel in SeaTac, Washington. In early October 2001, one man came up to me while I was parking my car and said: "Go Back to your country. We are coming over there to kick your ass". I explained to him that I was a Sikh who had been raised in India and then became an American citizen many years back. He did not care to listen to me and said, "We don't care. You all look the same".

"The same man returned to my motel on the morning of 19th October at 7:00 am and shouted at me: "You still here?" I told him: "Where else can I go? This is my country!" He got even more angry and agitated. He took out a metal cane and hit me on my head and shouted at me "Go to Allah." I bleed profusely, was taken to the hospital and received ten stitches in my head."

-Karnail Singh, Sikh American man from SeaTac, Washington

"I don t trust a single damn one of you"

"On the morning of June 18, 2002, I went to a drug store to pick up allergy medication. A woman who was angry that I had left one of my children in my car while I picked up the medication began berating me. She told me, I've learned all about you people [Muslims] over the last 10 months and I don t trust a single damn one of you. I tried to move away from her but the woman slammed me to the floor and began pulling at my hijab. I screamed at her to let me go, and that I was having trouble breathing, but the woman kept pulling on my hijab. In a panic, I pulled off my hijab in order to stop from choking. The woman then dragged me by my hair to the front of the store. The woman did not let me go until police arrived. My young children witnessed this sad event."

-FK, an American Muslim woman from Houston, Texas

Preface

More than two years have passed marking the anniversary of the 9/11 terrorist attacks on our nation, yet we are still recuperating from the shock that this sad and tragic event has caused us, as a society. The American people are still trying to make sense out of what happened.

Meanwhile, the public's interest to learn about Arabs and Muslims, in general, and Arab and Muslim Americans, in particular, has been unprecedented. The nation has been looking for means of self-healing and reconciliation.

To many Arab and Muslim Americans, 9-11 also represented a turning point in how America is struggling to accept them as a community with a distinct religious identity. The wave of anti-Muslim hate crimes after 9-11 was the worst in the nation's history. Although it has tapered off since the early weeks of the crisis, anti-Muslim agitation in television and radio has contributed to unprecedented acts of hate crimes.

"Islam and Muslims became a matter of public discourse in America. Along with major media organizations, mainline Protestants and Catholics, as well as members from the Black, Latino, Asian and Jewish communities have favored a position that distinguishes between extremists and mainstream Muslims. On the other hand, some conservatives and zealots have actively sought to drive a wedge between Arab and Muslim Americans and the nation. Members of these groups revived the defunct "clash of civilizations" thesis and have actively worked for the exclusion of Muslims from public forums, while continuing to argue for anti Arab & Muslim public policies." See Appendix III

Still, to the average citizen, there is a great deal of ignorance and confusion about the Arab World, the Middle East, and the Islamic world. The general public does not really know the difference between an Arab, a Moslem, a Persian, an Indian, where they came from? What do they worship? What are their issues and backgrounds?

"Fear of hate crime lingers; data show terrorist attacks spurred a burst of harassment; Arab and Muslims Americans are still afraid". Newly released statistics from police and government agencies document a sharp but short-lived spike up in threats and discrimination against Arabs, Muslims and people perceived to be Middle Eastern after Sept. 11. People are fearful of coming forward.

Arab and Muslim Americans have witnessed similar backlashes during the Gulf War, the Yom Kippur War, and conflicts related to the Middle East, and being victims generally of acts of bigotry committed by long known hate groups, or individuals who have their biases towards minority groups; the public outcry can come from the most unexpected sources.

Arab and Muslim Americans have witnessed and lived under similar hostile climates prior to the 9/11 backlash. " For the better part of the 1980s, the Arab Americans (and Muslims) lived in an increasing state of apprehension as the Reagan administration waged its war on "international terrorism". The fear reached its zenith in 1985 and 1986. The highjacking on June 14, 1985, of TWA flight 847 to Beirut by Lebanese Shiite gunmen highlighted the predicament. The incident received extensive coverage in the news media, much of it, unashamedly sensationalist and hysterical". See Chapter I

" The media hype may have contributed to the outbreak of violent attacks against Arab Americans and Middle Easterners that coincided with the highjacking, making 1985 a milestone in the history of violence against Arabs and Middle Easterners. *The crisis reminded many Arab and Muslim Americans that Anti-Arab and anti-Muslim racism continues to lie just beneath the service of society. And that as long as anti-Arab racism remains serviceable to government leaders, politicians, entertainers, the mass-media, and cultural institutions, it will continue to resonate unchecked and unchallenged at the popular levels of society."* See Chapter I

In the nineties, the same pattern of Anti-Arab and Anti -Mid Eastern violence continued to emerge. Many Arab Americans were put under surveillance. After the Gulf War, in early 1991, the Bush administration sent a crime bill to Congress that loosely defined a terrorist as any one who had raised money for any organization that had engaged in violence. The bill also effectively called for the establishment of a secret government tribunal to hear terrorist deportation cases and would also empower the government to detain suspects indefinitely.

Historically, violence against minorities in America is not a new trend. Arabs, Muslims or people of Mid Eastern ancestry were not the only ethnic groups that have received their share of home grown violence, or scapegoating. The pattern has emerged during similar crises, when the nation's security becomes threatened, and in times of economic recession, that some sociologists describe as a recurrent tide of Jingoistic *racism*.

According to Juan Perea, professor of Law at the University of Florida, "Nativism is the, intense opposition to an internal minority on the grounds of its foreign (i.e."un-American") connections". During Nativist times in the United States, democratic processes are turned against internal minorities deemed foreign or "un-American", resulting in discriminatory legislation they spawn. Nativist movements and the legislation they spawn, seek to rid the nation of perceived enemies of the "American way".

" We have been through all of this before. During the controversy of the Alien and Sedition Acts in 1798, the enemy took the form of the French ethnicity and ideology, and Americans associated with that ideology. The 1850s saw the vilification of the Irish "savages" who, for the first time had migrated in substantial numbers to the USA. In the years during and after the World War I yielded intense hatred of the Germans and German Americans among us. During World War II, the hatred of the Japanese enemy and of loyal Americans of Japanese ancestry, who looked like the enemy, resulted in the forced incarceration of seventy thousand Japanese American citizens, and between thirty and forty thousand Japanese aliens in domestic internment camps. During the 1950s, fear of the communist enemy was played out in the frequent interrogations of immigrants from Southern eastern European Countries, in suspicions regarding their ethnicity, and in the blacklisting of the Jews."

In general, 9/11 has negatively impacted the lives of Arab and Muslim Americans, other minority groups perceived to be of Middle Eastern origins, like Assyrians, Persians, Indians, and even Hispanics. Fear is looming, as we get closer to the 9/11 anniversary. Fear, not as much of the potential terrorist attacks against us, but fear from the enemy within. Fear of xenophobes, bigots; hate crime perpetrators, traditional hate groups, and the zealot next door. Fear of government legislations that can limit, or hinder our civil rights, or even our basic human rights, that might not after all make us feel safer.

Very few books have tried to answer the questions of: *Who are the Arabs? Who are the Muslims? Who are the Arab Americans? The Stereotypes around Arabs, and how did they evolve? Arab and Muslims in the United States, where do they live and how many are them? Do Arabs have a shared religion? When did Arab people come to the United States? Are Arabs a minority group? Are Arab Americans more closely tied to their country of origin, or to America? Arab Contributions to Civilization, if there is any?* Are Arab Americans active in U.S. politics? Have Arab Americans won major political offices? Who are some prominent Arab-American politicians? Nevertheless, no books that deal with the plight of Arab and Muslim Americans after 9/11 have been published yet.

"Silent Victims: The Plight of Arab & Muslim Americans in post 9/11 America ", answers the many questions that a great number of people are trying to find answers for. The increasing public's curiosity about the Arabs, Muslims and the Arab and Muslim Americans in the United States has been unprecedented. The book also explains the phenomenon of stereotypes stigmatizing Arabs and Muslims, and how it has affected their lives, a phenomenon that demonized and dehumanized almost two billion people in this world.

Chapter Outline

Part one starts with an introduction that describes the climate of fear in which Arab and Muslim Americans have been living in since 9/11. It documents the author's personal encounter with biases against Arab and Muslim Americans, and ignorance of the basic facts about Arabs and Muslims by the general public.

Chapter I, *"Arabs..go back home: Or, where does hatred come from?* " Explains the historical background that led to Arab and Muslim bashing and the wave of hate crimes against them in the United States after 9/11. It describes the role of Nativist politicians, the mainstream media, and other institutions in enflaming the public's outrage against a certain segment of society. It also explains the process of scapegoating other minority groups throughout the US history; the Irish, the French, the Germans, the Japanese, the Jews, Central and Latin Americans, and Asians.

Chapter II, "100 Years of anti-Arab and anti-Muslim stereotyping" explains how media stereotypes can lead to biases and the violation of one's civil rights. *"Jack Shaheen & the anatomy of Anti-Arab stereotypes: TV & Reel Bad Arabs"* provides insights on the phenomenon of anti-Arab and anti-Muslim stereotyping through the author's interview with Professor Jack Shaheen, the world's foremost expert on the media's stereotyping of Arabs and Muslims.

Part Two includes *Profiles of Distinguished Arab-Americans*, many of whom the author had met and interviewed, like: Poet Ahlam Shalhout, president of Arab American Institute Dr. James Zoghby, Prominent Arab American Poet, Naomi Shihab Nye, *Arab American Heart surgeon pioneer*, Dr. Michael DeBakey, Dr. Farouk El-Baz: *The Man Behind Apollo*, Secretary of Energy Spencer Abraham, Her Majesty Queen Noor, Congressman Nick Joe Rahall, *syndicated columnist and stand-up comic*, Ray Hanania, Congresswoman Pat Danner, *former secretary of health and human services, Donna* Shalala, *and others.*

Part two includes Appendices I & II & III. Appendix I is "A WHITE PAPER: PRELIMINARY REPORT ON HATE CRIMES AGAINST ARABS AND MUSLIMS IN THE UNITED STATES".

Appendix II, is the latest report about the " IMPACT OF THE SEPTEMBER 11TH ATTACKS ON THE FREEDOMS OF ARABS AND MUSLIMS ", PREPARED BY THE ARAB AMERICAN BAR ASSOCIATION.

Appendix III, is a detailed report about "AMERICAN MUSLIMS: ONE YEAR AFTER 9-11", PREPARED BY CAIR, Council on American-Islamic Relations.

Appendix IV, is a detailed report about "LATEST STATISTICS AND TRENDS ON HATE CRIMES, USING THE LATEST FIGURES IN THE FBI'S ANNUAL REPORT ON HATE CRIMES.

Appendix IV, is titled "WE ARE NOT THE ENEMY": Hate Crimes Against Arabs, Muslims, and Those Perceived to be Arab or Muslim after September 11th, 2001.

PREPARED BY: Amardeep Singh, Hate Crimes Researcher in the U.S. Program of Human Rights Watch.

In addition to the three million Arab Americans and seven million Muslim Americans, and many other communities in the United States that have been negatively affected by the backlash of 9/11, the tragic events have created an unprecedented curiosity to learn about Arabs and Muslims in general. Arab and Muslim American, and people of Middle Eastern ancestry will relate to the stories told in the book. The general American public will find it worth reading to learn for the first time that many of their favorite stars, like Paula Abdul, Selma Hayek, and Casey Casem, and, are Arabs and Americans, as well.

The book is also a detailed guide of Who's Who in the Arab and the Muslim communities in politics, medicine, entertainment industry, space discovery, and almost every endeavor of American live. The book is a useful tool for students in schools and colleges around the United States who would like to get a first hand account of who are the Arabs and Muslims.

The book is a very useful tool for cross-cultural presentations in corporate environments and to government officials involved in the debate over minority issues and legislations related to 9/11 and the Middle East.

Members of other ethnic communities in America, and immigrant communities around the world, including Canada, Australia, New Zealand and Western Europe will find the Arab and Muslim experience in the United States, somehow similar to theirs.

Readers in the Arab and Muslims worlds, as they have felt the heat reflected on them in terms of US foreign policies, general populations in these countries will find the book interesting to learn about the experience of people with common roots from that area, and their plight after 9/11 in their endeavor to achieve the American dream.

Acknowledgements

In the process of writing this book, I have been fortunate to enjoy unlimited support from so many individuals that makes it hard to mention all of them. I am deeply indebted to the unlimited support of those who assisted me during the last two years of preparing for this book, through research, providing material, references, agreeing to interviews, and providing photos from their own collections.

I also would like to give a big thank you to Jennifer Salan, director of media relations at the Arab American Institute for her assistance and patience answering all my questions, mail and demands. My thanks also go to Dr. James Zoghby, President & CEO of AAI Foundation for his relentless efforts in educating the public about Arab American issues.

Great help and assistance came from another source that is devoted to fighting bigotry and the defamation of Arab-Americans. The ADC, Arab-American Anti-Discrimination Committee and its former presidents, Dr. Ziad Asaly, and the late Dr. Hala Salam Maksoud, have been always at the forefront when it came to combating hate.

I cannot forget to mention the efforts of Hussien Ibish, the ADC media director, and his continuous appearances on major American media outlets educating the American public about Arab-American causes and exposing bigots who target Arabs in this country. Laila Al-Qatamia provided essential help with material from the ADC and was an essential source for that needed information.

A special thank you goes to the Honorable Judge William Haddad, Executive Director, Arab American Bar Association and Dr. Mohamed Nimer, Director of Research, CAIR Research Center, and Mr. Amardeep Singh, Hate Crimes Researcher in the U.S. Program of Human Rights Watch, New York City, for their contribution of the detailed reports about hate crimes against Arab and Muslim Americans and generously allowing me to include these reports in my book.

<u>Contributors</u>

- **William Haddad**

Executive Director, Arab American Bar Association

- **Dr. Mohamed Nimer**

Director of Research, CAIR RESEARCH Center.

- **Amardeep Singh**

Hate Crimes Researcher, U.S. Program of Human Rights Watch

Introduction

Where are you from? The Age-old question

During the many years that I have been writing and lecturing about the Middle East and the Arab World, in addition to public appearances on TV and radio talk shows, I have always been confronted with many questions about events in the Middle East, the Arab World, and the Muslim World. Most of these questions indicated the lack of the basic knowledge of the mere facts about these parts of the world, their people and their history.

I can still recall, the dinner speech given by Father Dahdal of the St. George Antiochian Orthodox Church in Cicero, Chicago, to welcome NBC Dateline correspondent, Hoda Kotbe, a prominent Arab-American, during her visit to Chicago. The dinner was hosted by former Chicago Sun Times reporter and executive director of the National American-Arab Journalists Association, Ray Hanania. Ray was born and raised in Chicago, and worships at Father Dahdal's Orthodox Church. That night, Father Dahdal told the crowd attending the dinner on Kotbe's honor a very interesting story.

Few years ago, a miraculous sighting of the Virgin Mary took place at his church in Chicago, which drove an outstanding number of people into his church. Father Dahdal would lead the amazed visitors into mass prayers and give them his blessings. One day, one of the visitors approached Father Dahdal and asked him about his origin.

Father Dahdal gracefully replied that he was born in the Holy City of Jerusalem, in the Middle East. The visitor was in total disbelief and amazement upon hearing that, and asked Father Dahdal: " Are you a Moslem?" The visitor could not comprehend that a man of Mid Eastern origin could possibly be a Christian, a priest, and above all lead the worshippers in masses in Chicago!

The reaction of the audience attending the dinner, and who were listening to Father Dahdal's story was a mixed one. In part, it was funny. It was a true story. But it was a sad one. It did not really come as a surprise to many of the attendees, because they have been into similar situations. But in a way, it was frightening. The amount of ignorance, confusion, and hostility towards that part of the world and its people, to many, including my self and many others attending that dinner was all too familiar to us, unfortunately.

That night, during the dinner, I sat next to Pete Dagher. Mr. Dagher was running for Congress in Chicago, and later on lost the election due to a negative ad campaign that aimed at tarnishing his image by his opponents and tying him to terrorism simply because of his ancestry. Mr. Dagher was born in the USA to Catholic parents who emigrated from the Middle East. He had an outstanding record. He worked in the White House during the Clinton administration, in addition to a track record in public service that was really impressive.

That dinner party, in which Father Dahdal told that story, took place about two months before the terrorist attacks on American soil on 9/11/01.

But, the moral lesson that Father Dahdal was trying to deliver to his audience was a complex one. *There is a great deal of ignorance and confusion about the Arab World, the Middle East, and the Islamic world. The general public does not really know the difference between an Arab, a Moslem, a Persian, or an Indian; where they came from? What do they worship? What are their issues and backgrounds?*

The general public has been always bombarded with a flood of negative images that come mainly from the media (10 o'clock news, when they are ready to go to bed) without really an explanation of who is doing what to whom? Who is who? And what's really going on? Most of the times, the mainstream media does not really bother or take the time to explain, or invite experts to shed some light on the events and enlighten the public.

As a journalist, and a frequent guest on several TV and Radio programs, I fully understand that working in the newsroom is a very stressful job, especially, in times of great crises. You have to say something to the public. This is why, most of the news items that we watch on the main TV networks, for example, look like identical twins! Same images, same quotes, same footage, and the same clips, over and over again. As Bill Meyers explained in his wonderful PBS documentary series, entitled: "The Public Mind"; we are living in the age of sound bites. Many forces really shape what we can see at the 10'clock news, and what we are really coerced into believing.

Every time something catastrophic happens in the Middle East, or elsewhere, that also might have ties to the Middle East, I receive calls from major networks, in the Chicago Land area, or sometimes from as far as Washington, DC, asking for a quote or a commentary on the events. The TV crew comes to my house, or office. The cameras roll, I answer the questions, and by the time my interview comes out of the editing room, it is reduced to 15 seconds. I do not blame the media for that. I fully understand the news business, and that there are so many other depressing stories that need to be covered that night and fed to the public, in addition to the sports and the weather forecast, of course.

But the question is: How can we expect the public to know and understand what's really going on somewhere without sufficient explanation? How would we expect someone to summarize the Arab/Israeli conflict, for example, in twenty seconds? There must be some other ways. Perhaps, through public libraries, social studies curriculums, learning some foreign languages, and/or tourism. How many of us really have access to these things? How many people out there are regular visitors of public libraries? Do we really want to know about other people of the world, their languages, history, culture or perhaps their food?

These are some of the questions that father Dahdal's story brought to the audience that night. He did not mean to entertain, or make fun of someone by merely telling the story, but he actually wanted to ring the alarming bells to the crowd of mostly Arab-Americans that night to pay attention to these issues.

Then on September 11th morning, the whole nation woke up in terror, literally. I remember that morning watching the news in total disbelief about what was happening. I left my house while I was still in denial, feeling that maybe it was a bad dream, or one of Hollywood's bad movies. By this moment, no body could really explain what was happening. I had a meeting by nine O'clock at one of the high rises in down town Chicago. The meeting was cut short and everyone in the building was ordered to leave and evacuate the whole down town area. It was rumored that another highjacked plain would target the Sears Tower in Chicago. The frantic, mass exodus of people and the nightmarish traffic was unprecedented.

Then, as media people and journalists, we had to come up with quick answers to the public.

All of a sudden, everybody became an expert on the Middle East, Islam and the Arabs. The public wanted to know who was the enemy? And the answers came too quick, too soon. The media added to the fury, anxiety, and confusion. Suddenly, inside our society, people looked around for traces of that enemy within. They were asked to be alert, vigilant, and on the guard. They were told that more attacks were to come. The War on Terrorism was officially declared on an evasive, sly, cunning enemy. It was a new "Crusade".

Suddenly, Arab and Muslim Americans found themselves on the defensive. They were looked down upon with distrust and sometimes with disgust by other fellow

American citizens. They became the new old targets of prejudice, bashing and sometimes ugly and horrendous hate crimes. Politicians and public officials had to come to the rescue. President Bush appealed to the public not to resort to any forms of violence or retaliation against other fellow Americans.

Nevertheless, acts of harassment, prejudice and hate crimes kept on happening on an unprecedented rate. Arab and Muslim-owned businesses, schools, Mosques and even Mid Eastern churches were visible targets as a "*collateral damage*".

For instance, after 9/11 groups of hooligans targeted the Harlem mosque and the elementary Aqsa school for girls in Bridgeview, Illinois waving the federalist flag and shouting racial slurs and obscenities against the Arabs and Muslims before the police was able to halt their advance. Hundreds of similar incidents took place around the country. (Full reports documenting these incidents will be included)

"Fear of hate crimes lingers; data show terrorist attacks spurred a burst of harassment; Arab and Muslims Americans are still afraid. " Newly released statistics from police and government agencies document a sharp but short-lived spike up in threats and discrimination against Arabs, Muslims and people perceived to be Middle Eastern after Sept. 11.People are fearful of coming forward. They don't want retaliatory acts, and they may be afraid of immigration consequences," said Cook County Assistant State's Attorney, David Stoioff. (1)

According to the Chicago Tribune, the data that several federal, state and local agencies recently made public document an outburst of ethnic hostility in the days after Sept. 11 directed against Arab and Muslim Americans. The numbers show, for example, that federal reports of discrimination against Muslims more than doubled than in previous years. Similarly, the Illinois State Police recorded five times as many anti-Arab hate crimes in 2001 as in 2000.

Taken together, the statistics cover everything from potentially deadly confrontations, some involving a knife or baseball bat, to reports of people being fired from their jobs or harassed at work. None of the local cases involved death or serious injury, officials say.

The numbers of reports of hate crimes involving Arabs or Muslims is small compared with other types of crime, but Seema Imam, an assistant professor of

(1) Richard Wronski, Tribune staff reporter, September 5, 2002.

education at National Louis University, is concerned that the real numbers will never be known.

Imam, a Caucasian American Muslim convert, who was born in Oklahoma and raised in downstate Illinois, said a stranger spat on her and swore at her in front of her children a few days after Sept. 11. Imam said she did not report the incident to police because she was embarrassed.

"If ever in my life I have seen fear, I see fear now," said Seema Imam, who is the vice president of the Hickory Hills-based Muslim Civil Rights Center, in Illinois.

The Chicago Commission on Human Relations logged 50 reports of anti-Arab incidents between Sept. 11 and 30. In September of previous years, the commission averaged 14 reports.

"Illinois State Police recorded 49 hate crimes against people of Arab descent in 2001. State police said they do not know how many of those occurred after Sept. 11, the total was far higher than in previous years. Nine crimes were reported in 2000, one in 1999, seven in 1998 and eight in 1997.In addition, state police classified 10 crimes as "anti-Islamic" in 2001, compared with one or two in the years before ". (2)

Nationally, the Federal Bureau of Investigation, FBI, began monitoring hate crimes against people perceived to be Muslim or Middle Eastern after Sept. 11 and opened 199 investigations between September and November. The agency had monitored hate crimes in general before Sept. 11, but it had not given special attention to those groups. Reports of the hate crimes began dropping after November, said Ross Rice, an FBI spokesman in Chicago.

The Chicago Police Department created a new category to document post-Sept. 11 incidents, counting 55 cases in the weeks after the attacks, said spokesman Pat Camden.

The U.S. Equal Employment Opportunity Commission recorded 497 discrimination complaints against Muslims related to their religion between Sept. 11 and May. During the same period a year earlier, 193 complaints were recorded. The EEOC also began tracking discrimination cases based on ethnicity against

(2) Ibid

people perceived to be Arab, South Asian or Sikh. As of May, the most recent figures available, there were 488 cases nationally. Illinois had 34 of them. (3)

A new poll conducted by the Washington-based Council on American-Islamic Relations, CAIR, a national Islamic civil rights and advocacy group, found that nearly half of the American Muslims it questioned said their lives have changed for the worse since Sept. 11. (4)

A handful of cases have received public attention, including that of a 25-year-old hospital clerk from Vernon Hills, Illinois, who filed a federal civil rights lawsuit in July, alleging he was fired after Sept. 11 because of his Muslim religion and Pakistani citizenship. Other cases have gone largely unnoticed, such as threats that Anwar Alhalabi and his family experienced in their Palos Hills apartment on Sept. 14.

According to police and prosecutors, a neighbor who lives above the Alhalabis began stomping on the floor and shouting threats and curses from his balcony, demanding that foreigners go home. The Alhalabis are U.S. citizens of Syrian ancestry. The neighbor eventually pleaded guilty in August to a weapons charge and was sentenced to 2 years probation and 20 hours of community service.

The Alhalabi case is one of six post-Sept. 11 hate crimes against people perceived to be Arab or Muslim that the Cook County state's attorney's office has prosecuted, said Assistant State's Atty. Neera Walsh. All of the defendants got probation.

Among those prosecuted were a Chicago man who threatened to blow up an Arab-owned grocery on the South Side; a Chicago Ridge man who threatened two Middle Eastern men with a baseball bat; and a Worth man who struck a Moroccan gas station attendant with the handle of a machete. (5)

To get a real sense of the amount of hate crimes against Arab and Muslim Americans in the USA after 9/11, we can simply multiply the above figures by the number of states in the union, taking into considerations that many hate crimes have gone unreported; sometimes for fear of reprisals, or simply out of shame, as in the case of Seema Imam who was featured by the Chicago Tribune twice since 9/11.

(3) Ibid
(4) CAIR
(5) Arab American Bar Association

Public officials tried vigorously to contain a wave of hate crimes in the United States after September 11, Human Rights Watch said in a report released recently. Nevertheless, anti-Muslim hate crimes in the United States rose 1700 percent during 2001. The report documents anti-Arab and anti-Muslim violence and the local, state and federal response to it. The forty-one page report, We Are Not the Enemy, draws on research with police, prosecutors, community activists, and victims of hate crimes in six cities (Seattle, Washington; Dearborn, Michigan; Chicago, Illinois; Los Angeles, California; Phoenix, Arizona; and New York, New York) to review steps taken by government officials to prevent and prosecute hate crimes after the September 11 attacks in New York and Washington, D.C. The report also examines the scope and extent of these hate crimes, which included murder, assault, arson, and vandalism. Government officials did not sit on their hands while Muslims and Arabs were attacked after September 11, said Amardeep Singh, author of the report and U.S. Program researcher at Human Rights Watch. But law enforcement and other government agencies should have been better prepared for this kind of onslaught.

In general, 9/11 has negatively impacted the lives of Arab and Muslim Americans, and also other minority groups perceived to be of Middle Eastern origins, like Assyrians, Persians, Indians, and even Hispanics. Fear is looming as we get closer every time to the 9/11 anniversary.

Fear, not as much of the potential terrorist attacks against us, but fear from the enemy within. Fear of xenophobes, bigots; hate crime perpetrators, traditional hate groups, and the zealot next door. Fear of government legislations that can limit, or hinder our civil rights, or even our basic human rights, that might not after all make us feel safer.

Such legislations that prompted my friends to advise me not to say much of anything, in general. It was perceived among the public that Arab and Muslim homes would be bugged, phone lines tapped, any mysterious looking mail would be reported to the authorities due to the TIPPS program that would turn mail carriers into eyes for the federal government. Even librarians, would be supposed to report on any ordering of suspicious book titles.

The post 9/11 climate sent shock waves through the Arab and Muslim communities in the USA, and to some extent in the Western World, in general. Thousands of Arab and Muslim young males in the US, mainly immigrants, were detained in undisclosed locations.

The government further announced its intentions of interrogating more than 10,000 young Arab and Muslim males- in their early twenties and mid thirties - that generally fit the profile of the usual suspect, whether they were legal or illegal immigrants. An uncertain number of the detainees were quietly deported, and some released. However, none were found having any ties to 9/11.

The continuation of using Secret Evidence, Military Tribunals and the Patriot Act in dealing with cases involving Arabs and Muslims have been disappointing to many legal experts and civil rights activists. These measures infuriated civil liberties organizations across the country, and resulted into joint lawsuits filed against the government by some of these organizations, mainly the ACLU and the ADC, American-Arab Anti-discrimination Committee.

With the Patriot Act, in particular, many people in the Arab and Muslim communities felt unsafe to go to their regular mosques and churches. Some stopped attending their religious institutions at all. Others stopped writing their usual charity and tithes checks that they used to. It is feared which religious institution would be the next to be doomed as tied to terrorist activities. Religious institutions are not the safe haven or the refuge that used to be to many people in the community, any more. In recent chilling TV ads, the American Civil Liberties Union, ACLU, depicted a pastor and his parishioners fleeing the church from the basement window after being told to be careful. After all, Walls have ears.

In the sixties, it used to be the Red Scare during the Cold War. In the post 9/11 era, it seems to many people that it is the "Green Scare", or Islamophobia, as dubbed by some observers. It is true that the perpetrators of the horrific terrorist attacks on 9/11 were all Arabs and Muslims from the Middle East. It is also true that nothing can justify these evil attacks against innocent civilians and the violation of the sanctity of a human life. But the fact is that the terror acts were single-handedly planned and declared by a crazed megalomaniac with a religious zeal, Usama bin-Laden, who could not be hated more by Arab and Muslim Americans. Not only because he spoiled it for them, tarnished their image and stole their American dream, but also because he turned their lives and the lives of many others into a nightmare, especially for the thousands of those who lost their loved ones in the terrorist attack - hundreds of them were Muslims.

Finally, the terrorist war was not declared by either the Arab or the Muslim Worlds. It was and has always been perpetrated by outcast, fringe, extremist groups rejected by their own societies and their governments.

Arab and Muslim Americans have proved their loyalty to their country-of-choice, the USA. In the wake of 9/11 tens of thousands of Arab and Muslim Americans volunteered to serve with US armed forces and law enforcement agencies, along with the tens of thousands of Arab and Muslim Americans who have been already serving for a long time. The process of reconciliation and self-healing might take us some time, but individual and collective efforts must be exerted in order to bring our society together, and stand strong against a common enemy that is set to destroy everything beautiful that we stand for.

Aladdin Elaasar, Chicago, Illinois, USA, February 29, 2004

Part I

Leaders of Arab & Muslim-American groups condemn the horrifying attacks on the World Trade Center and the Pentagon on September 11

On September 12, 2001, *Leaders of Arab-American and American Muslim groups met in Washington, D.C. and issued the following statement:*

"We condemn in no uncertain terms the horrifying attacks on the World Trade Center and the Pentagon on September 11. We are shocked and angered by such brutality and share all the emotions of our fellow citizens about these attacks, which target all Americans without exception. We firmly believe that there can be no justification for such horrible acts. We join with the nation in calling for the perpetrators of this terrible crime to be brought swiftly to justice. We commend the statements of Attorney General John Ashcroft, Secretary of State Colin Powell and the numerous senators and members of Congress who have cautioned against attempts to stigmatize the Arab-American and American Muslim communities or blame them for this tragedy. We urge our fellow Americans, the government and media to follow their example and not assign any form of collective guilt against communities for the crimes of individuals. " Signed by:

American-Arab Anti-Discrimination Committee (ADC)
Arab American Institute (AAI)
American Committee on Jerusalem (ACJ)
American Muslim Alliance (AMA)
American Muslim Council (AMC)
Center for Policy Analysis on Palestine (CPAP)
Council on American Islamic Relations (CAIR)

Aladdin Elaasar

Islamic Institute

American Leaders Speak out Against Backlash in Wake of September 11 Tragedy

President George W. Bush *remarked in a telephone conversation with NY Mayor Rudy Giuliani, September 12, 2001*

"I know I don't need to tell you all this, but our nation should be mindful that there are Thousands of Arab Americans who live in New York City, who love their flag just as much as the three of us do, and we must be mindful that as we seek to win the war, that we treat Arab Americans and Muslims with the respect they deserve. I know that is your attitude as well, certainly the attitude of this government, that we should not hold one who is a Muslim responsible for an act of terror. We will hold those who are responsible for the terrorist acts accountable, and those who harbor them."

And he said further in remarks at the Islamic Center in Washington, DC, on September 17, 2001 "the face of terror is not the true faith of Islam. That's not what Islam is all about. Islam is peace. These terrorists don't represent peace. They represent evil and war. When we think of Islam we think of a faith that brings comfort to a billion people around the world. Billions of people find comfort and solace and peace. And that's made brothers and sisters out of every race - out of every race."

U.S. Attorney General John Ashcroft, *September 12, 2001*

"[O]ur nation calls on us in times like this to be at our best. If we are to prevail in difficult times like this, we must be at our best. Since Tuesday, the Justice Department has received reports of violence and threats of violence against Arab-Americans and other Americans of Middle Eastern and South Asian descent. We must not descend to the level of those who perpetrated Tuesday's violence by targeting individuals based on race, religion, or national origin. Such reports of violence and threats are in direct opposition to the very principles and laws for which the United State of America stands, and such reports of violence and threats of violence will not be tolerated."

Robert Muller, Director of the FBI, *September 17, 2001*

Since the horrific attacks on September 11, dozens of retaliatory hate crimes have been directed at members of the Arab-American community, including assaults, arson, threatening communications and possibly-and I say "possibly"-ethnically motivated murders. Many of these criminal acts have been directed at Muslim houses of worship and at Muslim community centers.

I want to make it very clear: Vigilante attacks and threats against Arab-Americans will not be tolerated. We are all saddened by the recent acts of terrorism against our nation. Such acts of retaliation violate federal law and, more particularly, run counter to the very principles of equality and freedom upon which our nation is founded.

The FBI and the Department of Justice are committed to aggressively investigating and prosecuting violations of the federal hate crime laws. We, to date, have initiated 40 hate crime investigations, involving reported attacks on Arab American citizen and institutions.

Concurrent Resolution of the U.S. Congress, *September 12, 2001*

That the Congress-

1) Declares that in the quest to identify, bring to justice, and punish the perpetrators and sponsors of the terrorist attacks on the United States on September 11, 2001, that the civil rights and civil liberties of all Americans, including Arab-Americans, American Muslims, and Americans from South Asia, should be protected; and

(2) Condemns any acts of violence or discrimination against any Americans, including Arab- Americans, American Muslims, and Americans from South Asia.

Senator Tom Daschle, *September 14, 2001*

"We will be fierce in the defense of our ideals. We will make whatever material or physical sacrifice that is required of us to punish those who attacked our nation and to prevent future attacks. But we will not sacrifice the ideals that built this nation and have sustained us for more than two centuries. Just as we are united against the terrorists and their co-conspirators who carried out the attacks on our nation, we must also be united against acts of hate against innocent Arab- Americans and Muslims."

Senator Edward M. Kennedy, Massachusetts, *September 12, 2001*

"I know that the American Muslim and Arab communities share the nation's horror and outrage over yesterday's terrorist attacks. They have issued strong statements unequivocally condemning these vicious atrocities and expressing their condolences to the families of the innocent people killed...there is understandable anger across the nation. But it is wrong and irresponsible to jump to conclusions and make false accusations against Arabs and Muslims in our communities. Above all, we must guard against any acts of violence based on such bigotry."

Senator Russ Feingold, Wisconsin, *September 12, 2001*

"As we look for answers and we look for solutions and we look for things we must do, domestically as well as externally, we must continue to respect our Constitution...this should not be an occasion for ill treatment of Arab Americans, Muslim Americans, South Asians, or others in this country. It is wrong. They are as patriotic as any other Americans and are feeling extremely stressed as a result of this situation...we must stand together, all Americans of all background, to condemn these actions."

Senator Dick Durbin, Illinois, *September 12, 2001*

"As we identify the sources of terrorism, it is possible we will look to an Arab person, or a group of Arab people, or those of the Muslim faith. We should never allow those facts, if they turn out to be true, to cloud our judgment when it comes to our fellow Arab Americans and those who believe and practice the Muslim faith. Many of them share with us the pain and sorrow of yesterday's tragedy."

Representative John Conyers, Jr., Michigan, *September 12, 2001*

"Just as this horrendous act can destroy us from without, it can also destroy us from within. Pearl Harbor led to internment camps of Japanese-Americans, and today there is a very real danger that this tragedy could result in prejudice, discrimination, and crimes of hate against Arab-Americans and others. The lesson Oklahoma City taught us was the perpetrators of these acts of terror can be evil men of every race, nationality and religion as are the victims. We must ensure that these acts of terror do not slowly and subversively destroy the foundation of our democracy: a commitment to equal rights and equal protection."

Representative Hilda Solis, California, *September 12, 2001*

"I am heartened by the American people's extraordinary display of kindness and cooperation. I have been moved by how our diverse Nation has come together in a united show of support - men and women, children and adults, Christians and Muslims, Jews and Buddhists, Hindus and Catholics, Latinos and Caucasians, Asian and African Americans. However, I am concerned about reports of anti-Arab and anti-Muslim acts committed by some in our communities. American Muslims and Arab Americans share our commitment to the American ideals of freedom, justice, and democracy.... Acts of discrimination only serve to divide our Nation and weaken our strength. Our Nation is made stronger when we embrace our diversity."

Cari M. Dominguez, Chair of the U.S. Equal Employment Opportunity Commission, Urges Workplace Tolerance, *September 14, 2001*

"In the midst of this tragedy, employers should take time to be alert to instances of harassment or intimidation against Arab-Americans a Muslim employees. Preventing and prohibiting injustices against our fellow workers is one way to fight back . . . against the evil forces that assaulted our workplaces Tuesday morning . . . .Our laws reaffirm our national values of tolerance and civilized conduct. At this time of trial, these values will strengthen us as a common people . . . the nation's workplaces are fortified by the enduring ability of Americans of diverse backgrounds, beliefs, and nationalities to work together harmoniously and productively."

Paul Steven Miller, Commissioner, U.S. Equal Employment Opportunity Commission, *September 12, 2001*

"In light of the events this week, I recognize discrimination and harassment against Arab Americans and Moslems have become a much greater and more immediate threat today I want you to know that I and the EEOC are committed to combating any illegal discrimination against Arab Americans and Moslems that occurs in the workplace."

Robert A. Destro, Director, Interdisciplinary Program in Law & Religion, The Catholic University of America, *September 12, 2001*

"As we turn to the task of identifying those who supported the perpetrators of this callous murder of our fellow citizens, we must remember that Justice, not vengeance, is the basis for global solidarity and domestic tranquility. We must not, however, permit our righteous anger to lead us to forget the lessons of the past. Targeting any person - citizen or visitor - on the basis of his or her religion, nationality, or culture is evil, and at the root of our present crisis. Islam is not the enemy. Neither are our fellow Americans who are of Arabic origin or adherents of Islam. We must join together in this time of tragedy."

Union of American Hebrew Congregations, *September 12, 2001*

"We are concerned, in particular, with reports that some in our nation have directed their understandable anger at Tuesday's carnage at individual Arab Americans and Muslim Americans. We are outraged at reports of attacks on Arab Americans, Muslim Americans, and their mosques and businesses and condemn all such acts of lawlessness."

The Anti-Defamation League (ADL), September 14, 2001

In the aftermath of the terrorist attacks against the United States, the Anti-Defamation League (ADL), while calling on all Americans to maintain national unity, also urged that "no one be singled out for hatred, prejudice or blame based on their ethnicity or religion." Abraham H. Foxman, ADL National Director, issued the following statement:

"At this time of terrible tragedy, we must maintain national strength and unity while at the same time ensuring that no one is singled out for hatred, prejudice or blame based on their ethnicity or religion.

We are disturbed that a number of Arab Americans and Islamic institutions have been targets of anger and hatred in the aftermath of the terrorist attacks. At this time of profound anger and anxiety, no group in this country should be singled out for hatred, prejudice or blame based on their ethnicity or religion.

Threats, harassment or acts of hate-motivated violence against members of a group are un-American and must be forcefully condemned. In laying blame on an entire people, we undermine our nation's core values of equality and respect for the individual."

Korean American Coalition, *September 12, 2001*

"All of us remember the terrible mistakes we made as a country when thousands of innocent Japanese Americans were placed in internment camps during WWII in the hysteria following the attack on Pearl Harbor. Any attack on someone of perceived Arab ancestry is not only an attack on his or her civil rights, but also an attack on our country's sense of justice and equality." 3 of 4

Asian American Journalists Association, *September 12, 2001*

"Already, there is much concern within Arab American communities in our nation about the backlash that might result from Tuesday's attacks we can help ensure that the devastating events in New York, Washington, DC, and Pennsylvania do not lead to further injustices against other Americans." -

AFL-CIO, *September 12, 2001*

Even as we denounce this act, we must remember that this was an act of terrorists, not an Arab attack, and reject anti-Arab retaliation or discrimination. Now is the time to renew the values that bind us together as a nation.

Seniors USA, *September 15, 2001*

"Of more importance, in keeping with one of our most important cornerstones when our country was formed, we adhere to the principle to provide justice to all . . . In keeping with these beliefs, we must remember America's 7 million Muslims and 6 million Arab-Americans are Americans just as much as we are and are not to be viewed as a lesser American or any way different in our love for America."

Leroy D. Baca, Sheriff, County of Los Angles, *September 13, 2001*

"Unfortunately, there are those who would use this calamity as an excuse to blame a particular race or those practicing a specific religion. As a result, there have already been hate crimes committed against the Arab-American and Muslim-American communities. The terrorists, who attacked our nation, did so to divide us and create a climate of fear. If we allow prejudice and hate to separate our multicultural country, the cowards who planned and implemented this horror will have succeeded. We cannot allow history to repeat itself and make the same mistakes that were made following Pearl Harbor against loyal Americans of Japanese decent. Our nation is facing a grave challenge to our way of life and it s time to unite, as we have done time and again throughout our history."

Rod Paige, U. S. Secretary of Education, *September 19, 2001*

"In response to last week's events specifically, I urge you to make sure those assemblies, classroom discussions, and other school activities held to honor victim of the tragedies, do not inadvertently foster the targeting of Arab-American students for harassment or blame. Encourage students to discuss diversity constructively and to express disagreement over ideas or beliefs in a respectful manner . . . Through our words and the example of our own conduct, we must remind our children that harassment of and violence toward any individual because of his or her race or national origin is never acceptable. In addition, we must emphasize during this difficult time in our nation's history that our feelings of anger and sadness must not be directed at innocent Arab Americans, or other individuals having no connection to last week's events. Working together, we can make sure that our children get a good education in a safe environment that does not tolerate violence and hatred."

David Broder, The Washington Post, *September 18, 2001*

"This struggle will test the temperament of the American people for a long time. But one thing needs to be done right now. I have been talking with my friend Jim Zoghby, the president of the Arab American Institute, about the assaults and threats members of that community have experienced since September 11.

Vile words have been uttered on the street and on talk shows. Bullets and fist have flown. That cannot be condoned. The statements of condemnation from the Bush administration and the Senate have been strong. But they need to be echoed in local communities. It is not enough to remain silent. The bigots must be condemned, and gestures of support given to Arab American families. This too is part of our national character test."

Public Statement of Legendary American Boxer Muhammad Ali

"I am a Muslim. I am an American. As an American Muslim, I want to express my deep sadness and anguish at the tremendous loss of life that occurred on Tuesday.

Islam is a religion of peace. Islam does not promote terrorism or the killing of people.
I cannot sit by and let the world think that Islam is a killing religion. It hurts me to see what radical people are doing in the name of Islam. These radicals are doing things that God is against. Muslims do not believe in violence.

If the culprits are Muslim, they have twisted the teachings of Islam. Whoever performed, or is behind, the terrorist attacks in the United States of America does not represent Islam. God is not behind assassins. Anyone involved in this must pay for their evil acts. Hatred caused this tragedy and adding to the hatred that already exists in the world will not help. Instead, we should try to understand each other better.

Americans are warm, loving and hospitable people, and we share many of the same values. I ask that churches and synagogues all across the nation invite representatives of the Islamic faith into their places of worship, to better understand Islam. This could help us all respect each other more. I pray that God blesses the people and families of those who were killed, and our great country."

The chairman of Islamic Supreme Council of America, Shaykh Muhammad Hisham Kabbani Meets with President Bush and Endorses Bush's Call for Three Days of Prayer, *Friday, September 6, 2002.*

(Washington, DC 09/08/02) On Friday, September 6, the chairman of Islamic Supreme Council of America, Shaykh Muhammad Hisham Kabbani, together with a handful of religious leaders, was honored to join President George W. Bush in an intimate ceremony at the White House Roosevelt Room. The president used the occasion to proclaim that Friday, September 6, through Sunday, September 8, 2002, would be observed for the first time as "National Days of Prayer and Remembrance."

The president shared his personal religious convictions and called upon faith leaders of the nation to join him in observing religious services that honor the victims of September 11th, and to pray for the continued protection and safety of our country.

Expressing his feelings about the meeting, Shaykh Kabbani said, "While people around the world view President Bush as a great man of conviction and courage, very few get the unique opportunity to observe him as a sensitive, caring, religiously inspired individual. I expressed our community's deep sentiment and support for President Bush, to which he responded with a heartfelt embrace. I am truly blessed by that experience and will share his act of friendship with our millions of supporters around the world."

ISCA encourages its members, supporters and congregations around the world to join President Bush and people of all faiths in hosting services that commemorate the unspeakable tragedy our nation has endured. Further, we urge Muslims to let this first anniversary pass not only as a day of remembrance, but one of action.

On September 11, 2002, the Council unequivocally called on all leaders of traditional Islamic communities and Muslims at-large to immediately establish

"Community Watch" groups across the nation. While typically such groups are designed to prevent external threats, these community-based groups will protect our mosques, schools and centers from the threat within our ranks, the threat posed by extremist elements that attempt to hijack our peaceful religion. These watch groups will prevent extremists from using our places of worship for illegitimate and illegal purposes. We believe such action will demonstrate that Muslims are sincere, patriotic and upright citizens, committed to upholding the honor of traditional Islam and to preventing the Islamic faith from being manipulated by self-serving criminals.

We pray that our brothers and sisters throughout the Muslim world will see an end to the era of dictators and experience the same freedoms we cherish as citizens of this great nation. We also pray that traditional Muslims throughout the world will one day be liberated from the oppression of extremists who stifle universal human rights and destroy the sanctity of life.

As we approach the anniversary of September 11th, we at the Islamic Supreme Council of America stand united with our fellow Americans. We pray for swift victory in the war against terror and that all people will one day live in a world filled with peace, cooperation, and social justice.

American Jewish Committee Criticizes Rev. Pat Robertson For Comments Denigrating Islam, *Nov. 13, 2002*

NEW YORK -- The American Jewish Committee today sharply criticized the Rev. Pat Robertson for his sweeping condemnation of Islam. "..the Rev. Robertson's wholesale denigration of an entire faith, by calling Muslims 'worse than Nazis,' is outrageous," said David A. Harris, executive director of the American Jewish Committee. "Jews do not live under any illusions about the challenges before us, but we must always make distinctions between the extremists, with whom dialogue is impossible, and those committed to moderation and coexistence," said Mr. Harris. "By condemning all Muslims, rather than singling out those with twisted theology threatens all Christians and Jews alike, the Rev. Robertson has failed to make a distinction that is central to advancing inter-religious relations." The American Jewish Committee has launched a number of initiatives seeking to advance Muslim-Jewish relations, building upon decades of successful inter-religious work in dealing with Christian denominations. Mr. Harris also took umbrage at the recent statement by the Rev. Jerry Falwell, who had slandered an entire faith by calling the Prophet Muhammad a "terrorist."

President Bush reprimands some Christian-Right leaders over hateful Anti-Islamic rhetoric, *Nov 13, 2002*

WASHINGTON (Reuters) - President Bush on Wednesday took on the Christian right core of his political base, denouncing anti-Islamic remarks made by religious leaders including evangelist Pat Robertson.

Bush said such anti-Islamic comments were at odds with the views of most Americans. "Some of the comments that have been uttered about Islam do not reflect the sentiments of my government or the sentiments of most Americans," Bush told reporters as he began a meeting with U.N. Secretary-General Kofi Annan.

"By far, the vast majority of American citizens respect the Islamic people and the Muslim faith. After all, there are millions of peaceful-loving Muslim Americans," Bush said. "Ours is a country based upon tolerance ... And we're not going to let the war on terror or terrorists cause us to change our values."

Meanwhile, Secretary of State Powell said, "We will reject the kinds of comments you have seen recently where people in this country say the Muslims are responsible for the killing of all Jews. This kind of language must be spoken out against. We cannot allow this image to go forth of America, because it is an inaccurate image of America."

Bush did not identify conservative Christian leaders as his target, but White House officials said he was prompted by the anti-Islamic remarks of some of them, particularly religious broadcaster Pat Robertson, who reportedly said this week Muslims were "worse than the Nazis."

"He (Bush) wanted a clear statement," a senior White House official said. Spokeswoman Angell Watts of Robertson's Christian Broadcasting Network said she had no immediate comment. A representative of a Muslim-American civil rights group, which had stepped up calls for Bush to repudiate such remarks, welcomed Bush's words.

"Obviously, we'd like to hear him repudiate these people by name, but we appreciate that he's moving in that direction," said Ibrahim Hooper of the Council on American-Islamic Relations (CAIR). "It's encouraging to see that the president is finally addressing the issue of Islamophobia in America by addressing a specific attacks on Islam. This is a new stance, and it's one that we would encourage and support," Hooper said.

Bush's efforts to discourage a backlash over the Sept. 11, 2001 attacks, which were blamed on Islamic militant Osama bin Laden, have come increasingly into conflict with antipathy to Islam shown by some conservative Christians, a core of his support.

Robertson, a popular conservative commentator who sought the Republican presidential nomination in 1988, was criticized by CAIR and the American Jewish Committee for reportedly saying on his network Monday, "Adolf Hitler was bad, but what the Muslims want to do to the Jews is worse." Jerry Falwell, a Baptist minister and leading voice of the Christian right, in an October television interview described the prophet Mohammad as a "terrorist." Evangelist Franklin Graham, who gave the sermon at Bush's inaugural service in 2001, has also been criticized for comments on Islam.

Representative John Conyers, Jr., House Judiciary Committee, RENEWS CALL FOR PASSAGE OF HATE CRIMES LAW, *11/26/02*

"New Figures on Muslim Bias Make Need for Passage Compelling "

Representative John Conyers, Jr., the Ranking Democrat on the House Judiciary Committee, and lead author of hate crimes legislation in the last three Congresses issued the following statement In light of the FBI's annual hate crimes report finding that incidents targeting people, institutions and businesses identified with the Islamic faith increased from 28 in 2000 to 481 in 2001:

"These new statistics clearly make the case for passage of hate crimes legislation. If our nation is going to battle terrorism abroad, we must be willing to confront the domestic terrorism of hate crimes, and that means a willingness to make it a federal crime to harm or kill someone because of their race, religion or other factors. I am confident that we have bipartisan majorities in both the House and the Senate to pass such a law, but we need leadership from the White House to make this happen. I will reintroduce this bill when Congress returns early next year, and plan on making this a principal priority for the next Congress…

The increase in hate crimes against Muslims seen in the FBI report of 1,600 percent is truly shocking. Muslims previously had been among the least targeted religious group…

This increase is a direct consequence of the fear and suspicion that followed the Sept. 11 terror attacks. Sadly, the policies promulgated by the Administration and the Department of Justice may have contributed to the climate of distrust of Arab-Americans that is reflected in hate crimes data. Recently disclosed intelligence programs, such as the questioning and monitoring of thousands of Iraqi citizens and Iraqi-Americans, sends the message that these are untrustworthy people, not worthy of basic Constitutional protections...

Chapter I

Arabs.. go back home..
Or, where does hatred come from?
By
Aladdin Elaasar

On September 10, 2002, the eve of the first anniversary of 9/11, in a speech delivered at the Afghani embassy in Washington, DC, president George Bush addressed his audience saying:

"Bigotry is not a part of our soul. It's not going to be a part of our future. Sure, there may be some, but that's not the American way, and we must reject bigotry of all kinds in this great land. In order for us to reject the evil done to America on September the 11th, we must reject bigotry in all its forms. George Washington says, "America gives to bigotry no sanction; to persecution no assistance." And that is true today, we treasure our friendship with Muslims and Arabs around the world."

President Bush's message could not be more accurate and timely to calm the fears of the public towards their fellow Arab and Muslim Americans. 9/11 has created an atmosphere of fear among some "native' born Americans towards those who are deemed to be different, ethnic, or foreign in shape, attire, religious rituals, and life style, which can be summed into the "xenophobia syndrome". According to Eli Kedourie, " xenophobia is the dislike of the stranger, the outsider, and the reluctance to admit him into one one's group". (1) "Xenophobia is a term often associated with hostility to foreigners or to immigrants". (2)

(1) Eli Kedourie, *Nationalism*, New York: Prager, 1960, p 74.

14

But in the case of Arab and Muslim Americans, who have witnessed similar backlashes during the Gulf War, the Yom Kippur War, and conflicts related to the Middle East, and being victims generally of acts of bigotry committed by long known hate groups, or individuals who have their biases towards minority groups, the public bias can be ignited by the most unexpected sources.

- "We should invade [Muslim] countries, kill their leaders and convert them to Christianity." Columnist Ann Coulter, National Review Online, Sept. 13, 2001

- "Just turn [the sheriff] loose and have him arrest every Muslim that crosses the state line." Rep. C. Saxby Chambliss (R-GA), chairman of the House Subcommittee on Terrorism and Homeland security and Senate candidate, to Georgia law officers, November 2001

- "Islam is a religion in which God requires you to send your son to die for him. Christianity is a faith where God sent his Son to die for you."
  Attorney General John Ashcroft, interview on Cal Thomas radio, November 2001

- "(Islam) is a very evil and wicked religion, wicked, violent and not of the same god (as Christianity)." Rev. Franklin Graham, head of the Billy Graham Evangelistic Association, November 2001.

- "Islam is Evil, Christ is King."
  Allegedly written in marker by law enforcement agents on a Muslim prayer calendar in the home of a Muslim being investigated by police in Dearborn, Michigan, July 2002. (3)

The above statements were uttered by persons who either have held cabinet positions, are figures in public service, or persons with access to the mainstream media. These inflammatory statements were not the only statements with clear prejudice, but an indefinite number of similar statement were heard over the airwaves, printed by the press, or even used by religious leaders.

---

(2) Juan Perea, *Immigrants. Out!*, *The New Nativism and the Anti-Immigrant Impulses in the United States*, New York University Press, 1997, p 293
(3) Gary Leupp, *Challenging Ignorance on Islam: A Ten-Point Primer for Americans*

Aladdin Elaasar

According to a survey done by researcher Shelly Slade in 1980 after interviewing 600 people by phone in the US, Shelly concluded, " The Arabs remain one of the few ethnic groups who can still be slandered with impunity in America". (4)

Arab and Muslim Americans have witnessed and lived under similar hostile climates prior to the 9/11 backlashes. " For the better part of the 1980s, the Arab Americans (and Muslims) lived in an increasing state of apprehension as the Reagan administration waged its war on " international terrorism". "The fear reached its zenith in 1985 and 1986. The high jacking on June 14, 1985, of TWA flight 847 to Beirut by Lebanese Shiite gunmen highlighted the predicament." The incident received extensive coverage in the news media, much of it, unashamedly sensationalist and hysterical". (5)

" The media hype may have contributed to the outbreak of violent attacks against Arab Americans and Middle Easterners that coincided with the highjacking, making 1985 a milestone in the history of violence against Arabs and Middle Easterners. According to the Los Angeles Human Relations Commission, twelve out of a total of seventy-one religiously motivated incidents that took place in Los Angeles County in 1985" were directed against Islamic mosques, centers or individuals of the Islamic faith". (6)

With the Reagan administration in full gear against what he described as "the war on international terrorism", in November of 1981, president Reagan announced in front of the TV cameras that president Gaddafi of Libya had sent "hit teams" to the US to assassinate him, claiming " We have the evidence and he knows it ". " The allegations, which proved to be an utter fabrication, stimulated anti-Arab, anti-Mid Eastern hysteria among the news media and the public at large". (7)

The tension in American-Libyan relations continued to escalate during the eighties. In a nationally televised address, President Reagan announced that he had "direct, precise and irrefutable evidence" linking Libya to the La Belle disco bombing in Germany in 1986. He vowed to retaliate against " the mad dog of the Middle East" referring to Colonel Gaddafi of Libya. On April 14, a week later, US fighter planes bombed Libya in retaliation to Gaddafi's alleged involvement in the disc bombing.

(4) Ernest McCarus, *The Development of Arab American Identity,* The University of Michigan Press, 1997, p 159.
(5) Nabeel Abraham, *Anti-Arab Racism and Violence in the United States*, included in *The Development of Arab American Identity*, The University of Michigan Press, 1997, p 161.
(6) Ibid p.161
(7) *Washington Times*, interview of FBI Assistant director, Oliver B. Revel in January 1986 in which he dismissed the allegations that Gaddafi sent suicide terrorists as " a complete fabrication.

" In an interview on April 28 with a reporter for the US Army journal *Stars and Stripes*, Manfred Ganschow, chief of the Berlin Staatscutz and head of the 100-man team investigating the disco bombing, stated that " I have no more evidence that Libya was connected to the bombing than I had when you first called me two days after the act. Which is none." (8)

Whether the allegations were accurate, or not, more anti-Arab violence erupted in various parts of the country. Two days before the US bombing of Libya, five Arab students from the University of Syracuse, New York, "were beaten by a gang of Americans in a bar", where one student almost lost an eye. (9) In the Detroit suburb of Westland, a smoke bomb was thrown into the house of a Palestinian family with the words " *Go Back to Libya*" daubed on one of the walls.

In the nineties, the same pattern of Anti-Arab and Anti -Mid Eastern violence continued to emerge. Many Arab Americans were put under surveillance. After the Gulf War, in early 1991, the Bush administration sent a crime bill to Congress that loosely defined a terrorist as any one who had raised money for any organization that had engaged in violence. The bill also effectively called for the establishment of a secret government tribunal to hear terrorist deportation cases and would also empower the government to detain suspects indefinitely.

Historically, violence against minorities in America is not a new trend. Arabs, Muslims or people of Mid Eastern ancestry were not the only ethnic group that have received their share of home grown violence, or scapegoating. The pattern has emerged during similar crises, when the nation's security becomes threatened, and in times of economic recession, that some sociologists describe as a recurrent tide of Jingoistic *racism*.

Jingoistic racism is "a curious blend of knee-jerk patriotism, and homegrown white racism toward non-European, non-Christian dark skinned people. It is racism spawned by political ignorance, false patriotism, and hyper-ethnocentrism". (10)

According to Juan Perea, professor of Law at the University of Florida, "Nativism is the intense opposition to an internal minority on the grounds of its foreign (i.e." un-American") connections". (11) During Nativist times in the United States,

(8) Nobel Abraham, *Anti-Arab Racism and Violence in the United States*, included in *The Development of Arab American Identity*, The University of Michigan Press, 1997, p 172.
(9) *Harassment and violence Log Sheet*, US Congress, 1988, 67-69.
(10) Ibid p 193.
(11) Juan Perea, *Immigrants. Out!*, *The New Nativism and the Anti-Immigrant Impulses in the United States*, New York University Press, 1997, introduction, also see John Higham, Strangers in

democratic processes are turned against internal minorities deemed foreign or "un-American", resulting in discriminatory legislation they spawn. Nativist movements and the legislation they spawn, seek to rid the nation of perceived enemies of the "American way".
(12)

" We have been through all of this before. During the controversy of the Alien and Sedition Acts in 1798, the enemy took the form of the French ethnicity and ideology, and Americans associated with that ideology. (13) The 1850s saw the vilification of the Irish "savages" whom, for the first time had migrated in substantial numbers to the USA. (14) In the years during and after the World War I yielded intense hatred of the Germans and German Americans among us. (15) During World War II, the hatred of the Japanese enemy and of loyal Americans of Japanese ancestry, who looked like the enemy, resulted in the forced incarceration of seventy thousand Japanese American citizens, and between thirty and forty thousand Japanese aliens in domestic internment camps. (16) During the 1950s, fear of the communist enemy was played out in the frequent interrogations of immigrants from Southern-eastern European Countries, in suspicions regarding their ethnicity, and in the blacklisting of the Jews." (17)

"Other targets of today's Nativism wear Mexican, Central American and Asian faces". Professor Juan Perea believes that: "as a society, we have declared legislative and border war both on undocumented and legal aliens alike. Undocumented aliens have been the most useful and productive enemy. Governor Wilson of California enjoyed great political success blaming the economic atrophy in his state on immigrants.

"Conservative Republican politicians make use of immigration reform as one of their prominent political issues. The undocumented make easy targets; they lack the power to vote and so they lack political legitimacy, clout and voice". (18)

---

the Land, (2nd ed.; New Brunswick, N. J.:Rutgers University Press, 1988).

(12) James Aho, *This Thing of Darkness: Sociology of the Enemy* (Seattle: University of Washington Press, 1994).

(13) Ibid p 2, also see James Morton Smith, Freedom's Fetters12, 20-21 (Ithaca, N.Y.: Cornell University Press, 1956)

(14) Ibid p 2, also see Joe R. Feagin, " Old Poison in New Bottles: The Deep Roots of Modern Nativism, chapter two.

(15) Ibid p 2, also see Higham, Strangers in the Land.

(16) Ibid p 2, also see Ronald Takaki, A different Mirror 378-85(Boston: Little Brown, 1993); Allan R. Bosworth, America's Concentration Camps 18 (New York: W. N. Norton, 1967).

(17) See, Juan F. Perea, " Demography and Distrust: An Essay on American Languages, Cultural Pluralism, and Official English," 77 Minnesota Law Review 269, 337-40 (1992).

(18) Juan Perea, *Immigrants Out! The New Nativism and the Anti-Immigrant Impulses in the United*

Immigrants become the new threat to national security and identity, filling the void left by the loss of the old enemies after the collapse of the Soviet Union and the end of the Cold War. "In this respect, the anti-immigrant discourse of the 1990s corresponds to the new vision of " America First" put forward by Pat Buchanan and increasingly touted by some Republican presidential candidates". (19)

To some observers "much of the anti-immigrant diatribe is socially constructed by political, business, and media leaders as well as white-collar executives who have organized anti-immigrant groups. The elites and anti-immigrant activists intentionally, according to immigration scholar Wayne Cornelius, " prey upon the fears and the lack of knowledge of the average citizen, creating a doomsday "Third Worldization" scenario of a jumble of unrelated facts and unsubstantiated assertions". (20)

The Arab and Muslim American dilemma seems to be connected unwillingly to the Neo-Nativism movement that keeps on bursting often, especially in crises times. Throughout American history, many ethnic groups have taken the burden to be the next scapegoat. The backlash can affect other immigrant or ethnic groups that get caught in the crossfire.

Yet, Arab-American writer, Nabeel Abraham, found that " *the Gulf Crisis of August 1990..reminded many Arab Americans that Anti-Arab (anti-Muslim, as well) continues to lie just beneath the service of society. And that as long as anti-Arab racism remains serviceable to government leaders, politicians, entertainers, the mass-media, and cultural institutions, it will continue to resonate unchecked and unchallenged at the popular levels of society.*" (21)

States, New York University Press, 1997

(19) Juan Perea and John Higman

(20) Wayne Cornelius, "Perspective on Immigration; Neo-Nativism Feed on Myopic Fears; No Industrial Country Is Able to Keep Foreign Workers From Settling In, They become "Our Own", Los Angeles Times, July 12, 1993, Metro, p. B7.

(21) Nabeel Abraham, *Anti-Arab Racism and Violence in the United States*, included in *The Development of Arab American Identity*, The University of Michigan Press, 1997, p 208

Chapter II

"100 Years of anti-Arab and anti-Muslim stereotyping"
By
Aladdin Elaasar

- **Media Stereotypes and Civil Rights***
- **Jack Shaheen & the anatomy of Anti-Arab stereotypes: TV & Reel Bad Arabs**
- **"The Instant TV Arab Kit "**

*Some of the divergent identity options chosen by Arab Americans can be placed to the treatment of Arabs and their culture in the United States. In both popular culture and government policy, anti-Arab stereotypes since the 1970s have affixed a stigma on Arab ethnicity in America. The first wave of immigrants did confront Nativism, ignorance, and anti-foreign sentiments of the prewar period, but they were rarely singled out. This changed with the development of the Arab-Israeli conflict, which created a highly charged political arena in which the United States became a strategic player and a strong supporter of the state of Israel. Because public exposure to Arab history and culture was often shaped only by old stereotypes of Arab sheiks, harems, and camels, it was not difficult for this cultural bias to deepen in direct proportion to U.S. interests in the Middle East.

New negative stereotypes emerged in and permeated throughout advertising, television, and movies, particularly those of the nefarious oil sheik and the terrorist. The Arab as villain has been a favorite scapegoat of popular American culture, thereby setting the stage for acts of discrimination and bigotry that have affected Arab Americans at home and resulted in a range of reactions (see the most recent reports of hate crimes). In the most assimilated circles, personal pride in Arab heritage did not always reach the public realm, where the stigma of unpopularity and controversy motivated some to mask their ethnicity, particularly in such arenas as the entertainment, media, and academic fields.

Stereotypes also seeped into public policy. Beginning in the 1970s a number of government investigations, executive orders, and legislative provisions aimed at combating terrorism had an impact on Arab American activism and violated the rights of some Arabs living in the United States. A more activist response emerged as Arab-born intellectuals, students, and professionals coalesced to counter the bias they saw in American policy and culture. Organizations to educate and to advocate the Arab point of view laid the groundwork for the first publicly engaged movement to represent the needs and issues of Arab Americans and to create a national sense of community and common purpose. Organizations such as the National Association of Arab Americans, the Association of Arab-American University Graduates, the American-Arab Anti Discrimination Committee, the Arab American Institute and others were founded to respond to these political, civic, and cultural challenges.

Recent anti-terrorism policies of airline-passenger profiling and the use of secret evidence by immigration judges have disproportionately affected Arabs and Muslims and have raised the concern of selective prosecution. The secret-evidence provisions of the Illegal Immigration Reform and Immigrant Responsibility Act, enacted by the U.S. Congress in 1996, have been challenged by constitutional-rights advocates and through bipartisan legislation slated to reverse this policy that was introduced in the 106th Congress in 2000.

When the relative invisibility of the broader Arab American community is contrasted with highly volatile political events, the most visible members and their institutions can be vulnerable to scapegoating. One prominent example was the 1995 Oklahoma City bombing tragedy in which initial suspicions of a Middle-Eastern link prompted incidents of anti-Arab backlash.

* Source: Arab American Institute Foundation

Jack Shaheen & the anatomy of Anti-Arab stereotypes: TV & Reel Bad Arabs

Throughout its history, Hollywood has been criticized for the its stereotypical portrayal of minority groups: the "incompetent black", the "savage" Native American, the "sinister" Asian. But while the film industry has evolved to more

21

accurately depict most of these groups, Jack Shaheen argues that Arabs remain the "bad guys" of the silver screen.

From Bedouin bandits to gun-toting terrorists, Shaheen says Arabs are not fairly represented on the big screen. Shaheen examines the roots of Hollywood's anti-Arab bias and suggests that this bias has tainted Americans' view towards the Middle East.

Jack Shaheen, a Fulbright scholar, is the author of *Reel Bad Arabs: How Hollywood Vilifies a People*, a former CBS News consultant on Middle East affairs, and Professor Emeritus of Mass Communications at Southern Illinois University in Edwardsville. He is also the author of the award-winning *TV Arab,* and *Arab and Muslim Stereotyping in American Popular Culture. He also wrote Reel Bad Arabs, How Hollywood Vilifies a People.* Howard Rosenberg, Los Angeles Times TV critic describes *Reel Bad Arabs* as: "Jack Shaheen continues to be a piercing laser of fairness and sanity in pointing out Hollywood's ongoing egregious smearing of Arabs."

Reel Bad Arabs: How Hollywood Vilifies a People is a groundbreaking book that dissects a slanderous history dating from cinema's earliest days to contemporary Hollywood blockbusters that feature machine-gun wielding and bomb-blowing "evil" Arabs. Award-winning film authority Jack G. Shaheen, noting that only Native Americans have been more relentlessly smeared on the silver screen, painstakingly makes his case that "Arab" has remained Hollywood's shameless shorthand for "bad guy," long after the movie industry has shifted its portrayal of other minority groups. In this comprehensive study of nearly one thousand films, arranged alphabetically in such chapters as "Villains," "Sheikhs," "Cameos," and "Cliffhangers," Shaheen documents the tendency to portray Muslim Arabs as Public Enemy #1- brutal, heartless, and uncivilized Others bent on terrorizing civilized Westerners. Shaheen examines how and why such a stereotype has grown and spread in the film industry and what may be done to change Hollywood's defamation of Arabs

"100 Years of anti-Arab and anti-Muslim stereotyping"

Mazin Qumsiyeh, director of Media Relations for the American Arab Anti Discrimination Committee, NC, describes the phenomenon that he calls **"100 Years of anti-Arab and anti-Muslim stereotyping"**, as follows: "Hollywood has had a consistent record of Arab stereotyping and bashing. Some in the Arab (& Muslim) American community call this the three B syndrome: Arabs in TV and movies are portrayed as either bombers, belly dancers, or billionaires. Thomas

Edison made a short film in 1897 for his patented Kinetoscope in which "Arab" women with enticing clothes dance to seduce a male audience. The short clip was called Fatima Dances (Belly dancer stereotype).

The trend has shifted over the years and was predominated by the "billionaires" for a short while especially during the oil crises in the seventies. However, in the last 30 some years, the predominant stereotype by far has been the "Arab bombers." In the latest movies G. I. Jane and Operation Condor viewers chant as a hero blows away Arabs. In G. I. Jane, Demi Moore plays a Navy Seal officer who gains her stripes killing Arabs. In Operation Condor starring Jackie Chan, we have Arab villains and a money grubbing inn-keeper (no good Arabs). Another scene shows Arabs praying and then cuts to an auction where Chan's women companions are being auctioned".

Jack Shaheen has spent years investigating these trends and this is well documented in his book *The TV Arab*. According to Shaheen over 21 major movies released in the last ten years show our US military killing Arabs. This includes such "hits" as Iron Eagle, Death Before Dishonor, Navy SEALs, Patriot Games, the American President, Delta Force 3, Executive Decision, etc. Not since the heyday of the cowboys-killing-Indians streak of films have we had such an epidemic. New York columnist Russell Baker wrote, "Arabs are the last people except Episcopalians whom Hollywood feels free to offend en masse." It is very interesting that a lot of what we see as offensive is released by subsidiaries of Disney, a so called family value company run by Mike Eisner.

It is not surprising then that Disney and Operation Condor received a "Dishonor Award" at the national convention of the American Arab Anti-discrimination Committee (ADC). The ADC and CAIR have been at the forefront in combating stereotypes and negative portrayal of Arabs in the media. The successes are there but the challenge is very large indeed. Some in the Arab and Muslim community in the US believe that there is a widespread effort now to create the "Muslim terror" as the replacement enemy now that communism is not a threat. In other words, to justify our continued massive military and the billions of dollars we send to Israel every year, we need a demonstrable enemy who will not go away.

The Arab and Muslim community in the US feel especially vulnerable because the energy and center of the Anti-Arab and anti-Muslim media movements are concentrated here. How else would we explain that the New York Times runs a cartoon with a bomb-wielding, mean-looking Arab and a caption that reads "Orthodox.. conservative...reform... what's the DIFFERENCE." Such cartoons have not been rare in Europe since the Nazi era.

"The harm is not only psychological (insult to a culture or a religion) but helps feed into actions that are physically harmful. Didn't we see this before, dehumanizing a group first before attacking it? A law was passed by Congress recently on airport "profiling" which is really stereotyping and racism. The idea is that you can identify "risky" people based on the countries they traveled to in the past (thus Arab Americans) and search them more thoroughly than the "normal" people. This leads to one line at the airport for Arabs and Muslims and one line for others. The double standards and hypocrisy of the media is everywhere".

"How is it that they are portrayed collectively as terrorists bent? The Arab and Muslim community in North America are vibrant and thriving, but are in distress over these issues. We are doctors, business people, engineers, scientists, judges, humanitarians, advocates for human rights, and in short a productive segment of the fabric of this great society. Western civilization would not have developed without the influence of the Arab civilization (just think of the bridge and continuity that the Arab civilization had between ancient European civilizations and the renaissance of western civilization after the "Dark Ages"), Shaheen says.

"The Instant TV Arab Kit "

"It is generally well recognized that Arabs have come under a renewed focus as the villains of Hollywood, the latest in a series of enemies threatening the foundations of American society and values. Arabs have been represented as villains since the dawn of Hollywood era, and recent stereotypes of Arabs abound, as terrorists with political aims, religious zealots, and uni-dimensional, or even portrayals of submissive, helpless women. There is some evidence, however, of an emerging voice in American entertainment that questions the negative and value laden representation of Arabs", Professor Jack Shaheem explained.

Jack Shaheen has initiated a dialogue on those issues affecting Arabs with media celebrities." It seems that they all agree on the existence of a prejudicial pattern of portraying Arabs in the Media", Shaheen in his books *"TV Arab"*, *"Arab and Muslim Stereotyping in American Popular Culture "*. " When our view is clouded with stereotypical images it can have a profound effect on our perception of people and their problems. Television creates lasting images. Too few people, these days, take the time to read newspapers and magazines. Most of us depend on television for news!", said Ed Bradley of CBS news.

When asked about how Arabs are portrayed in American media (1), professor Shaheen, so eloquently summed up the decades he devoted watching and monitoring American media as follows:

"Turn to any channel, to any show and they are always full of Arab baddies - billionaires, bombers, belly dancers, etc. An episode of popular entertainment program may be seen by 40 million people the first time it is telecast. With returns, the program may attract a total of 150 million viewers.

Television tends to perpetuate four basic myths about Arabs: they are all fabulously wealthy; they are barbaric and uncultured; they are sex maniacs with a penchant for white slavery; and they revel in acts of terrorism. After all, Arabs, like every national or ethnic group are made up of good decent people, with the usual mix of one-percentners, the bad apple found in any barrel.

Television executives permit the stereotypes because they do not know much about Arabs, or their nations, nor have they taken the time to find out. The image can be best described as " The Instant TV Arab Kit." The kit suitable for most TV Arabs consists of a belly dancer's outfit, headdress (which looks like tablecloth pinched from a restaurant), veils, sunglasses - to add to the faceless mystery, you add oil wells, and limousines driven beside a herd of camels!

This odious phenomenon, the stereotype, is defined as " a standardized conception or image invested with special meaning. But more often than not, the stereotype has other connotations attributed to groups of people, as persona- non-grata!"

1) Author's interview with Shaheen at Cinemayat Arab Film Festival at Berkeley, California, September 2000.

Part II

Profiles of distinguished Arab & Muslim Americans: -
By
Aladdin Elaasar

In Literature & Human Studies:

Poet Naomi Shihab Nye & The Language of Life

Naomi Shihab Nye attracted national attention when she was featured on Bill Moyer's PBS' series *"The Language of Life"* in the summer of 19995 reciting some of her poetry.

Nye's poetry books include *Different ways to pray, Hugging the Jukebox, Red Suitcase, Words Under the Words, This Same Sky, and What Have You Lost.*

Naomi was born in St. Louis, Missouri, in 1952, to a Palestinian father and an American mother. She received her BA from Trinity University in San Antonio, Texas, where she still resides with her family. She is the author of six books of poetry, including Hugging the Jukebox (1982), red Suitcase (19940, and Fuel (1998).

She traveled to the Middle East with the Unites States Information Agency promoting international goodwill through the arts. Nye has received awards from the Texas Institute of Letters, the Carity Randall prize, and the International poetry forum. Her poems and short stories have appeared in various journals and reviews throughout North America, Europe, and the Middle and Far East.

Naomi was recently awarded an honorary doctorate by Saint Mary-of-the-woods College in Indiana. The college is the oldest institution of higher learning for girls in the US. Her poetry is being taught in colleges and schools throughout the United States.

Among the other awards she reaped was the Arab Arts Award at the ADC 17th National convention in Washington, DC on June 2000.

Naomi lives in San Antonio, Texas, with her husband attorney-photographer Michael Nye, and their 13-year-old son, Madison.

In her poem *Sewing, Knitting, Crocheting* she gives tribute to her grandmother who lived in the Old City of Jerusalem, and whom, in her own simplicity had inspired her tremendously...

A small stripped sleeve in her lap,
Navy and white,
Needles carefully whipping in yarn
From two sides.
She reminds me of the wide-angled women filled with calm
I pretended I was related to in crowds.

In the next seat
A yellow burst of wool
Grows into a hat with a tassel.
She looks young to crochet.
I'm glad history isn't totally lost.
Her silver hook dips gracefully.

And when the last time you saw
Anyone sew a pocket onto a gray linen shirt
In public?
On Mother's Day
Three women who aren't together
Conduct delicate operations
In adjoining seats
Between La Guardia and Dallas.
Miraculously, they never speak.
Three different kinds of needles, three snippy scissors,
Everybody else on the plane
Snoozing with The Times.

When the flight attendant
Offers free wine to celebrate, you'd think they'd sit back,
Chat a minute,
Tell who they're making it for,
Trade patterns,
Yes?

But a grave separateness
Has invaded the world.
They sip with eyes shut
And never say
Amazing
Or
May your thread
Never break.

Poet Nathalie Handal and the " *The Poetry of Arab Women*"

Poet Nathalie Handal was born on July 29, 1969. She has lived in the United States, Europe, the Caribbean, and has traveled extensively in the Middle East and Eastern Europe. Poet, writer, playwright, editor and literary researcher, she finished her postgraduate studies in English and Drama at University of London, United Kingdom, her MFA in Creative Writing and Literature at Bennington College, Vermont, her Master of Arts in English and her Bachelor of Arts in International Relations and Communications at Simmons College, Boston. She has taught creative writing workshops worldwide, was one of the Chairs at the Pushkin Club, London (Russian Literary Center) and the Program Director of Summer Literary Seminars in the Dominican Republic.

Her work has appeared in numerous magazines/literary journals in United States, Europe and the Middle East, namely, The Literary Review, Orbis, the Brooklyn Review Ambit, Stone Soup, Sable, Jusoor, Visions-International, Al Jadid, Al Karmel, Post-Gibran (Syracuse University Press), and in various anthologies, most recently, 110 Stories: New York Writes After September 11 (New York University Press), This Bridge We Call Home: Embodying the Spirit of This Bridge Called My Back, ed. Gloria Anzaldua and Ana Louise Keating (New York: Routledge), and she is the title poet of an anthology edited by Naomi Shihab Nye, The Space Between Our Footsteps (Simon & Schuster). Her work has been translated into French, Spanish and Arabic; and Sargon Boulos is currently translating her book of poetry into Arabic. Handal has also interviewed numerous writers including Allen Ginsberg, Charles Simic and Mahmoud Darwish. She has read/performed poetry and given talks on Arab-American and Ethnic-American literature and theatre in the United States, Europe, and the Arab world, namely, La Sorbonne, University of London, McGill University, City University of New York, Yarmouk University, University of Jordan, and numerous other universities and conferences in America and England.

Her poetry book, The Never Field (1999) is published by The Post-Apollo Press, California; and Traveling Rooms (1999), a CD of her poetry and improvisational music by Russian musicians, Vladimir Miller and Alexandr Alexandrov, is produced by ASC Records in the United Kingdom. She is the editor of The Poetry of Arab Women: A Contemporary Anthology (Interlink, Massachusetts, 2000), an Academy of American Poets bestseller. Handal is presently editing two anthologies, Arab-American Literature and Dominican Literature and co-editing along with Tina Chang and Ravi Shankar, Risen from East: An Anthology of South Asian, East Asian and Middle Eastern Poets. She is finishing a play, The Raining Room and her poetry book, Strangers Inside Me, is forthcoming.

Elmaz Abinader: A one-woman-show about memories and identities

Elmaz Abinader is a rare jewel, as her name literally means in Arabic. Elmaz is a sparkling author, poet and performance artist, who was born and raised in America, a product of baby boomers, and roots going back to Lebanon.

In her quest to rediscover her Arab-American heritage, Elmaz has been an influential voice in American Literature for over a decade. Her work, from her memoir to her poetry to her performance work, resonates with the complications of the history of America, its relationship to other cultures and itself.

Abinader makes no secret of her concerns in her writing. She wants to bring the story of Arab-Americans to the literature of inclusion in this country and she uses every mean she can master, from writing to acting.

With an M.F.A. in poetry from Columbia University, where she studied with Philip Levine and a Ph.D. in Creative Writing, Abinader won a Post Doctoral Fellowship in Humanities where she worked with Nobelist Toni Morrison on her first major work, Children of the Roojme, A Family's Journey from Lebanon (Norton, 1991,University of Wisconsin, 1997). Early in her career, she won an Academy of American Poets Award and most recently, A Fulbright Scholarship in Egypt.

Country of Origin, the storytelling performance Abinader has written and performed throughout the States and the Middle East, has won two Drammies,

Portland's Critic's Circle Awards for Theatre. This compelling, three-act, one-woman show portrays the lives of three Arab-American women struggling with cultural conflict and expectations. The original music for Country of Origin was composed by Tony Khalife.

Now with In Country of My Dreams. Abinader brings together a lifelong collection of her poetry. Many of these works have appeared in anthologies and journals and won several awards .Her poetry was first introduced to the public in Grape Leaves, A Century of Arab-American Poetry, edited by Gregory Orfalea and Sharif Elmusa (University of Utah Press, 1988). She has been commissioned to write several pieces, as well: two commemorating the centennial of Gibran Khalil Gibran and another honoring the works of musician Marcel Khalife.

Elmaz Abinader's years as a creative writing teacher has prepared her for public presentation and exiting and accessible performing. Throughout her career, she has focused on the stimulation and growth of young writers-of-color, particularly through her participation in the Houston -Wright Writers' week West and The Voice of Our Nations Foundation.

Country of Origin brings alive the stories of women lost in the cultural shuffle. Three tales are told that reminds us of our dependence on our home and our identities.

Country of Origin brings the audience into the lives of these women who illuminate yet another story of being the "other, the strangers; the foreigners." As Elmaz animates each voice, you travel to her time and join her in the challenge of keeping her identity her own .In her last performance in Chicago, before the Arab-American Writers Conference, Elmaz brought the audience into tears.

In her storytelling poetry, Elmaz speaks for so many people:

My life is filled when hearing them
And knowing the stillness of memory
Must be stirred to find the pleasure in our history.
But I remember I am an Arab, too, looking for a home
Of my own, unoccupied, without siege. I need my first quiet
My pockets empty; my water bottles full and cool.
At night I watch the moon that passed across Lebanon
Before it came to this sky.

Elmaz performances have been met with advanced praise. Her voice will resonate for a long time to come.

Ahlam Shalhout: Rediscovering Stolen Dream

Ahlam Shalhout is one of those rare, prolific and versatile personalities that you do not meet everyday. A mathematician by trade, a passionate cook and dancer, and a poet by hobby.

Ahlam is a first generation Palestinian-American. She holds her undergraduate degree from the University of Connecticut and her MBA from Rensellaer Polytechnic Institute. She carved a robust career with the U. S. Department of the Navy in the sciences and Program Management.

Her writing career began when poetry came to her in her dreams and meditations. Her first book of poetry entitled Recovering Stolen Dreams was published in its first edition in 1999. It is currently in its second edition and is an epic entailing a path of self-realization. Recovering Stolen Dreams unveils a path of emerging self-awareness and self-empowerment through the process of overcoming one's fears.

Her path of healing began in early adulthood when she acknowledged her manic-depressive patterns. Choosing to meditate rather than medicate, she stumbled upon a spiritual path that prescribed holistic healing. Soon afterwards, she began practicing yoga which then lead her to tai chi. She is currently a tai chi instructor in Southeastern Connecticut and a speaker on the benefits of complementary medicine in the form of art therapy, meditation, yoga and tai chi. Drawing on her personal experiences, she leads discussions on exploring one's creativity while overcoming one's fears.

Ahlam goes beyond those boundaries and walls that people draw around themselves. In Recovering Stolen Dreams, Ahlam dives deep down in a journey into the human psyche and hers especially, in a unique autobiographical style. She dives deep into the oceans of hidden memories, and suppressed dreams.

Ahlam is a unique personality. Her background is so colorful. She was born and raised in St. Thomas, US Virgin Islands that gave her that Caribbean flare and passion for life. On the other side, her parents came to the US as immigrants from Palestine with a rich heritage from the Biblical land of Milk and Honey and strict rules of upbringing. The family moved to Connecticut, a move that galvanized Ahlam in her early days with the East Coast way of living and cultural traditions.

31

As if this cultural exposure was not enough, Ahlam made another move in her life that left some imprint on her. She relocated to the West Coast, crossing different time zones, to make California, and San Diego in particular, her home.

In her poetry, Ahlam successfully attempts to bring into harmony, memories of the past, dreams for the future, individual and collective dreams, the scientific and the literary, all married in the most perfect marriage.

In her poetic tradition, life style, and life endeavors, Ahlam is truly a renaissance woman with a clear vision for her life and socially conscious, gasping for a poet's dream of a Utopian paradise that hardly exists on earth, but good to dream of.

"Her poetry weaves a tapestry of emotion set in the past, present and future time. Her gift is the expression that gives birth to a touch of healing. She lures us to touch the pain that propels use into motion. This motion that generates energy for action sets us apart from our self- importance long enough to disentangle the ego from the true self".

Her poetry speaks volumes about everybody's stolen dreams:

Open Gaze
Emerging from the state of the womb
I enter into the state of vulnerability
And fear
I slip into a trough
And emerge into a
Healing..
Understanding..
Knowing ..

The jagged edges of the shell
Are memories of the past?
The struggle is all too familiar.

With those lines, Ahlam touches a familiar cord inside everybody; days of childhood, the warmth of the womb and the process of molding those inner feelings into a common language. As a poet, Ahlam went through that process of virtual pregnancy and delivery that is similar to a good earth that needs to be tiled and watered to bring out the most desired fruit.

Ahlam's *Recovering Stolen Dreams* is an epic that depicts a path of emerging self awareness and self empowerment by overcoming one's fears. The poems have been inspired by the author's dreams and meditations as well as walks in nature. The audio book is used globally for art therapy and psychoanalysis. It is also used by artists of all types as a catalyst for creative expression. It is being integrated in college curricula for women's studies programs in multicultural settings. No wonder: Her name *"Ahlam"* means *"dreams"* in Arabic!

Ray Hanania: First Arab-American Syndicated Columnist

For some people, Ray Hanania looks like a terrorist. When he returned from a vacation outside the U.S., immigration agents in Miami International Airport pulled him out of a long line. But once they cleared him, they allowed him to proceed to the exit, ahead of the crowd.

"When I walk through airports, people look at me funny", he says with a sardonic chuckle. "I don't hate them .I know I look like one of those guys. What can you do?"

Although Ray was born and raised in the U.S., and speaks a pure Chicago accent, yet he fits the "profile"! He has dark eyes, dark complexion, prominent nose, long hair and bushy moustache.

Ray Hanania, 45, is a Palestinian-American journalist, a syndicated columnist, and stand-up comic, was born on Chicago's south side.

His father who came to the U.S. in the 1920s was born in Jerusalem. His mother is from Bethlehem. They are Orthodox Christian Arabs. They spoke Arabic to each other, but English to their children. They also gave them American names; it was important to "fit in".

In 1973, just few months before the Yom Kippur War, Ray joined the U.S. Air Force. One of his fellow servicemen asked him: " If we go to the Middle East to kick some Arab a . . , whose side are you gonna be on?"

About patriotism and loyalty, Ray has a distinctive view: *"I didn't have to buy an American flag to hang in front of my home on the dreadful morning of September 11, 2001. I already owned one. I didn't have to learn a lesson about patriotism, because I consider myself to be a patriot. I wonder who are those people who send me email saying they hate me because I am Arab? I am Arab American and I am proud of that. Both sides of the hyphen. I didn't hesitate to serve this country in*

33

the armed forces. I was about to be drafted while I was in college and I decided not to wait. I enlisted in the U. S. Air Force for four years during the Vietnam War. And when the Vietnam War ended, I received an Honorable Discharge and I then entered the Illinois Air National Guard where I served for nine and one-half years, receiving another Honorable Discharge when I left".

"I learned that patriotism from my father, George Hanania, who immigrated to this country in 1926 and proudly served in the U. S. 5th Army in Europe fighting the Nazis during World War II to defend Democracy, to defeat the enemies of freedom, to free those who were subjugated by Nazism and Facism, including the Jewish people. He did it proudly. My uncle, Moses Hanania enlisted in the U. S. Navy and fought during World War II, also. Those people who hate me because I am Arab are wrong. That's not patriotic. It's un-American. Because I know that I am the image of patriotism in this country and I am not ashamed of that."

In 1976, Ray became a reporter with the South Town Economist, his beat was City Hall. Later, he became a reporter for the Chicago Sun Times and was nominated for a Pulitzer Prize in 1991.He also won a Society of Professional Journalism Column Writing Award in 1985.

Though he established himself with the Chicago media, Ray still has a problem with the American media. "Editors always believed it was all right to send a Jewish reporter to cover issues involving Arabs and Israelis. But they always told me it was improper for me to write about being an Arab, or to cover Arab-Israeli events". Hanania finds that aggravating, biased and unacceptable.

Moreover, according to a public survey done by Urban Strategies Group, most Americans view Arabs negatively. "When you ask them to associate three words with the word Arab, 47 percent said; "terrorists", 11 percent said: "foreigners", and 7 percent said; "store owners". "

In 1992, he quit professional journalism. Now he is the media consultant for many major corporations, a stand-up comic, the publisher of The Arab American View, and executive director of NAAJA, National American-Arab Journalists Association. But he is "greatly disappointed to see the failure of his community to understand how important public relations is to the success of an effort".

This is why he organized the National Professional Literary Conference on Arab-American and Ethnic Writing in Chicago every year. The conference will have a wide variety of speakers, Arabs and non-Arabs, and journalists from overseas sponsored by the U.S. Information Agency. The conference will tackle a wide range of topics; from cultural labor of writing, to the mechanics of getting published, finding an agent, and networking.

By studying debate techniques, Ray believes that in order to tell a story, you have to win over the confidence of your audience first. "If they don't identify with you, they will never hear your message no matter how just or righteous that message is".

Ray went the extra mile to introduce his nagging issues to the public by authoring several books. He wrote: " I'm Glad I look Like a Terrorist: Growing up Arab in America/Humor and Reality in Ethnic American Experience." He also wrote: "The Grape leaves of Wrath", "The Door to God; The Story of Arabs in America and a History of Chicago Arab American Community".

Nihad Dukhan: *The dilemma of the sacred and the experimental*

With the rise of Islam in the seventh century, Arabic calligraphy became recognized as an art form, and elaborate, meticulous and decorative Arabic calligraphy became synonymous with the culture. It is said that the written word is a talisman, and the process of writing is a magic connected not only to the master's technique and skill, but also to his spiritual and moral character. If true, it explains Arabs' fascination with calligraphy. It's hard to find a mosque, a home or a store in a Muslim land that does not have wall hangings of decorative Qur'anic calligraphy. It is believed to drive away evil and invoke blessings and protection.

Arabic calligraphy aims at a mystic balance of meaning and beauty, using strokes that flow from right to left with energy similar to the ecstasy Sufis and dervishes experience. Classic calligraphy can be grouped into two broad categories: "dry styles" (Kufic) created with heavy, horizontal strokes; and "moist styles" written with soft, cursive strokes. Throughout history, masters handed down personal styles of Arabic calligraphy to their devoted pupils.

Therefore, the challenge is greater for rebel calligrapher Nihad Dukhan, who violates the rules of traditional calligraphy. Dukhan has invented his own domain; one so striking that even a non-Arab eye can see the difference. He doesn't fit any of the traditional schools of calligraphy; he does not even try or aspire to.

Unlike traditional calligraphy, Dukhan's designs incorporate the meaning of the written word without compromising the general shape of the letters. His designs, though highly stylized and innovative, remain legible, however, and their tremendous simplicity immediately puts viewers at ease. As he puts it, his

35

goal is "not only to attract the Arabic speaking audience, but to cross barriers and touch other languages and cultures." His works have been exhibited in New York, Chicago, San Francisco, and Washington, D.C.

Dukhan's interest in calligraphy began in the sixth grade when a teacher taught him basic rules, and since then, it has been his way of expressing himself. In 1967, when he was 3, his birthplace Gaza Strip fell to Israeli troops along with neighboring Sinai, the West Bank and the Golan Heights. So as a teenager, he used calligraphy as an elaborate form of graffiti on Gaza's walls, perhaps his only way of rebelling. Maybe that's why he chose words like freedom, mother and pen to experiment with in his calligraphy.

Dukhan later studied at the University of Toledo's College of Engineering in Ohio, where he received his Ph.D. in mechanical engineering in 1996. Soon after graduation, he was appointed a lecturer in Thermo/Fluid Sciences and Visiting Professor of mechanical engineering.

In Medical Discovery:

Dr. Michael DeBakey, an Arab American Heart surgeon pioneer

Dr. Michael Debakey is a renowned Arab American heart surgeon. He performed the first successful coronary bypass operation in 1964, and made the first Dracon artery grafts in the 1950s using his wife's sewing machine, and has led work on artificial heart-assist devices since the early 1960s.

Dr. Debakey is chancellor emeritus of Baylor College of Medicine in Houston, Texas -USA .He has treated statesmen and celebrities like former Russian president, Boris Yeltsin, the Duke of Windsor, and Hollywood actress Marlene Dietrich. After he treated her successfully, Dietrich presented him with an autographed picture of herself; in a very slinky outfit-as Dr. Debakey described it laughingly.

At the age of 91, Dr Debakey continues to pursue a remarkable diversity of interests that long ago catapulted him to the heights of the medical profession. Not only is he a highly respected figure in the medical community worldwide, but he has become a living icon and a "medical statesman", as well.

Dr. Debakey came to Chicago to accept the Global Conference institute's Healthcare Humanitarian Award. Dr. Debakey has always fought for the welfare of his patients and for a more humanitarian treatment against what he describes as " organized medicine". " I have been criticized for a number of things and had to stand my ground. For example, organized medicine and the American Medical Association were strongly opposed to Medicare when President Kennedy first introduced it and was trying to get support. And I openly disagreed with organized medicine - I thought it was a very good thing, the whole concept. And I think that more of that thing is needed to support those who cannot afford medical care. I mean, they are our fellow human beings, and in general, we are a compassionate society. But, I was severely criticized at this time for being a renegade", Dr. DeBakey said.

Dr. DeBakey has also fought for giving access to the public for medical references and records. He led the movement since the late forties to establish the National Library of Medicine, which has already started to give access to the public, and also through the Internet .A review of DeBakey's list of accomplishments, from his innovations in open-heart surgery to his recent pioneering work in the field of telemedicine, is a catalog of many of the greatest accomplishments in the history of medicine.

Dr. Debakey is still keeping a busy schedule. He is involved right now with the development of an artificial heart pump through NASA.

Dr. Farouk El-Baz: The Man Behind Apollo

While circling the moon for the first time during Apollo mission 15, astronaut Alfred Worden said, "After the King's (Farouk's nickname) training, I feel like I've been here before". In the series "From Earth to the Moon", produced by Tom Hanks for HBO, El-Baz role was featured in a segment entitled "The Brain of El-Baz". To his honor, too, ""Star Treck: The Next Generation" featured a shuttlecraft named "El-Baz'.

This notable scientist is Research Professor and Director of the Center for Remote Sensing at Boston University, MA, and USA. He is also Adjunct Professor of Geology at the Faculty of Science, Ain Shams University, and Cairo.

Dr. El-Baz was born on January 1st, 1938, in the Nile Delta town of Zagazig. He received his B.Sc. in Chemistry and Geology from Ain Shams University, Cairo. His excellence in science won him a scholarship at the Missouri School of Mines and metallurgy, where he received his M.S. in 1961, and won membership in the honorary society of Sigma Xi.

He received his Ph.D. in geology from the University of Missouri after conducting an advance research at the Massachusetts Institute of Technology (MIT),

Cambridge, MA. In 1989, Dr. El-Baz received an honorary Doctor of Science degree from the New England College, Henniker, NH.

From 1967 to 1972, El-Baz participated in the Apollo program as Supervisor of Lunar Science planning at NASA headquarters. He became Secretary of the Landing Site Selection Committee for the Apollo missions to the moon. El-Baz also worked as Principal Investigator of Visual Observations and Photography, and Chairman of the Astronaut Training Group.

After the Apollo program ended in 1972, Dr. El-Baz joined the Smithsonian Institute in Washington, DC to establish and direct the Center for Earth and Planetary Studies at the National Air and Space Museum. He was also elected as a member of the Lunar Nomenclature Task Group of the International Astronomical Union.

In 1979, El-Baz visit to the deserts of China was chronicled in the National Geographic and the Explorers Journal, thus earning him a Fellowship at the American Association for the Advancement of Science. He was also featured as an authority in by many News-Media outlets such as: CBS, CNN, BBC, New York Times, Washington Post, Boston Globe, Time and Newsweek.

From 1978 to 1981, El-Baz served as Science Advisor to late Egyptian president Sadat. Now, El-Baz is a senior Advisor to the world Bank/UN World Commission on Water for the 21st century. He authored 12 scientific books.

In Politics & Community Activism:

Her Majesty Queen Noor: *Destined to be a queen*

Her Majesty Queen Noor of Jordan was destined to be a queen. She came from a notable Arab-American family. Her father is Najeeb Halaby, former director of the Federal Aviation Authority in the Kennedy administration. As a child she shook hands with presidents and celebrities, and the stars have been always guiding her to fame and ascendancy.

Queen Noor was born on 23 August 1951 as Lisa Halaby. She went to schools in Washington, D.C., and New York City and graduated from Concord Academy in Massachusetts before entering Princeton University. In 1974, she graduated with a BA in Architecture and Urban Planning.

Destined to be a queen, she met King Hussein of Jordan for the first time in Amman while she was working on a project to develop the Arab Air University. She joined the Royal Jordanian airlines as Director of Planning and design Projects. When she met late King Hussein, it was love at first sight.

Their Majesties, the late King Hussein and Queen Noor were married on 15 June 1978. Their happy marriage lasted till the last day of the life of the late King Hussein. She stood by his bedside till the last moment, and she has been working ever since to preserve the legacy of her late husband and beloved King.

Since her marriage to King Hussein, Queen Noor has been very active on the Jordanian and the international arena working on many humanitarian issues that she's passionate about. Queen Noor has directed and sponsored many projects in the areas of mother and child health care, environmental protection and many others.

Queen Noor is an advocate and patron of Landmines Survivors Network. She patronized the first international conference on landmines. She is also a member of the international advisory board of the Nobel Prize winning International Campaign to Ban Landmines. The queen is also an active member of the International Alert's Women and Peace-building campaign, which focuses on women's role and contribution to peace-building and conflict resolution.

Since her ascendancy to the throne of Jordan as queen, she has played an active role in the fields of arts, social reform, women and family welfare and children in particular. She still maintains that active role today as Mother Queen, as all Jordanians are looking up to her for inspiration, guidance and assistance .The legacy of the late King Hussein lives on through her relentless endeavor to make the world around her a better place to live in.

Secretary of Energy Spencer Abraham:

The last Arab voice in the US Senate

Former Senator Spencer Abraham of Michigan was the only US Senator of Arab origin in the Senate. Since his admittance in the US Senate, Senator Abraham has made a difference with regard to Arab, and Arab American issues that had been historically neglected.

Listening to his speech before the ADC National Convention in Washington, DC, one could not help but wishing that Arab Americans would have more voices representing them with the administration, with the caliber of Senator Abraham. The Senator was not only representing or defending Arab causes in the Senate, but he is a passionate and relentless crusader of human rights issues in the US and issues affecting his constituents in his home state of Michigan, as well.

Since the early nineties, America has witnessed a tide of anti-immigrant sentiments promoted by right wing demagogical politicians who played the tunes of xenophobia to win cheap victories. The recession of the early nineties played a major role in the resurgence of hate groups that felt that immigrant minorities were a threat to their welfare and status, intentionally ignoring the economic facts of that era. The sad thing is that many uneducated, unsuspecting people bought into that. The media also played a major role in demonizing and bashing immigrants, ignoring the fact that America has been built by the hands of early settlers and immigrants, and America has always been a nation of immigrants.

But suddenly, amidst that darkness and the hype about immigration came a voice of reason, along with others. That voice was Senator Spencer Abraham. Proud of his heritage as the grandson of immigrants from the Arab World, Senator Abraham is the Chairman of the Immigration Subcommittee, where he has fought to toughen enforcement measures against illegal immigration while making sure to keep the door to America open to legal immigrants seeking the American dream, contributing and enriching American society.

Splitting with his party, Senator Abraham led the effort to make a strong pro-immigrant case during the Judiciary Committee and full Senate debate over the Immigration Reform Act of 1996, introducing and helping pass an amendment to split the bill to consider legal and illegal immigration separately. Because of his efforts, the amendment passed overwhelmingly.

The Senator also worked to defeat an amendment, which would have reduced legal immigration by cutting overall "family preference" immigration by 60%. Again, thanks to Senator Abraham, the Senate rejected the amendment by a vote of 80-20.

The Senator has fought and crusaded relentlessly for other issues of importance. In one of the biggest legislative victories, the Senator was able to get $15 million earmark for Lebanon to help build the infrastructure. In addition, the Senator was successful in getting report language in the bill that assists the American University in Beirut in the amount of $4 million.

The Senator has been successful in assisting a Michigan humanitarian organization to secure a license to ship humanitarian goods- food, medicine and clothing - to innocent civilian population in Iraq.

For more than four years, Senator Abraham had tried to rectify an injustice that has befallen on immigrant communities, and especially, the Arab community. In 1996, the Senate passed the Anti-Terrorism law after a mass hysteria following the World Trade Center and the Oklahoma bombings. The law, which has been stigmatized unfair and unconstitutional, gives some law enforcement agencies the power to detain immigrants under secret evidence provisions without allowing them, or even their attorneys to know what the charge, or the evidence is! More than twenty immigrants and asylum seekers had fallen victims to that notorious law; most of them were Arabs.

For all his efforts in defending Arab, humanitarian and immigrant causes, Senator Abraham was targeted viciously by anti-immigrant, anti-Arab hate groups that raised millions of dollars and ran negative ads and commercials, claiming that the Senator would like to bring terrorists like Osama Bin Laden to the US, presuming that any Arab immigrant is a potential terrorist, unless proven otherwise. Ironically, that group is called FAIR, the Federation for American Immigration Reform!

An ultra-zealous Nativist, anti-immigrant organization like FAIR with 70,000 supporters and unlimited funds puts defenders of immigrant and human rights under threat. With the rise of such groups, common sense seems to be at leave, and the future of harmony and peace in society at stake.

Senator Abraham lost his seat in that election due to negative and ugly ads, nevertheless he was chosen by President Bush to head the US Department of Energy.

Congressman Nick Joe Rahall, II: Keeper of the Flame, and Friend of the Earth

In addition to serving his constituents in his home state of West Virginia and causes on the national level, Congressman Rahall has been a watchdog for civil liberties of Arab Americans and others. He has been focusing public attention to threats on those rights, including cases from the Gulf War, anti-terrorism legislation and airline passenger profiling regulations that unfairly target Arab Americans.

Congressman Nick Joe Rahall, II of West Virginia is a passionate and relentless crusader for many causes close to his heart.

41

The descendant of Arab immigrants from Lebanon, he led the US Congress in the cause of Palestinian human rights and supported lifting the US travel ban to Lebanon. In 1998, Rahall headed the first Arab American delegation to Lebanon and Syria to promote better understanding and cooperation with USA. In 1996, he led the Arab American Observer Mission to the first Palestinian National elections.

Congressman Rahall was born in May 20, 1949 at Berkley, West Virginia. He received his BA from Duke University in 1971.Rahall has spent most of his career serving his home state of West Virginia over 22 years in the US House of Representatives. Rahall served on the Resources, Transportation &. Infrastructure committees. He has been deeply involved in the development of numerous water resources, Rahall is responsible for many US Army Corps of Engineers flood control and related projects in southern West Virginia including the establishment of the Environmental Infrastructure Program.

Rahall also took on the cause of greater protections for coalfields by twice spearheading legislation to extend the Abandoned Mine Reclamation program, which provides funds to combat health, safety and environmental threats from old mine sites.

He is also a sponsor of legislation to promote the remaining of lands previously mined for coal. He also co-authored the amendment to the Export-Import Bank Reauthorization prohibiting the financing of foreign mining ventures and the National Geologic Mapping Act of 1992.

Numerous states and national organizations have recognized Rahall for his work. He received the 1991 Citizen's Coal Council Award", the 1996 "Keeper of the Flame", and "Friend of the Earth"" Outstanding Environmental Stewardship".

In the arena of transportation, Congressman Rahall received the American Road & Transportation Builders Association Award in 1997, the Public Service Award in 1997, and the Highway Safety Leader Award.

In addition to serving his constituents in his home state of West Virginia and causes on the national level, Congressman Rahall has been a watchdog for civil liberties of Arab Americans and others. He has been focusing public attention to threats on those rights, including cases from the Gulf War, anti-terrorism legislation and airline passenger profiling regulations that unfairly target Arab Americans.

Politics of Exclusion: James Zoghby and unifying Arab American Community

James Zoghby's mission is to unify and bring together the Arab American community, as an influential force on the American arena, a task that many people have doomed impossible on the American arena, a task that many people have doomed impossible. But James Zoghby has no illusions about it.

James Zoghby is the founder and president of the Arab American Institute that since 1985 has led the efforts to secure the Arab American Political empowerment. He hosts " A Capital View", a weekly TV-call in program, broadcast by the Arab Network of America and simulcast by the Middle East Broadcasting Company, MBC.

Since 1992, Zoghby has been writing a weekly column on the US politics for major newspapers in the Arab World. He is also a lecturer and a commentator on Arab issues who frequently appears on TV and radio networks.

Dr. Zoghby received his doctorate degree from Temple University in 1975. He received his BA from Le Moyne College, which named him outstanding alumnus, and later awarded him an honorary doctorate in 1997.

Zoghby, a descendant from Arab immigrants and a third Arab American generation, became involved in Arab American affairs by reflex, as he describes it. Back in the seventies, as he grew up as a kid in upstate New York, he was working with a precinct captain passing out cards at the polls on Election Day. Later, he became involved in the civil rights movement and anti-war movements. One day, he was speaking at an anti-war rally and somebody shouted: " Why are they letting the Arabs speak? Thanks to that person, from that day on, it was the turning point that made James Zoghby decide to dedicate himself to Arab causes.

Arab immigrants to the US, who came after 1967, were more vocal about Arab issues more than other previous Arab waves of immigrants that wanted simply to blend in.

In the Mid-1970s James was pondering means of making Arab issues an American concern. In 1984, he had an opportunity to work with the Reverend Jesse Jackson for his presidential campaign as a deputy campaign manager. James learned a lot of from Jackson. He learned how to frame issues, how to mobilize a constituency, and above all, how to maintain a positive attitude.

But James Zoghby has always tried to assure the bi-partisanship of the Arab American Institute. He feels that Arabs need to be involved in the political arena in order to be able to be fairly represented. They need to be in both major political parties, in the Democratic and the Republican parties, alike. For example, Arab Americans should not exclude themselves from the Republican Party, especially after the resurgence of right wing, Nativist and isolationist currents inside the party that can be a threat to immigrants and minorities.

By 1992, Arab Americans were excluded from participating in election campaigns and contributions." There was a point when the Democrats were even returning Arab American campaign contributions. In fact, there were those who wanted to keep us out of the Clinton Campaign, but we fought and we got in. Bill Clinton recognized us from day one. Actually, it was Senator Joe Liberman who called George Stephanopoulos, who invited me in ", Zoghby explains.

James Zoghby, chaired the Ethnic Council in the Democratic Party, and also chaired the ethnic leadership meetings in the White House with President Clinton. For Zoghby, Clinton had been the first American president that gave Arab issues a priority, attention and understanding. He had shown more sensitivity and dedication to minority and ethnic groups in the US more than his predecessors have.

For the past three decades, Dr. Zoghby has been involved in a full range of Arab American issue. A co-founder and chairman of the Palestine Human Rights Campaign in the late 1970s, he later co-founded and served as the Executive Director of the American-Arab Anti-Discrimination Committee. In 1982, he co-founded Save Lebanon, Inc., a private non-profit, humanitarian and non-sectarian relief organization which funds health care for Palestinian and Lebanese victims of war, and other social welfare projects in Lebanon. In 1985, Zoghby founded AAI.

In 1993, following the signing of the Israeli-Palestinian peace accord in Washington, he was asked by Vice President Al Gore to lead Builders for Peace, a private sector committee to promote U.S. business investment in the West Bank and Gaza. In his capacity as co-president of Builders, Zoghby frequently traveled to the Middle East with delegations led by former Vice President Gore and late Secretary of Commerce Ron Brown. In 1994, with former U.S. Congressman Mel Levine, his colleague as co-president of Builders, Zoghby led a U.S. delegation to the signing of the Israeli-Palestinian agreement in Cairo. Zoghby also chaired a forum on the Palestinian economy at the Casablanca Economic Summit in 1994. After 1994, through Builders, Zoghby worked with a number of US agencies to promote and support Palestinian economic development, including AID, OPIC, USTDA, and the Departments of State and Commerce.

Dr. Zoghby has also been personally active in U.S. politics for many years. Most recently, Zoghby was elected a co-convener of the National Democratic Ethnic Coordinating Committee (NDECC), an umbrella organization of Democratic Party leaders of European and Mediterranean descent. On September 24, 1999, the NDECC elected Dr. James Zoghby as its representative to the DNC's Executive Committee.

A lecturer and scholar on Middle East issues, U.S.-Arab relations, and the history of the Arab American community, Dr. Zoghby appears frequently on television and radio. He has appeared as a regular guest on all the major network news programs. After hosting the popular "A Capital View" on the Arab Network of America for several years, he now hosts " on Abu Dhabi Television, which can be seen Friday afternoons from 2:00-3:00pm EST.

Since 1992, Dr. Zoghby has also written a weekly column on U.S. politics for the major newspapers of the Arab world. His columns are currently published in 14 Arab countries. He has authored a number of books including two recent publications, "*What Ethnic Americans Really Think*" and "*Arabs: What They Believe and What They Value Most.*"

Dr. Zoghby has testified before U.S. House and Senate committees, has been guest speaker on a number of occasions in the Secretary's Open Forum at the U.S. Department of State, and has addressed the United Nations and other international forums. He recently received a Distinguished Public Service Award from the U.S. Department of State "in recognition of outstanding contributions to national and international affairs."

Dr. Zoghby is also active professionally beyond his involvement with the Arab American community. He is a board member of the human rights organization Middle East Watch and currently serves as a member of the Council on Foreign Relations. In January 2001, he was selected by the President to be a member of the Central Asian-American Enterprise Fund and serves on its Board of Directors. Additionally, he recently attained a position with polling firm Zoghby International as Senior Analyst.

In 1975, Dr. Zoghby received his doctorate from Temple University's Department of Religion, where he studied under the Islamic scholar Dr. Ismail al-Faruqi. He was a National Endowment for the Humanities Post-Doctoral Fellow at Princeton University in 1976, and on several occasions was awarded grants for research and writing by the National Endowment for the Humanities, the National Defense

Education Act, and the Mellon Foundation. Dr. Zoghby received a Bachelor of Arts from Le Moyne College. In 1995, Le Moyne awarded Zoghby an honorary doctoral of laws degree, and in 1997 named him the college's outstanding alumnus.

Donna Shalala: Serving with a Big Heart

Former US secretary of health and human services, Donna Shalala is not only the first woman to hold that high cabinet " position, but she is the first woman of Arab origin to be elevated to that height and recognition by a U.S. administration, as well.

In 1993, Donna Shalala was selected by President Bill Clinton to be secretary of health and human services. A dynamic and charismatic leader, she outlined five major policy initiatives for her first year: revision of health-care financing, expansion of the Head Start program for preschool children, universal childhood immunizations, expansion of AIDS research, and welfare reform.

Donna Shalala was not only the first woman to hold that high cabinet position, but she was the first woman of Arab origin to be elevated to that height and recognition by a US administration, as well.

Shalala was born in Cleveland, Ohio, in 1941 and educated at Western College. After graduating in 1962, she served for two years in the Peace Corps in Iran, and then returned to the United States to attend Syracuse University. After graduating from Syracuse in 1970, she taught political science at Bernard Baruch College in New York City, then taught politics and education at Columbia Teacher's College.

In 1975 Shalala became director and treasurer of the Municipal Assistance Corporation, which helped reverse New York City's financial collapse. In 1977 she became assistant secretary for policy research and development at the Department of Housing and Urban Development (HUD) in Washington, D.C. At HUD she promoted women's issues, working toward the creation of battered women's shelters, mortgage credits for women, and anti-discrimination measures.

In 1980, at the age of 39, she became president of Hunter College. At Hunter College, she added to her reputation as a committed humanist by overseeing dramatic increases in the percentages of female and minority faculty and administrators.

Shalala was born in Cleveland, Ohio, in 1941 and educated at Western College. After graduating in 1962, she served for two years in the Peace Corps in Iran, and then returned to the United States to attend Syracuse University. After graduating from Syracuse in 1970, she taught political science at Bernard Baruch College in New York City, then taught politics and education at Columbia Teacher's College.

In 1975 Shalala became director and treasurer of the Municipal Assistance Corporation, which helped reverse New York City's financial collapse. In 1977 she became assistant secretary for policy research and development at the Department of Housing and Urban Development (HUD) in Washington, D.C. At HUD she promoted women's issues, working toward the creation of battered women's shelters, mortgage credits for women, and anti-discrimination measures.

In 1980, at the age of 39, she became president of Hunter College. At Hunter College, she added to her reputation as a committed humanist by overseeing dramatic increases in the percentages of female and minority faculty and administrators.

In 1988 she became the chancellor of the University of Wisconsin at Madison, one of the largest universities in the United States. Confronted by a campus afflicted with racial tension, she

As one of the nation's foremost advocates for children and families, Shalala served on the board of the Children's Defense Fund, becoming its chair in 1992.

Most recently, she co-chaired the U.S. delegation to the United Nations Fourth World Conference on Women in Beijing. In addition, Shalala is spearheading the Clinton administration's initiatives in welfare and healthcare reform; preschool immunization; women's health; biomedical research; and AIDS research, treatment, and prevention.

Congresswoman Pat Danner: Fighting for Ordinary People

In recognition of her commitment to saving taxpayer dollars, Congresswoman Danner has been presented with the Grace Caucus Award by Citizens Against Government Waste (CAGW). CAGW commended Danner on her" front-line work in the fight to restore fiscal responsibility to the federal government.

Congresswoman Pat Danner was rated by Money Magazine as one of the most outstanding members of Congress when it comes to understanding pocketbook issues and standing up for working Americans' financial interests. Of 435 members of the US House, Danner tied for 9th best on "pocketbook issues" in an analysis conducted by Money Magazine".

In recognition of her commitment to saving taxpayer dollars, Congresswoman Danner has been presented with the Grace Caucus Award by Citizens Against Government Waste (CAGW). CAGW commended Danner on her" front-line work in the fight to restore fiscal responsibility" to the federal government.

Congresswoman Danner was born January 13, 1934, in Louisville, KY. She attended public schools in Bevier, and graduated cum laude from Northeast Missouri State University (B.A., in political science). She worked as a District Assistant to Congressman Jerry Utton, 1973 - 1976. She was appointed to a sub-cabinet position in the Carter Administration in 1977. She was also the first and only woman to serve as chair of a regional commission in 1982. In 1992, Danner was elected to the US House of Representatives.

Danner achieved many legislative victories during the first session of the current 106th Congress aimed at providing millions of Americans an access to emergency assistance, and solving one age-old problem.

One of the most memorable moments for Congresswoman Danner came during the session of the 106th Congress when House Speaker J. Dennis Hastert recognized her with a unique honor. Hastert commended Danner for her outstanding bi-partisan by an overwhelming majority in the House of Representatives.

Committed to the philosophy of fiscal responsibility, Congresswoman Danner established " The Danner Scholarship Award" for constituents who wish to continue their educational endeavors.

The Late Dr. Hala Salaam Maksoud: Giving to the last moment

The late Dr. Hala Salaam Maksoud was the former President of the American-Arab Anti-Discrimination Committee (ADC), the largest Arab-American national grassroots organization in the United States. She has been actively involved with ADC since its inception in 1980, having worked closely with the founder, Sen. James Abourezk, and with other board members. Throughout her professional life, she worked relentlessly for the rights of her fellow Arab Americans.

Dr. Maksoud held a Doctorate in political theory, and a Master's Degree in government from Georgetown University, as well as a Master's Degree in mathematics from the American University of Beirut. She taught courses on international relations and the Middle East at George Mason University and on Arab women's issues at Georgetown University.

She had also published numerous articles in American journals and the Arab press, as well as several monographs. In her effort to educate the public about Arab causes, she lectured extensively on the Arab world, the condition of Arab Americans, Arab women, Islamic political thought, and the Arab-Israeli conflict. She has appeared on numerous television and radio shows in the United States, Europe and the Arab world.

As a prominent and active member of her community, Dr. Maksoud held the position of Secretary of the American Committee on Jerusalem, Treasurer of the Committee for the Preservation of Palestinian Heritage, past president of the Association of Arab-American University Graduates, as well as a founding member and past president of the Arab Women's Council. She was also on the advisory board of many journals on the Middle East.

Dr. Maksoud's activities and accomplishments had earned her a reputation as a prominent community leader and an advocate for the rights of Arab Americans and the Arab peoples.

Dr. Ziad J. Asali: ADC president: Championing the Arab-American Rights Cause

Ziad J. Asali, M.D., is the President of the American-Arab Anti-Discrimination Committee (ADC), the largest Arab-American grassroots civil rights organization in the United States. Dr. Asali is also the Chairman of the American Committee on Jerusalem (ACJ), which was founded in 1995 to develop and promote educational and informational activities on the heritage and future of Jerusalem.

Dr. Asali has been a long-time activist on Arab-American issues. He served as the President of the Arab-American University Graduates (AAUG) from 1993-1994, and was a member of the Board of Directors of the Council for the National Interest (CNI), and as a member of the Chairman's Council of ADC since 1982.

Dr. Asali has contributed and written for the *Los Angeles Times, Detroit Free Press, Washington Post, Boston Globe, Miami Herald* and *Daily Star.* He has provided television commentary and interviews for CNN, Hardball, MSNBC, FOX News, BBC, Voice of America and numerable syndicated cable programs. Dr. Asali has also appeared on several Arabic television networks, including Al Jazeera, Nile

TV, ART, Egyptian TV, Abu Dhabi TV and the Dubai satellite channel. Newspaper interviews in Arabic include *Al-Hayat, Al-Ahram, Al-Raii, Jordan Times* and *Akhbar Al-Arab*. In addition, he is a regular speaker at international conferences, Arab-American conventions, academic groups and community gatherings.

Asali is the author of several publications that include: *"Coronary Artery Spasm Causing Myocardial Infarction"* (1983), *"Expedition to Jerusalem"* (1990), *"Zionist Studies of the Crusades"* (1992) and *"From Crusades to Zionism"* (1993).

Dr. Asali is in continuous contact with high-ranking foreign policy makers, Middle East leaders and other officials in Washington, D.C.

Dr. Asali was born in Jerusalem, where he completed his elementary and secondary education. He received a B.S. from the American University of Beirut (AUB) in 1963 and an M.D. from AUB Medical School in 1967. He completed his residency in Internal Medicine and Endocrinology at the Latter Day Saints Hospital in Salt Lake City, Utah.

Dr. Asali practiced medicine in Saudi Arabia and Jerusalem before returning to the US in 1973. Dr. Asali was the Medical Director, Laboratory Director, and Chairman of the Board at the Christian County Medical Clinic and St. Vincent Memorial Hospital in Taylorville, Illinois, until he retired in 2000. He remains licensed to practice medicine in Illinois, Virginia, and Washington, D.C. Dr. Asali has certifications from the Educational Council for Foreign Medical Graduates, the American Board of Internal Medicine and the American College of Physicians. He is a member of several medical societies such as the American Medical Association, the American Society of Internal Medicine and the American Academy of Medical Director.

Dr. Shibli Sawalha, GOP committeeman

Dr. Shibli Mansour Sawalha Born in Madaba/Jordan 1936 immigrated to Palestine 1945 and completed his secondary education in Jerusalem. 1965 he came to Chicago, Illinois as a student at DePaul University to study Medicine. He shifted careers from premed to management. He received his Master degree in health care management from Roosevelt University in 1973 and his Doctorate degree in Health care management and Hospital Administration in 1980 from Century University in California.

He became active in Arab American Activities and after graduation in 1968 he was elected as president of the Arab American Congress. During his tenure with the assistant of Dr. Bassiouni, R. Ihasan Diab, Dr. Mahdi and Dr. Abu Lugud, a conference on the Palestinian struggle was conducted for three days with many notable speakers and academics to highlight the Palestinian issues. That conference exposed to the American media the plight of the Palestinians and their right for arm struggle and the establishment of a homeland.

In that year Dr. Clovis Maksoud was invited at a fund raising at the University of Illinois Technology on the same day the astronaut landed on the moon.1976 was the year he became involved in State and National politics by joining the ranks of elected officials in Will County. He was elected as vice president of the homeowner association as then as a GOP committeeman in Homer Township. He was active in the Arab American Community by organizing the Arab American Republican Federation in 1980. The Arab American Community became a member of the Heritage Council and the Board of the Ethnics in Illinois with the help of then Senator Judy Topinka. The Arab American Republican Federation was active in the campaign to elect Ronald Regan as President. The Arab American community received the personal thanks of President Regan through a meeting with his Daughter Maurine who delivered the personal message.

Their first activity locally was in the campaign to elect a Cook county Sheriff and for Governor. It was a successful campaign and James Ogrady was elected as the Republican Sheriff. Governor James Thompson was elected Governor. Dr. Sawalha worked with the Chairman of the city of Chicago GOP The Hon. Lou Casper, Former Governor Ogelbvy and State Chairman Adam Smith during that campaign and introduce them to the Arab American community by attending the ADC function. Jim Edgar was the first Secretary of State and an American top official to attend our functions. In 1980-85 many notable elected officials from the Mayor, Senators, State Representatives and Aldermen began attending our functions and seeking our support.

In March of 2002 he sponsored a conference for Arab American Journalist in the US with Mr. Ray Hanania a Journalist and an Arab Activist to discuss the effect of 9/11 on the Moslems and the Arab community as a whole. It was a very successful event with over 35 journalists from around the USA, BBC, WBM, NBC and Al Jazeera TV.

Dr. Sawalha currently is a GOP committeeman in Will County, A member of the Finance Central Committee and a member of the Candidate Selection committee. He is the Chairman of the Arab American Republican Federation and Campaign coordinator for Jim Ryan in Homer Township.

He is married to Manuela, his wife since 1969 and has two children and one grand-daughter. His daughter Tara is an attorney graduated from Ohio State University in 1996, and his son Mark a civil engineer graduated from the University of Illinois on Champaign 1997.

Imam Senad Agic: A Community and Spiritual Leader

Imam Senad Agic is a very prolific person: He's a community leader and organizer, a Muslim scholar, a writer/commentator, and a lexicographer, as well. He was born in the town of Novi Travnik in central Bosnia-Hercegovina. After receiving his Islamic education at the oldest educational institution in the Balkans (founded in 1537), Gazi Husrev Beg Medresa, he received his higher education at the University of Sarajevo, where he studied Islamic civilization and the languages of Arabic, Persian, Turkish and their literature.

In 1988 he published his comprehensive collection of names used by Muslims emphasizing the importance of personal names in the preservation of the Islamic identity. (This work has been very popular since the war started and it has entered its fourth printing).

At the Headquarters of the Islamic Union of Bosnia-Herzegovina, Croatia and Slovenia (1985-1989); Publishing Department; Imam Agic worked on the Arabic text of the first (Serbo-Croatian-Bosnian)-Arabic dictionary of 50,000 words; edited many texts published that involved Arabic language; published comprehensive collection of names used by Muslims with introduction on the importance of personal names in the preservation of the Islamic identity. This work entered its sixth printing.

In 1989, Imam Agic was appointed as Imam, Spiritual leader and Administrative director to the Islamic Cultural Center of Greater Chicago (1989-to this day). Later on, he was chosen by the Supreme Authority of the Islamic Community in Bosnia-Herzegovina to be Head Imam of the Bosnian Muslim community in the USA.

Imam Agic is the author of a book and 29 scholarly articles, in addition to many translation works and interviews on titles and topics such as: the Qur'an, Arabic Literature, Religion and Violence in Bosnia, Mystical Sufi Traditions, September 11 and the Struggle for the Soul of Islam. He discussed peace and conflict within and among religions on "National Public Radio, NPR", on the Voice of America", "Free Europe", "Deutche Walle"; and was consultant and participant in the 2001 ABC Oprah Winfrey Show on Islam. He also spent years on studying the issue of inter-religious and intercultural representation with a focus on Bosnia and Israeli/

Palestinian conflict, and worked with Muslim and non-Muslim scholars, clerics and students to find a way that the human face of Muslims and Islam, the diversity of viewpoint that humanizes religion, may be better communicated.

Since his arrival to Chicago in 1989, Imam Agic has initiated, promoted, and participated in interfaith activities both within and outside of Northbrook. His continuous and laudable interfaith efforts have attracted more than one thousand visitors to ICC every year. Furthermore, these interfaith activities have led to some important notable events. In 1996, a Jewish synagogue in Northbrook was invited to use ICC for their services while they were in the process of constructing a new synagogue for their use. In 1998, while hosting the Catholic-Muslim Dialogue, Cardinal Francis George, Archbishop of Chicago, participated in the dialogue and breaking the fast during the month of Ramadan at ICC. The Cardinal is planning to make a return visit during the month of Ramadan in 2003. The ICC held this year's annual Northbrook Interfaith Thanksgiving Service on November 27, 2002.

Imam Agic was elected vice-president of the Northbrook Clergy Association this year. He will serve as president of the Northbrook Clergy Association in 2003. He is also a member of the Islamic Supreme Council of America, Interfaith Council of Parliament of the World Religions in Chicago, and is a founding member of Averroes Academy in Northbrook and the Islamic Association of Bosniaks in North America, and Vice president of Northbrook Clergy Association.

Professor Cherif Bassiouni: An International Legal Expert

Human Rights versus War Crimes

Professor Cherif Bassiouni is a renowned and distinguished legal expert and authority on International Law. He is a teacher of Law at DePaul University since 1964; a 1970 Fulbright-Hays Professor of International Criminal Law at the University of Freiburg in Germany; a 1971 Visiting Professor of Law at N.Y.U.; and a 1972 Guest Scholar at the Woodrow Wilson International Center for Scholars, Washington, D.C. He is non-resident Dean of The International Institute of Higher Studies in Criminal Sciences (Siracusa, Italy) since 1976.

He studied law in the three major legal systems of the world: civil law, common law, and Islamic Sharia, at Dijon University, France, The University of Geneva Switzerland, and the University of Cairo, Egypt. His degrees are: J.D., Indiana University; LL.M., John Marshall Law School; S.J.D., George Washington University. In 1981, he was awarded the degree: Doctor of Law Honoris causa (Dottore in Giurisprudenza) from the University of Torino, Italy, and in 1988, the degree: Doctor of Law Honoris causa (Docteur d'Etat en Droit) conferred at The University of Pau, France.

He is the author of twenty-two books on U.S. Criminal Law and International and comparative Criminal Law and over 100 law review articles. Active in several scholarly and professional organizations, he has served as the Secretary-General of the International Association of Penal Law since 1974; chairman of the International Law Section of the Illinois State Bar Association for several years, and chairman of several committees of the Chicago Bar and American Bar Associations.

A frequent lecturer at distinguished universities in the U.S. and abroad, he has also been a frequent U.N. consultant: Fifth U.N. Congress on Crime Prevention (1975) where he was elected Honorary Vice-President of the Congress; Sixth U.N. Congress (1980) where he presented a Draft International Criminal Code; U.N. Division of Human Rights in 1980-1981 for which he prepared a Draft Statute for the Creation of an International Criminal Court; Seventh U.N. Congress, for which he chaired two preparatory meetings of committees of experts in 1983-1984. He also served in 1978 as co-chairman of the committee of experts, which prepared the U.N. Draft Convention of the Prevention and Suppression of Torture, and chairman of the committee of experts, which prepared the U.N. Draft Convention on the Prevention of Unlawful Human Experimentation.

He was also a consultant to the Departments of State and Justice on projects relating to international traffic in drugs (1973) and control of terrorism (1975 and 1978) and the defense of the U.S. hostages in Iran (1979).

Among the distinctions and awards he received are: 1956, Order of Merit, Egypt; 1977, Order of Merit, Italy (Rank of Commendatore); 1978, Order of Merit, Italy, (Rank of Grand' Ufficiale); 1984, Order of Sciences, Egypt), (Rank of First Class). Also among others: 1967, Outstanding Citizen of the Year of Metropolitan Chicago; 1970, Outstanding Educator of America; 1973, Gold Medal of the Italian Press (Rome, Italy).

He has been admitted to practice the law in Illinois and Washington, D.C. and before the United States Supreme Court, the Second, Fifth, Seventh, and Eleventh Circuits of the U.S. Courts of Appeals, the United States Court of Military Appeals, and the United States Court of International Trade. Since 1973 he has served as member of the Board and President of the MidAmerican Arab Chamber of Commerce.

Dr. Seema Imam: Fighting Prejudice with Education!

"If ever in my life I have seen fear, I see fear now," said Seema Imam, who is the vice president of the Hickory Hills-based Muslim Civil Rights Center, in Illinois.

Imam, a Caucasian American Muslim convert, said a stranger spat on her and swore at her in front of her children a few days after Sept. 11. Imam said she did not report the incident to police because she was embarrassed. She was featured by the Chicago Tribune twice since 9/11.

Dr. Seema Imam was born in Oklahoma and raised in downstate Illinois as a Methodist. Early in her college life she embraced Islam and since the 70s has been leading in a variety of community development projects. She has a Bachelor of Arts in Elementary Education, a Master of Arts degree in Reading, a Master of Arts degree in Educational Administration, and a Doctorate in Curriculum and Social Inquiry, which she completed at National-Louis University located in Evanston, Illinois.

Dr. Seema Imam has nearly 30 years of experience in education. She is currently instructing and supervising teachers in the Master of Arts Program at National-Louis University where she has worked for the last 7 years. She teaches History and Philosophy of American Education, as well as Practicum courses, Student Teaching seminars, student teaching supervision and Reading and Language Arts Methods. She has more than 16 years experience as a public school teacher in Chicago public school system and was the first and founding principal of Universal School in Bridgeview from 1990 to 1995. The Universal School is an Islamic School, grades Pre-K to High School located in Bridgeview, Illinois. Seema has helped various schools in their development and is currently working on a school project in Northwest Indiana.

Seema has volunteered extensively in citywide events both in the Muslim Community and the Community at large. She is the Vice President of the Muslim Civil Rights Center and the President of the Organization of Islamic Speakers, Midwest. Dr. Imam serves as a Reader for the Quran Project, a Quran translation and interpretation nearing completion, by Dr. Ahmad Zaki Hammad, a premiere Islamic scholar and President of the Quranic Literacy Institute. She is a human rights commissioner for the past 7 years and is appointed until 2005 by the Mayor of Hickory Hills. She serves on the Board for the Independent Coalition for Non-Public Schools. She served on the Catholic-Muslim Dialogue Committee project and was a founding member of UMAA. Dr. Imam has worked with international schools in staff development; teacher recruitment and curriculum as well as helping school officials in Kuwait achieve school accreditation. Seema recently participated in a 3 day International Diversity Training session for United Auto Workers and Delphi Automobile Parts union employees.

Seema has her doctorate in Curriculum and Social Inquiry. Her Doctoral Dissertation was entitled, "Six Muslims Living in the Midwest in the Presence of the Negative Public Curriculum". It includes experiences of Muslims living their lives within the mass media's depiction of Muslims as well as a discussion of how Muslim children are effected by the mass media and the public curriculum when they go to public schools.

Seema is the mother of five children; Aisha, Khalid, Yousuf, Mujahid and Ibrahim and grandmother of two grandsons; Hamza Ghori and Samir Ozaki. She strives to enhance the image of Muslims and to rectify the social injustices experienced by many American minorities. She works effectively with her husband, Syed Shahab Imam in various educational and community projects. She believes that education is key to making social change, and she is very active in public engagements where she speaks on various educational topics and aspects of Islam.

Dr. Sayyid Muhammad Syeed, Secretary General of the Islamic Society of North America (ISNA),

Dr. Sayyid M. Syeed, Secretary General of the Islamic Society of North America (ISNA), a national community leader, is chief executive officer of this Plainfield, IN, a suburban Indianapolis-based national umbrella organization which has more than 300 affiliates all over the U.S. and Canada.

A naturalized American citizen, Dr. Syeed obtained his Ph.D. in Socio-linguistics from the Indiana University at Bloomington, Indiana, in 1984.

As President of the Muslim Students Association of USA & Canada (1980-1983), he pioneered its transformation into the Islamic Society of North America (ISNA). During 1984-1988, he was Secretary General of the International Islamic Federation of Student Organizations (IIFSO) in which capacity he traveled widely through the former Soviet Union, and Europe, Africa, Asia, the Caribbean, and South America.

In his last appointment, Dr. Syeed was Director of Academic Outreach (1984-1994) at the International Institute of Islamic Thought, near Washington, D.C. Dr.

Syeed has been General Secretary of the Association of Muslim Social Scientists (AMSS), a national professional organization founded 31 years ago.

Dr. Syeed, one of the founders of the quarterly American Journal of Islamic Social Sciences (AJISS), served as its Editor-in-Chief (1984-1994). During his tenure AJISS grew from a twice a year to a quarterly publication, simultaneously published from Washington, D.C., Kuala Lumpur, Malaysia, Islamabad, Pakistan, and in Turkish from Istanbul, Turkey. Today AJISS has acquired a respectable niche in academia and is quoted with recognition in professional and scholarly researches. It is widely recognized as the foremost journal in its field globally. Dr. Syeed is also a member of the Board of Advisory Editors for the Middle East Affairs Journal and a member of the Board of Advisors for the Council on American-Islamic Relations (CAIR). In his present position Dr. Syeed is also chairman of the Editorial Board of Islamic Horizons, the flagship magazine of ISNA, a position he held previously during 1982-1984.

Dr. Syeed has been actively involved in fostering understanding among the world's religions and has participated in interfaith dialogues at different levels in the U.S.A. and Canada. A frequent speaker at interfaith dialogues, he has served as a member of the Board of Trustees of the Council for a Parliament of the World's Religions.

In recognition of his contribution to inter-religious understanding and harmony, Dr. Syeed was awarded an honorary doctorate of letters by the Graduate Theological Foundation, Donaldson, Indiana on May 4, 2001. He received the Lifetime Achievement Award for distinguished service in furthering the Islamic tradition in North America and for promoting inter-religious understanding and harmony from the Catholic Heritage Foundation, Louisville, Kentucky on November 18, 2001.

On January 5, 2002, Mr. Frank O'Bannon, the Governor of Indiana, in his State of the State Address, recognized Dr. Syeed's "work to educate Americans about the Muslim faith in the wake of the September 11 terror attacks, along with your life's work to encourage tolerance and racial healing has marked you as a great leader in Indiana."

Dr. Syeed has been invited to speak on Muslim and Islamic issues on the national TV channels, NBC, CBS, CBN, ABC. He was interviewed on PBS on the McNeill-Lehrer Report and appeared on the "Today Show" and CNN's "Crossfire" and on the national televisions of Turkey, Malaysia, Sudan, Pakistan and Saudi Arabia on matters related to Islam and Islam in America.

Part III: Appendices

Appendix I

WHITE PAPER: PRELIMINARY REPORT ON HATE CRIMES AGAINST ARABS AND MUSLIMS IN THE UNITED STATES

By
William J. Haddad
Executive Director
ARAB-AMERICAN BAR ASSOCIATION OF ILLINOIS, INC.

Introduction

On September 11, 2001, using hijacked airplanes as weapons on targets in New York City and Washington D.C., terrorists attacked the United States of America, destroying the lives and property of American citizens. The murder victims included citizens, nationals, rescue workers and policemen of Arabic ancestry or of the Muslim faith.

Since it is believed that the terrorists were Middle Eastern and/or Muslim, civil disturbances have erupted throughout the United States targeting Americans of Arabic descent, Americans of the Islamic faith, and Americans who were stereotyped as "looking like" Arab/Muslim-Americans. Some of the disturbances erupted during sanctioned civil marches at or near mosques in the Chicago area and Dearborn, Michigan. Others were pre-meditated criminal acts of vandalism, arson, and murder---three such murders victimized persons who looked like Arab or Muslim Americans, but in fact were not (i.e. A Sikh man in New Mexico, a Pakistani man in Texas, and a Coptic man in California).

Since the targets of these crimes were Americans of Arabic ancestry and Muslims---or persons who resemble them, the Arab American Bar Association of Illinois made a preliminary investigation to determine the extent of the hate crimes, the response of government and media, the likelihood of an escalation of the violence, and the effect all of this may have on the civil liberties of the ethnic and religious minorities loosely characterized as Arab Americans and Muslim Americans.

This is not the first report of its kind. This Association issued a report in 1992 in the aftermath of a civil disturbance that followed a world championship basketball game in Chicago. After the completion of a telecast depicting a Chicago sports victory, wide scale civil disturbances erupted on the west and south sides of Chicago. Many retail establishments were looted, vandalized, and burned during this disturbance. 139 Arab-American owned businesses were victimized, accounting for a majority of the $14 million in losses from the disturbance.

II.
Arab/Muslim Americans in the United States of America

According to the Economist (10/14/00) and the Washington Post (10/16/00), there are 3.5 million Arab-Americans in the United States "unusually concentrated in industrial states such as New Jersey, Pennsylvania, Ohio, Illinois and Michigan. There are about 300,000 ethnic Arabs in the Detroit metropolitan area, the biggest concentration of Arabs anywhere in the world outside the Middle East". Although there are 7 million Muslims in the United States, all Arab-Americans are not Muslim. Indeed, many are Catholic, Orthodox and Protestants who can trace a continuous line of Christian faith back to the first converts in the Church.

Among notable Americans of Arabic Ancestry are presidential candidate Ralph Nader, Secretary of the Interior and former Senator Spencer Abraham, former Senate Majority Leader and Ambassador George Mitchell, former White House Chief of Staff during the Gulf War and Governor John Sinunu, Candy Lightner who was the founder of Mothers Against Drunk Driving, Colonel James Jabara who was the first "jet ace" in the Korean War, General George Joulwan who was the former Commander of NATO, Nobel Prize winners Ahmed Zewail (Physics) and Elias Corey (Chemistry), Dr. Farouk El-Baz of NASA, and school teacher/

astronaut Christa McAuliffe who perished on the space shuttle "Challenger". 36% of Americans of Arab ancestry have college degrees.

III.
The Extent of the Hate Crimes

A reading and interpretation of the data supplied by the news media, churches, mosques and community organizations indicates that the commission of hate crimes targeting Arab-Americans is widespread throughout the United States and numbers in the thousands. It has resulted in a loss of life and property in the Arab-American community with many of the targets being women and children, churches and mosques, and occasionally Pakistanis and Hispanics. Some of the targets bear ancestry to the very nations who are allied with the United States Government in its war against terrorism.

CNN reported on September 17, 2001 multi-state shooting deaths of a Sikh (Indian of Hindu faith) wearing a turban and a Pakistani garage attendant; both deaths are believed related to the backlash against Arab/Muslim-Americans.

ABC News reported through correspondent Derek Thomson the following incidents as of September 14, 2001:

> Hours after the attacks on Tuesday, the Islamic Institute of New York received a telephone call threatening the school's 450 students, said manager Azam Meshkat. The caller "said he was going to paint the streets with our children's blood," The school is closed, but continues to receive several threats a day.

> On Wednesday, a well-dressed young Manhattan couple yelled insults at a Lebanese-American who was desperately searching for survivors from the arts center he had run on the 92nd floor of the World Trade Center's north tower. "They told me, 'You should go back to your country, you f...ing Arabs, we should bomb the s... out of you".

> A mosque in Denton, Texas, was firebombed, and another in Lynnwood, Washington had its sign defaced with black paint. In Huntington, N.Y., police say a 75-year-old man tried to run over a Pakistani woman in a shopping mall parking lot.

> Khaled Ksaibati, the faculty adviser for the Muslim Student Association at the University of Wyoming described the attack on the Muslim family at a

Laramie Wal-Mart. "The people who screamed in her face wanted her to go back to her country," he said. "This is her country. She was born here."

In Bridgeview, Ill., a suburb of Chicago, police stopped 300 marchers as they tried to march on a mosque. Marcher Colin Zaremba, 19, told The Associated Press, "I'm proud to be American and I hate Arabs and I always have."

CBS (and CNN) News, Los Angeles and Atlanta, 9/20-21/01. In Los Angeles a 48-year-old father of three and a Christian (A. Karas) was murdered at the store he owned for 20 years by what investigators believe to be a hate crime.

A Virginia woman was accused of a bomb threat against a Mosque. In Seattle, a man with a gun was arrested for suspected arson outside a mosque. In San Diego, an explosion outside a mosque forced worshipers to evacuate. In Middlebury, Ohio a man drove his car into the entrance of a Mosque at 80 miles per hour.

In Evansville, Indiana, a 28-year-old man drove his car into a Mosque. In Huntington, N.Y. a drunk driver tried to run over a Pakistani lady at a shopping mall parking lot and then chased her into a store threatening to kill her for "destroying my country." (CNN and CBS reports). In Fair Haven, Michigan windows were shot out of a gas station believed owned by an Arab-American.

In Gary, Ind., a man in a ski mask fired a high-powered assault rifle at the gas station where a U.S. citizen born in Yemen was working.

In Austin, Texas an incendiary device was thrown at a Pakistani (Muslim)-owned gasoline station. In Salt Lake City a man attempted to burn down a restaurant owned by a Pakistani.

During the past week passengers and flight crews on United, Northwest and Delta airlines on separate occasions ejected previously boarded passengers who looked Arabic because they made others "uncomfortable" and therefore posed a "security threat". All of the passengers passed security checks and none of the ejected passengers were arrested. One of them was an Egyptian-American and another who was a 15-year-old Saudi teen.

[It is noteworthy that an ABCNEWS/Washington Post poll conducted Thursday, "43 percent of Americans" said they thought the attacks would make them "personally more suspicious" of people who appear to be of Arab descent.] Newsweek, 9/24/01 issue.

In Washington, D.C., Muslim women have had hijab scarves snatched from their heads.

A mosque in San Francisco was splattered with pig's blood. A bomb threat at a mostly Arab school in Dearborn, Mich., sent frightened teens running into the streets. Internet and talk radio became a hothouse for hate. "You are the true coward now sand n---r."

"Police won't protect Muslims now," raged one email to a Muslim organization in Florida.

Radio jocks are amping up callers with comments like, "Death to ragheads." Even legitimate journalists have vented rage. Political analyst Ann Coulter wrote in an op-ed: "We should invade their countries, kill their leaders and convert them to Christianity."

Reports from the Chicago area Muslim Community through United Muslim American Association as of September 16, 2001 are as follows:

Arab-American deli owner in Ardsely, New York asked if he was Arab by one customer. When he responded honestly, the customer cursed and yelled at him. The customer then sprayed the deli owner with pepper spray when the deli owner attempted to escort him out of the store.

At a gas station in Dearborn Mich., a female customer was insulted by a man driving by in a car who yelled, "Get out of America, Get out of America."

The public school system in Jefferson Parish, New Orleans closed down due to the attacks on Arab and Muslim students.

Rockville, Maryland- A rug company was set on fire during the night of the 11th. The Palestinian owner had been renting the building to another Palestinian and an Iranian. The men reported threatening phone calls Tuesday.

Six bullets fired through windows of Dallas area mosque, overnight Tuesday (tolerance.org) Carrollton, TX mosque (Madinah Masjid) has windows shattered late Tuesday, or early Wednesday (Tolerance.org and BBC).

A woman was on her way to pick up her son from school in Brooklyn, New York, when she was approached by an older Caucasian man who threatened her (CAIR).

Two girls were on their way home from school when they were approached by a group of adults and teenagers who began to threaten them and threw stones at them. (CAIR)

Texas, a woman was sent home from work Wednesday following a meeting with her boss who had singled her out because of her Palestinian heritage. He commented that he didn't know if she would be celebrating the death of Americans in the office.

Waverly, TN, two Arab American clinic workers received threatening phone calls telling them to "go home and get out of our country" and calling them "foreign fags." Their daughter in Atlanta, GA received threatening phone calls.

In Brooklyn, New York, an Arab-American grocer was subjected to a litany of racial slurs and threats. This transpired after the grocer was attempting to pay the balance of his bill in cash and the delivery person suggested that the grocer call into the main office of Derlie Farms and the manager who answered the call began spewing racist venom. This incident was reported to the police.

The Arab-American Anti-Discrimination Committee reported in Washington, D.C., on September 19, 2001 that comments were made by United States Congressman John Cooksey (R-LA) on Louisiana radio stating that "someone who comes in that's got a diaper on his head and a fan belt wrapped around that diaper on his head, that guy needs to be pulled over'." The Anti-Discrimination Committee has received a reported 250 alleged hate crimes and harassment on college campuses alone. Some of the targeted students were actually Hispanic and African-American. CNN in Atlanta reported on September 21, 2001 specific instances of the backlash on college campuses:

Boston University student was stabbed in the back and arms after leaving an off-campus fundraiser for victims of the World Trade Center attacks.

Women students have been spat at and had their traditional hijab scarves pulled off. [See Newsweek report that a Virginia college student was detained by a police officer who demanded that she remove her headscarf and searched her car.] Male students have had turbans plucked from their heads or been targeted because of their beards.

A Muslim Student Association reports threats: You people are going to die. The Holy War has begun. Go home. CBS News reports University of California, Berkeley campus newspaper publication of a cartoon depicting demonic caricatures of Muslims burning "in hell".

A Muslim student at Colorado University was approached as she entered the campus library by four men dressed in black who asked 'What are you doing in this country?' and used racial epithets. The library's six columns were then spray-painted with graffiti: "Arabs Go Home," "Nuke sand niggers"

Examples of hate mail and voice messages received at the Arab-American Anti-Discrimination Committee in Washington D.C. on September 11-12, 2001.

Baby killers, spineless worms, dirt of the mothers womb...

God f...ing damn you

I now enjoy watching Arabs and Muslims die

F...ing Arabs go to hell. You will pay.

Americans are no longer sympathetic to you, your cause, or your people.

You should start acting like Americans and not terrorists.

You are either American or Arab. Arab-American is an oxymoron.

I am usually a levelheaded person, but now I believe your organization should shut down, and I will refrain from going to any Arab owned businesses. Now Arabs all over the world will suffer.

Go Home! You people act violently towards Christian nations.

Die bastards.

You Muslims must die.

Get out of our country...you ignorant pieces of crap!

You will all die at the hands of Americans.

Go fuck yourself you raghead f....

Get out of our country.

I will enjoy watching your countries and people burn.

I hope Bush kicks you bastards out of my f...ing country.

I really enjoyed watching the footage of that Palestinian man with his son, right before they were shot by Israeli troops...he died like (all) Arabs should." A Chicago Tribune article by Noreen Ahmed Ullah and Don Terry on September 15, 2001 reports that:

Mosques and Islamic institutions have been vandalized in the days after terrorist attacks in New York and Washington, and Muslims have faced harassment and even violence. Fearing for their congregation's safety, a few mosques across the country decided to close Friday. Officials at the Mosque Foundation in Bridgeview seriously considered it after nightly confrontations with protesters.

CNN reports that:

The head of Arab-American Anti-Discrimination Committee claims that Arab-American community is "keeping its head down for the moment... don't want to be conspicuous right now. Being inconspicuous for most members means staying home, not going to work, not even going out to shop".

At an Arab-American Family Support Center in Brooklyn, a counselor reports to CNN on September 16, 2001 that they have received "hundreds of calls from Arab-Americans who have been threatened by people who blame the community for the attacks. The center also has documented reports of physical assault in the Atlantic Avenue area, which has a large population of Americans from Yemen, Lebanon and other Arab nations.

Brooklyn police confirm presence of armed guards to protect one retail establishment after numerous death threats to the Arab-American proprietor. Local police now guard his office and walk him to and from work every day.

65

A 17-year-old Palestinian American student reported that her health teacher told her class at a high school in Brooklyn that "Palestinian children all want to become terrorists."

Maher Saleh, a News York City schoolteacher, said he had Arab-American friends who were New York City police officers and firefighters helping in the rescue effort, as well as a Marine who was called up for duty today. "I had friends and family who worked in the World Trade Center." Even though he was born and raised in his Brooklyn neighborhood, Saleh said he found himself being shunned today by some non-Arabs. "A lot of people I usually talk to, they turn away their faces".

The Chicago Sun Times reported on September 15, 2001 that:

The Chicago police said they have received 13 reports since Tuesday of hate-related incidents targeting Muslims and Arabs. On Thursday afternoon a man walked into a grocery store at 4326 S. State carrying a briefcase. "I'm going to blow up this store the same way the World Trade Center was blown up," he told the Arab-American owner, according to police.

The United Muslim Americans Association said a Palos Hills Islamic organization has received more than 50 death threats in e-mails and phone calls. Most Muslim and Arab children in the Chicago area are staying home from school, the association said.

ABC News/ WBEZ Radio, Chicago:

Evanston, Illinois police reported an Arab-American cab driver and his passenger who resembled an Arab-American were chased by two motorcyclists and beaten. One of the assailants was a corrections officer with the Sheriff of Cook County (Chicago), Illinois who said, "This is what you get, you mass murderer."

A Muslim school was firebombed the morning of September 12, 2001 with no damage or injury to the children.

CNN New York, 9/19/01

A San Francisco man from India was severely beaten up and his girlfriend "Robin" was stabbed by a gang of young men made anti-Arabic epithets.

A turbaned Sikh in New York was chased into a subway station by a group of young men who called him a "terrorist" and threatened to kill him.

Finally, on Sunday, September 23, 2001, while a prayer vigil took place at Yankee Stadium in New York urging persons of all faiths to show restraint, Fox News of Chicago flashed a report that an arson fire was set at St. John Assyrian Catholic Church in Chicago with a property loss of over $200,000.

IV
Government & Media Response to Backlash

After the attacks last week law enforcement and public officials have been unified and clear in cautioning Americans to refrain from taking vengeance against their fellow citizens who may be Muslims or of Arabic Ancestry. President Bush cautioned Americans to refrain from reprisals against innocent Arab/Muslim-Americans. Indeed, all of our former Presidents, Ford, Carter, Bush, Sr., and Clinton, have urged restraint and promoted the rule of law. The Governor of New York and the Mayor of New York City have urged their citizens to refrain from using violence, and Chicago's Mayor Richard Daley very passionately appealed to Chicagoans to obey the law, stating that Arab-Americans are among Chicago's most prominent and loyal citizens. Members of Congress and religious leaders have also spoken out. Finally, local law enforcement have publicly announced criminal complaints against individuals accused of hate crimes in an effort to deter more of them.

The media has by and large been diligent and fair in reporting these messages of restraint and deterrence to the public. Moreover, the media has aired public interest stories showing the impact of discrimination on a personal level. For example, on September 18, 2001 ABC's Nightline aired a piece depicting the funeral of a murdered Muslim husband and father in Texas and then presented interviews with children at a Muslim school, ending the piece with a little girl's hope that some day "we can play together again and be normal".

Although media coverage of the human impact of the atrocities and the statements of government leaders has greatly reduced the violence, the violence has continued and, with the continuing arrests of terrorist suspects bearing Arab/Muslim names and the prospect of a prolonged war, there is a reasonable basis to believe that the atrocities against Arab/Muslim Americans will increase.

Adding to the danger is the prospect that the United States is on a "war footing" and, therefore, law enforcement will necessarily be preoccupied with the security and defense of our country.

V. Overview of Government's Legal Duty to Act

The Constitution of the United States guarantees all Americans the right to "life, liberty and the pursuit of happiness". The American Bar Association's Standards for the Administration of Criminal Justice outlines certain rights and duties concerning the police. Clearly, the duty to enforce laws and protect property is inherent constitutional and statutory requirements of a law enforcement agency. What the police actually do in a given situation is determined by several factors. (1) Is there a legislative mandate to act? (2) Do the police have the authority and means to enforce the Law? (3) Are the police sensitive to community needs? That is, do they demonstrate their duty to "create and maintain a feeling of security in the community" and, further "to promote and preserve civil order"? ABA Standards, 2.1

The legislative mandate of most municipalities is similar to Chicago's Municipal Code, 2-84-220 (General Duties of the Police), which requires that the Chicago Police "preserve order, peace, and quiet and enforce the laws and ordinances throughout the city". Section 2-84-280 of the Code provides that a policeman who "shall refuse or neglect to perform any duty [so as to] tend to hinder, obstruct or impair in any way the proper and strict enforcement of any law... is hereby declared to be no longer qualified to be a member of the police force, and shall be discharged...."

Most states have laws similar to the ones in the books in Illinois. These laws mandate the police's duty to preserve life and property. See 720 ILCS 5/7-1 et seq (use of force), paragraph 33-1 ("mandatory duty"), and paragraphs 107-1 et seq (power of arrest). Under Chapter 125, Section 82, the legislature specifically directs peace officers to "suppress all riots and unlawful assembling and to keep the peace..." Under Chapter 129, paragraph 220.83 the Governor is empowered to use military force when necessary to the degree that the governor "may deem to aide civil authorities in suppressing riots and unlawful assemblies. (See also paragraphs 265 and 266) .

The ABA Standards provide that law enforcement should "take appropriate action to prevent disorder... and to deal properly and effectively with disorder when it occurs". ABA Standards, 3.3 (iv). Police are granted wide discretion, particularly in areas of selective enforcement, investigative techniques, and enforcement methods. ABA Standards, 4.3

Despite the authority to act, can law enforcement act quickly, decisively, and effectively [and should they]? The Report of the National Advisory Commission on Civil Disorders, New York Times Ed., 1968 (pages 325-334), maintains that success is often based upon the sufficiency of the manpower to control a crowd and the speed with which the manpower can arrive to the scene of the civil disturbance. There must be a pre-constructed strategy for this. See also, Violence in the City -- An end or a beginning?

A report by the Governors Commission on the Los Angeles Riots in 1965.

Recommendations:

The Arab-American Bar Association is recommending that Federal, State and local governments develop contingency plans for the enforcement all laws applicable to those suspected engaging in widespread hate crimes against Arab/Muslim Americans. Based upon a plan implemented in Chicago after the June 1992 civil disturbance, the Arab-American Bar Association is recommending the following:

a. That law enforcement be very vigilant during highly sensitive events that may impact upon minority citizens;

b. That law enforcement act upon any intelligence information gathered through inquires and reports to the police of hate crimes;

c. Where widespread hate crimes are foreseeable, the Government should make available adequate personnel and equipment and emergency communications to deal with it. Law enforcement should plan to alert and/or re-deploy a maximum complement of personnel and resources from other districts and towns or the state at sensitive times to sensitive areas.

d. Courts, prosecutors, and correctional facilities must all be prepared for any such event(s).

e. Society and Government, through the media and through community service projects, should endeavor to educate the public to defuse the hatred. (e.g. Chicago Sun Times and Detroit Free Press full page Ads dated September 24, 2001 entitled "12 Answers to Questions About Our Arab American Neighbors")

VI.
Findings

1. On September 11, 2001, using hijacked airplanes as weapons on targets in New York City and Washington D.C., terrorists attacked the United States of America, destroying the lives and property of American citizens.

2. Included among the victims of this attack were citizens, nationals, rescue workers and policemen of Arabic ancestry or of the Muslim faith.

3. The acts of the terrorists are condemned as crimes against humanity and must not go unpunished, as required under the law.

4. Since it is believed that the terrorists were Middle Eastern and/or Muslim, civil disturbances involving the widespread commission of hate crimes have erupted throughout the United States targeting Americans of Arabic descent, Americans of the Islamic faith, and Americans who were stereotyped as "looking like" Arab/Muslim-Americans. These crimes include murder, arson, bombings, aggravated assaults and batteries (using weapons such as handguns, pepper spray, stones, and motor vehicles), vandalism to businesses, schools and religious sights, mob violence, looting, death and bomb threats, school closings, job discrimination, workplace violence and harassment.

5. Therefore, the threat of widespread hate crimes and civil disturbances against Americans of Arabic Descent and Muslim Americans who comprise an ethnic/religious minority in the millions is unprecedented and dangerous.

6. There are approximately 3.5 million Americans of Arabic ancestry and 7 million Muslims in the United States who have served their country as Congressmen, Senators, Governors, Cabinet members, Mayors, Soldiers, Firemen, Policemen, Scientists, Bankers, Businessmen, Doctors, Lawyers, and Educators.

7. In an attempt to enforce the Constitution and the Rule of Law, public officials and religious clerics have acted responsibly in cautioning Americans to refrain from taking vengeance against their fellow citizens who may be Muslims or of Arabic Ancestry.

8. There has been responsible media coverage of the human impact of these hate crimes, including reports of public statements condemning them.

9. As more U.S. resources are used to search for, apprehend and punish the terrorists, impacting our economy, there is reason to believe that more potential resentment, discrimination and violence could be triggered against Americans of Arabic Descent and Muslims.

10. The Constitution of the United States guarantees all Americans the right to "life, liberty and the pursuit of happiness". The American Bar Association provides Standards that provide that law enforcement should "take appropriate action to prevent disorder... and to deal properly and effectively with disorder when it occurs".

VII.
Resolutions

This Association requests that other professional bar groups join us in the adoption of the following resolutions:

1. The threat of widespread hate crimes and reprisals against blameless Americans of Arabic Ancestry and Muslims (and those who resemble them) constitutes a danger to the liberties of all Americans.

2. In addition to the law enforcement's response to hate crimes, Government should: (a) develop and coordinate preventive measures to protect the rights of Arab-American and Muslim citizens, and (b) develop and coordinate pre-constructed strategies to protect the lives and property of Arab-American and Muslim citizens in the event of an escalation of hate crimes against Americans of Arabic descent and Muslim Americans.

3. Society and Government, through the media and through community service projects, should endeavor to educate the public to defuse the hatred.

4. It is recommended that Government not act in haste to enact special legislation that may negatively impact upon the civil liberties of all Americans.

5. It is recommended that Americans continue to speak out against this backlash of hate crimes and that the media report it.

6. It is recommended that the Government of the United States bring the terrorists and those who aided and abetted the terrorists to justice, and proceed to use all

reasonable and necessary measures to protect the people of the United States of America.

7. It is recommended that other Arab-American and Muslim organizations present this Report to local government to document the danger and to begin a dialogue to defuse the danger.

VIII.
Conclusion

Those who would harm others because of their ethnicity or religion become accomplices to the terrorists. Those who embrace the innocent become accomplices to Freedom. The goal of our enemies is to destroy our Freedom

Appendix II
IMPACT OF THE SEPTEMBER 11TH ATTACKS ON THE FREEDOMS OF ARABS AND MUSLIMS

Presented to the MARSHALL LAW SCHOOL in Chicago
on Wednesday, September 11, 2002
By
William J. Haddad, Executive Director
Arab-American Bar Association of Illinois

"None are more hopelessly enslaved than those who falsely
believe they are free."

Johann Wolfgang von Goethe

Introduction

The Arab-American and Muslim communities in the United States were severely affected by the criminal attacks upon the United States of American on September 11, 2001 (9/11) by terrorists. First, as U.S. citizens, Arab-Americans and Muslims were horrified by the colossal loss of life. In fact several hundred victims and rescue workers in New York were Arabs and Muslims. Although not well reported, each and every organization, society, mosque and church in these communities condemned the attacks. Second, Arab-Americans and Muslims were again victimized by a massive backlash of retaliation and blame. This took three forms: (1) visible, criminal attacks against these communities; (2) insidious social and employment discrimination; and (3) special governmental measures and legislation were enforced against them. The Arab-American Bar Association issued a warning in its "Preliminary Report on Hate Crimes" on September 26, 2001 that it was concerned about the protection of life and property in the event of another terrorist attack.

However, new concerns have been voiced by jurists, local police, foreign governments, the American Bar Association, and even the Foreign Intelligence Surveillance Court about new measures adopted after 9/11 that empower the government to: (1) arbitrarily choose foreign or domestic organizations suspected of supporting terrorism, and then---using "secret evidence--- jail or deport anyone who gives them "material support"; (2) jail those who commit minor criminal offenses deemed "dangerous to human life" whose intent is to "intimidate" society or "influence government policy", (3) detain U.S. citizens and non citizens suspected of being "enemy combatants" without bail, *in communicado*, without access to an attorney; (4) prepare "citizen camps" to incarcerate U.S. citizens, and (5) try such individuals before military tribunals.

This presentation is merely a message of these concerns.

1. The Backlash Against Arab-Americans and Muslim Citizens

Crimes and acts of discrimination against Arabs and Muslims in the United States rose immediately following the 9/11 attacks. News reports in Washington, Texas, California, Michigan and Illinois were replete with stories of murder*, armed assault and battery (guns, knives, pepper spray, cars, trucks, and rifles), arson and firebombing and vehicular driving attacks upon schools, mosques, and churches.

In an ABCNEWS/Washington Post poll conducted days after the attacks, 43 percent of Americans said they thought the attacks would make them "personally more suspicious" of people who appear to be of Arab descent. A national poll reported by the Council on American-Islamic Relations from Washington indicated that "nearly 75 % of Muslim-Americans either know someone who has or have themselves experience of anti-Muslim discrimination." (See usnewswire.com, 6/11/02) Some of the inflammatory rhetoric directed against Muslims was reported in the media, as excerpted below from Alherwar Magazine (See Alhewar.com, 8/17/02):

> * "We should invade [Muslim] countries, kill their leaders and convert them to Christianity." (Columnist Ann Coulter, National Review Online, Sept. 13, 2001)

> * "Just turn [the sheriff] loose and have him arrest every Muslim that crosses the state line." (Rep. C. Saxby Chambliss (R-GA), Chairman of the House Subcommittee on Terrorism and Homeland security and Senate candidate, to Georgia law officers, November 2001)

> * "Islam is a religion in which God requires you to send your son to die for him. Christianity is a faith where God sent his Son to die for you." (Attorney General John Ashcroft, interview on Cal Thomas radio, November 2001)

* "(Islam) is a very evil and wicked religion wicked, violent and not of the same god (as Christianity)." (Rev. Franklin Graham, head of the Billy Graham Evangelistic Association, November 2001.)

* "Islam is Evil, Christ is King." (Allegedly written in marker by law enforcement agents on a Muslim prayer calendar in the home of a Muslim being investigated by police in Dearborn, Michigan, July 2002.)

---

*The post 9/11 backlash has resulted in several suspected murders of Arab-American, Muslims and those who resemble them. According to Collateral Compassion, the Council on American Islamic Relations, and the American-Arab Anti-Discrimination Committee some of the victims are Nirmal Singh Gill, Vancouver, B.C., Sukhpal Singh Sodhi, Balbir Sodhi - Meza, AZ, Adel Karas - San Gabriel, CA, Ali AlMansoop - Lincoln Park, MI, Ali Ali-Minneapolis, MN, Yasser Al-Ghurazy - Clovis, CA, Saed Mujtahid - Dallas, TX, Mohammad Omary - Denton, TX, Kimberly Lowe - Tulsa, OK, Jawed Wassel - Queens, NY, Ibrahim Mohammad - Chattanooga, TN, Waqar Hasan - Dallas, TX, Jayantilal Patel - Haines City, FL, Surjit Singh Samra - Ceres, CA, Abdo Ali Ahmed - Reedly, CA, Abdullah Mohammed Nimer - Los Angeles, CA, Vasudev Patel - Mesquite, TX, Ramez Younan - Los Angeles, CA

> * "Muhammad was a demon-possessed pedophile [and Allah] is no Jehovah either. Jehovah's not going to turn you into a terrorist that'll.. take the lives of thousands and thousands of people." (Rev. Jerry Vines, former President of the Southern Baptist Convention, to conventioneers at the annual gathering of the SBC last June; CAIR, 6/11/02)

In Chicago, where the police reported four documented hate crimes against Arab-Americans in all of 2000, thirteen were reported within days of the 9/11 attacks. (See Chicago Police Department Hate Crimes Report) One example involved a man who walked into a south side grocery store carrying a briefcase, saying to the Arab-American proprietor: "I'm going to blow up this store the same way the World Trade Center was blown up." A south suburban Muslim group reported 50 death threats via phone and e-mails and advised parents to keep their children at home. Evanston, Illinois police reported an Arab-American cab driver and his passenger who resembled an Arab-American were chased by two motorcyclists and beaten. One of the assailants was a corrections officer who said, "This is what you get, you mass murderer." A mob in Bridgeview marched on a mosque carrying confederate flags and pelting Arab-American owned grocery stores with rocks and bricks, reminiscent of the "brown shirts" seen decades ago in Germany.

Arsons were committed at a north side Assyrian Catholic Church and a south side Muslim community center.

Two recent reports of discrimination exemplify how the hate crimes have moved from the streets to public accommodations. On August 15, 2002 the Justice Department announced the settlement of a claim filed by the Chicago based Midwest Federation of Syrian Lebanese Clubs against Marriott for cancellation of a contract to hold a convention at the Des Moines Marriott. The Midwest Federation was established in 1936 with associated members such as Danny Thomas (who used it as a springboard to establish St. Jude Children's Research Hospital in Memphis), James Shalala (whose daughter Donna was Secretary of Health and Human Services), and Spencer Abraham (Secretary of Energy). On August 27, 2002 Chicago comedian, Ray Hanania, was cancelled as the opening act at local comedy club "Zanies" reportedly because a nationally known headliner, Jackie Mason, refused to appear at the same time with a "Palestinian". (A.Buchanon, AP & Chicago Tribune, A.P. 8/28/02). Hanania is an Arab-American who was born in Chicago, but also served as a sergeant in the U.S. Army.

2. Workplace Discrimination

First reports of discrimination in the workplace came from the American-Arab Anti-Discrimination Committee, a watchdog group in Washington, D.C. They reported that discrimination against Arab and Muslims in the United States had resulted in more than 400 reports of employment discrimination. (Chicago Tribune, "Americans on Alert for Terror", K. Brandon & D. Glanton, 11/25/01)

Reports of discrimination against Arab-Americans and Muslims in the workplace more than tripled after 9/11. Between September 11, 2001 and May 7, 2002 the Equal Employment Opportunities Commission reported that their field offices received 497 charges of religious bias against Muslims in the workplace (compared to 193 cases in the previous year), and 488 charges of ethnic discrimination against Arab-Americans in the workplace (with none noted the previous year). (See EEOC's May 15, 2002 Press Release)

The Council on American-Islamic Relations (CAIR) from Washington reported 1516 claims of denial of religious accommodation, harassment, discrimination, bias, threat, assault and several murders since 9/11. According to a study conducted by the John J. Heldrich Center for Workforce Development: "About 20% of people say Arab-Americans are the employees most likely to be treated unfairly in the workplace" which surpasses "the number who said women or Hispanic workers were most likely to be unfairly treated".

3. Measures to Stop Hate Crimes and Discrimination

In the aftermath of 9/11, President Bush was joined by all of America's living past Presidents, and by a host of Mayors, Governors, and law enforcement officials to condemn the hate crimes perpetrated against the life and property of Americans of Arabic ancestry and Muslims. Some major bar associations have focused upon discrimination, profiling, and rights issues, as seen at the American Bar Association's forum on February 3, 2002 in Philadelphia, "Confronting Racial/ Ethnic Profiling...The Dilemma of Arab Americans the Individual of Muslim Faith" and the ABA's decisions in January and August to officially question measures taken by the Justice Department (*infra*).

Within a month after 9/11, over 65 hate crime complaints were filed by state and local law enforcement, while in the same period, the Federal Bureau of Investigation had launched 350 investigations nationwide. A variety of federal prosecutions resulted, including charges against a Tallahassee man who drove his pickup truck into a mosque, two California men who tried to bomb a mosque and murder a U.S. Congressman of Lebanese descent, a Utah man who attempted to arson- bomb a restaurant owned by a Pakistani-American, and a Washington man who shot two Muslim worshipers when trying to firebomb their mosque. (See Dept of Justice Website, 8/02 and Arab-American Institute Report, 2/13/02).

Since 9/11 the President dispatched the Director of the Federal Equal Employment Opportunities Commission to major cities to invite Arab-Americans and Muslims to file job discrimination complaints. The President also ordered the Justice Department's Civil Rights Division to canvass grass roots groups in the Middle Eastern/American community, inviting them to report discriminatory activity and hate crimes. Consequently, Justice filed several civil rights complaints.

Other agencies, such as the US Commission on Civil Rights are seen as providing the public with information through websites and forums. Federal, State and local government have also held forums and discussions, including the meetings held by Chicago Police Superintendent Hillard, and community meetings hosted by various civil rights organizations.

In an effort stop the violence, the Arab-American Bar Association of Illinois issued its "Preliminary Report on Hate Crimes Against Arabs and Muslims in the United States," with findings and resolutions (See arabbar.org) on September 26, 2001 at a news conference joined by the Cook County State's Attorney and the Presidents of the Illinois State Bar Association, the Chicago Bar Association, and the Jewish Judges Association. Representatives of the American Bar Association, the Decalogue Society of Jewish Lawyers, the Justinian Society of Lawyers, and the Ethnic Bar Coalition also attended, as did all the major broadcast and print news media.

Among the resolutions announced at the news conference by the Arab-American Bar was a warning that, should there be another attack perpetrated by Middle Eastern criminal terrorists, then it is likely that a more severe backlash will result that may cause massive loss of life and property in the Arab-American and Muslim communities. The resolution called for law enforcement agencies to prepare pre-constructed strategies and plans to deal with civilian insurrections that may follow such an attack.

4. Patriotism of Arab-Americans and Muslims in the United States.

There are about 3 million Arab Americans living in the United States according the United States Commission on Civil Rights. Most of them are Christians-many of whom came here about a hundred years ago. There are major concentrations in California (Los Angeles), Michigan (Detroit/Flint) and New York (Brooklyn), Illinois (Chicago), Maryland, Massachusetts, New Jersey, Ohio, Texas and Virginia. (US Commission on Civil Rights) There are 5 to 7 million Muslims in the USA, most of whom are not from the Middle East. (*The Economist,* 10/14/00 and *The Washington Post,* 10/16/00) In the Chicago area alone, there are over 400,000 Americans of Arabic descent and Muslims.

Experts say that Americans of Arabic descent are among America's best-educated and most affluent citizens. Notable Arab-Americans include scientists such as: Nobel prize winners Elias Corey and Ahmed Zewail, famed M.D. Michael Debakey; Apollo/Nasa scientist Farouk El-Baz; Business leaders such as Jacques Nasser of Ford, John Mack of Morgan Stanley, Joseph Aboud, and J.M. Hagger; Political leaders like Senators George Mitchell, Spencer Abraham (Department of Energy), James Abourezk, and James Abdnor; Congressmen Nick Rahall, Pat Danner, Ray Lahoud; John Sinunu, Selwa Roosevelt, Donna Shalala, Phillip Habib, and Ralph Nader; Sports figures such as Doug Floutie, Jeff George, Bill George, Ron Sheikaly, Bobby Rahall, and Joe Robbie; Entertainers such as Danny Thomas, Paul Anka, Frank Zappa, Paula Abdul, Tiffany, Casey Kasem, Rosalind Elias, Jamie Farr, Khrystne Hage, Kristy McNichol, Tony Shalhoub, Kathy Najimy, Salma Hayek, and F. Murray Abraham. Only one other ethnic minority has more medical doctors in the United States than Arab-Americans. (Arab-American Business Magazine, 8/02)

Arab-Americans have fought for the United States in every war in the 20th Century. The last of them to have died in the service of America was Albert Haddad (USMC) of Lewisville, Texas, who perished in the Gulf War. The first jet ace in Korea, Colonel James Jabara, was an Arab American. Others were four star General George Joulwan who commanded NATO and Christa McAuliffe, the "first teacher in space" who died in the space shuttle Challenger.

5. Governmental Measures and Special Legislation affecting Arab-American and Muslim Citizens

The United States is said to be "at war". Previous administrations in time of war have engaged in massive expulsion of foreign nationals, massive detention of ethnic minorities, and the eradication of due process of law to its citizens. During America's "undeclared war" with Napoleonic France in 1798, President John Adams signed The *Alien and Sedition Acts*. Historian David McCullough describes the atmosphere in the United States:

There was rampant fear of the enemy within. French émigrés in America... by now numbered 25,000 or more... In addition to the French there were the "wild Irish," refugees from the Irish Rebellion of 1798 who were thought to include dangerous radicals.

The *Alien Act* authorized the President to "expel any foreigner he considered "dangerous" and the Sedition Act made it a crime to make any "false, scandalous, and malicious" writing against the government...". [N.B. a clear violation of the First Amendment.]

Even where there was no legislative authority, America's Presidents have suspended rights when national security was threatened. Abraham Lincoln's unilateral proclamations without an act of Congress in 1861 during the Civil War suspended the right to seek a writ of *habeas corpus* and created military style tribunals, those tribunals were sometimes utilized to punish draft resisters, Southern sympathizers, and critics of the Civil War. In 1866 the Supreme Court in *Ex Parte Milligan,* 71 U.S. 2 (1866), seemingly outlawed Lincoln's use of military style tribunals.

America's early "suspicion" of foreigners was evident in the Civil War, particularly so during the Battle of Chancellors Ville when Ohio's XI Corp of German born

79

solders were wiped out because Union General Lewis Howard refused to sacrifice his reserves to protect the right flank of "foreigners". After the sneak attack on Pearl Harbor, President Franklin Roosevelt interned 120,000 American citizens of Japanese ancestry. Roosevelt's use of military tribunals, which led to the execution of foreign saboteurs, was upheld by the Supreme Court. Even relatives of saboteurs were not protected from governmental suspicion as seen in Chicago where relatives of an executed spy were all charged and quickly convicted of treason. Their convictions were all reversed on appeal. (See Chicago Magazine, February 2002)

Today, some fear that measures enacted after 9/11 have empowered the government to: (1) indiscriminately choose foreign or domestic organizations suspected of supporting terrorism and then jail or deport anyone who gives them "material support" on the basis of "secret evidence"; (2) jail those who commit minor criminal offenses that it deems as "dangerous to human life" where the perpetrators intend to "intimidate" society or influence government policy, (3) detain U.S. citizens and non citizens suspected of being "enemy combatants" without bail, *in communicado*, without access to an attorney; (4) prepare "citizen camps" to incarcerate U.S. citizens, and (5) avoid the justice process by trying such individuals before military tribunals. Here are some of those measures.

a. The Anti-Terrorism and Effective Death Penalty Act of 1996:

Discrimination and special laws did not begin in the aftermath of 9/11. One reason for the establishment of the Arab-American Bar Association in 1990 was in response to the backlash during the Gulf War. In 1992 Chicagoans pillaged Arab-American owned businesses after the Bulls Basketball team won its first world championship, causing over $10 million in damage. After the Oklahoma City bombing of 1995, Congress reflected its suspicion of Arab-Americans and Muslims in the passage of the *Anti-Terrorism and Effective Death Penalty Act of 1996* which created "designations" of foreign terrorist organizations. Although the 1995 Oklahoma bombing was not committed by "foreign terrorists", the 1996 law has since been largely enforced against Middle Eastern aliens and citizens. (See International Law Section Forum on Secret Evidence, ABA Convention, Chicago, August 5, 2001) At the time the law was criticized by civil liberties organizations, law professors, and constitutional rights advocates as "one of the worst assaults on the Constitution in decades." Illinois has been accused by the ACLU of passing its own version of this "special legislation" with the enactment of an *International Terrorism Bill* in 1995. (720 ICLE 5/29C-10).

In his election campaign of 2000, President Bush (and many congressmen) had candidly objected to the "secret evidence" provisions of the *Anti-Terrorism Act of 1996,* saying that it was an instrument of "profiling". The Immigration and Naturalization Service had successfully avoided constitutional scrutiny of the INS provisions of the Act by relying upon administrative court proceedings under the *Immigration Responsibility Act of 1996*, rather than proceeding in federal district courts where it would be duty-bound to charge aliens as "terrorists" and prove that they "engaged in terrorist activity". However, in those rare administrative instances that did reach the scrutiny of a federal district court, the so-called "secret evidence" was found to be flawed or non-existent. (See International Law Section, ABA Convention, Chicago, August 5, 2001).

The negative impact of the *1996 Anti-Terrorism Act* upon the Muslim community was demonstrated in a poll conducted by Zoghby International in June of 2000 which showed that 87% of Muslims polled expressed a strong belief that the Muslim community was the main target of "the Immigration and Naturalization Service's controversial authority to use secret evidence in its proceedings against persons accused of unlawful immigration."

The criminal provisions of the *Anti-Terrorism and Effective Death Penalty Act of 1996* outlaw contributions of material support to any "foreign" group deemed a threat to our "national security", and thereby "designated" by the Secretary of State as a "terrorist organization". Although the Secretary must confer privately with legislative principals and other members of the Cabinet prior to making the designation official, it is ultimately the Secretary of State who makes the "designation". Any challenge to that designation may be in the form of an "appeal" within 30 days and only the "foreign organization" has standing to raise that appeal. At trial defendants cannot raise a defense or object on the basis that the foreign organization was, in fact, not a terrorist group. It is sufficient to prove only that the defendant knew that the group was "designated" as a terrorist organization. Therefore, if funds from a church bingo game reached the Irish Republican Army and the players knew such funds directly, indirectly, partly or entirely reached the IRA, then the players would conceivably be guilty of violating this law if the IRA was "designated". If the Secretary "designated" an overseas Muslim religious organization, or a Jesuit mission organization in South America, or a University in China---rightly or wrongly---as terrorist, then material support by Americans would be unlawful.

The *1996 Anti-Terrorism Act* is replete with limitations upon discovery and the admissibility of evidence at trial where it may impinge upon what is deemed "classified". This "secret evidence" has been cause for concern.

On July 8, 2002 a North Carolina man, Mohammad Hammoud, became the first person to be convicted under the 1996 law as a result of funneling profits from a cigarette-smuggling ring to Hezbollah, a designated terrorist organization based in Lebanon. However, on the date of Hammoud's conviction, a federal judge in Los Angeles declared the same law unconstitutional and threw out a March, 2001 indictment against seven people accused of directing charitable donations to an Iranian group "designated" as a terrorist organization. The judge questioned the failure to afford due process scrutiny of the "designation" status by the Secretary of State, or at the trial stage. The law, often called the "material support statute" will also be challenged by a New York attorney and her translator who were accused of relaying messages from a convicted terrorist to his terrorist associates overseas. (A.P., Tim Whitemire, 7/8/02)

b. The USA Patriot Act:

The passage of the *USA Patriot Act* shortly after 9/11 provoked further protests from civil liberties groups such as the American Civil Liberties Union. Here is a brief discussion of some of the controversial provisions of that Act.

(1) Prosecution of Designated Domestic Terrorist Groups: This provision empowers the Secretary of State and the Attorney General to "designate" domestic groups as "terrorist organizations". The Act declares it a crime for anyone to knowingly make a material contribution to a "designated" terrorist group, and the Act permits the use of "secret evidence" at trial.

(2) The Crime of Domestic Terrorism ("The Greenpeace-Right to Life Provision"):
Section 802 of the *USA Patriot Act* now defines "domestic terrorism" to include any criminal act in the United States that is "dangerous to human life" which appears to be "intended to intimidate or coerce a civilian population" or to "influence the policy of a government by intimidation or coercion", or to "affect the conduct of government. The ACLU believes that this provision could be applied to any minor criminal offense perpetrated by an activist group such as Greenpeace and the Right to Life proponents. Indeed, most acts of civil disobedience during the 1960s civil rights struggle or the anti-war protests during the Vietnam conflict might now be considered "domestic terrorism" under this Act.

(3) Detention of Immigrants: The Attorney General may "certify" the detention of non-citizens for seven days based upon reasonable grounds to believe that he

endangers national security. After seven days criminal or immigration charges must be filed to continue the detention. Where the non-citizen is deported, but no nation will accept him, he may be detained indefinitely.

(4) Electronic Surveillance: Where there is a customary criminal investigation with a relationship to significant foreign intelligence gathering, then there will be expanded electronic surveillance of private persons with minimal judicial supervision. Such surveillance includes access of business records, the Internet, and wiretaps.

(5) Expansion of "Secret Searches": Rather than the required notification of the execution of a search warrant, there will be expanded secret searches of individuals by law enforcement in criminal cases.

Last month, the Foreign Intelligence Surveillance Court (FISA), a secretive federal court that approves spying on terror suspects in the United States, refused to give the Justice Department broad new powers under the *USA Patriot Act*, saying the for the past two years the government abused existing laws and misled the court dozens of times (including 75 applications for search warrants and wiretaps). FISA approves about 1000 warrants a year. Legal standards for FISA warrants are much lower than for traditional criminal warrants. The *USA Patriot Act* included measures that softened the standards for obtaining intelligence warrants, requiring that foreign intelligence be a significant, rather than primary, purpose of the investigation. The Court turned down a Justice Department request to authorize the counterintelligence community, which operates outside most Constitutional restraints, to share information with domestic law enforcement, which operates within Constitutional restraints. Attorney General Ashcroft appealed the ruling, the first such appeal in the 23-year history of FISA. Stewart Baker, former general counsel of the National Security Agency, called the Court's opinion "a public rebuke.... The message is you need better quality control," Baker said. "The judges want to ensure they have information they can rely on implicitly." In light of the fact that FISA was previously criticized as a "rubber stamp" for the government, this public rebuke is unprecedented.
(D. Eggen & S. Schmidt, *Washington Post*, 8/23/02)

c. Detentions of Non-Citizens:

One of the first measures of concern was the Justice Department's authorization of the detention of over 1100 immigrants (while the vast majority of these were persons of Arabic descent, some were Jews). As of February 2002, 1400 people had been jailed, while only some 440 of them remained in INS custody in March. (Monitor, 3/27/02, See also the Chicago Daily Law Bulletin, 2/13/02)

The detentions raised widespread media and congressional concern. ABC reported that detainees were being held in isolation, denied access to legal representation, suffered beatings, sleep deprivation, and blindfolded during interrogations. (ABC, "National Security vs. Citizens' Rights", Bill Blakemore) One detainee was the Health Commissioner of Chester, PA, Dr. Irshad Shaikh, a John Hopkins educated immigrant who was released after the FBI broke down his door and mistakenly arrested him for suspicion of anthrax terrorism. Former FBI Director, William Webster, was among eight former ranking FBI officials who said that these detentions might constitute an "abuse of civil liberties" because it "carries a lot of risk with it". (Washington Post, 11/28/01) Those detentions were supported by new rules issued by the Justice Department and the INS that allowed for the detention of non-citizens who were otherwise adjudged eligible for release from custody by immigration judges where there is "reasonable grounds to believe he is engaged in any activity that endangers the national security of the United States." (See New York Times, "Bush's New Rules", Matthew Purdy, November 25, 2001).

News reports indicated that the detainees were initially held *in communicado* without access to anyone, including lawyers, and their identities were reportedly kept secret; except in the case of Mr. Mohammed Rafiz Butt, a 55 year old Pakistani detainee who, according to the Chairman of the Senate Judiciary Committee Patrick Leahy, died in his cell of a heart attack. His incarceration was later admitted to be "a mistake". (See Comments of Senator Patrick Leahy on "Meet the Press", National Broadcasting Company, 11/25/01) United States Senator Russ Feingold called "unsatisfactory" the Justice Department's early claim that the publication of the identities of the detainees would invade their privacy, could impede the criminal investigation, or deter suspects from cooperating. (ABC, "Justice Declines to Identify Sept. 11 Detainees", Josh Gerstein, 11/21/01)

At the American Bar Association Convention this past August (2002), a measure was passed demanding that the government reveal the identities of the detainees still held in custody, and further to explain why they were not allowed legal representation.

d. Detentions of U.S. Citizens:

Two American citizens who are Muslims are now being held in detention as "enemy combatants" Jose Padillo of Chicago and Yasser Esam Hamdi of New Orleans. Last month U.S. District Court Judge Robert Doumar in Virginia criticized the Assistant Solicitor General for the continuing incarceration of Hamdi as an "enemy combatant" who now resides in to the brig in Norfolk. (AAI, Washington D.C.; N.Y.Times, K.G. Seelye). The Judge stated:

> This case appears to be the first in American jurisprudence where an American citizen has been held incommunicado and subjected to an indefinite detention in the continental United States without charges, without any finding by a military tribunal, and without access to a lawyer. (D. Levenosky, Casper Star-Tribune, 8/18/02)

The government maintains that "anyone detained in connection with the war on terrorism was an enemy combatant and had no right to a lawyer" (N.Y.Times, Seelye) Some believe that the Bush administration has declared war on the doctrine of separation of powers in defying judicial orders concerning Hamdi. (D. Levenosky, Casper Star-Tribune, 8/18/02).

e. Ashcroft's "Citizen Camps":

On August 8, 2002 the Wall Street Journal broke a story that Attorney General John Ashcroft had announced a desire to establish camps for United States citizens who he deems to be "enemy combatants". (See reports in LA Times, Turley, 8/14/02; Wall Street Journal, 8/8/02; CNN.com, Findlaw, Prof. A. Ramasastry - Washington Law School; and R. Goldstein, Internment Camps, 8/26/02) Internees in these special camps will be treated just as Padilla and Hamdi have been so far -- as if they did not possess the basic, traditional rights that can be invoked by U.S. citizens suspected of crimes. (CNN.com, Findlaw, A. Ramasastry, 9/4/02) Jonathon Turley, a constitutional law expert from George Washington University, commented on Ashcroft's plan:

> Few would have imagined any attorney general seeking to reestablish such camps for citizens. Of course, Ashcroft is not considering camps on the order of the internment camps used to incarcerate Japanese American citizens in World War II. But he can be credited only with thinking smaller. (LA Times, Turley, 8/14/02)

Such a policy raises questions of who qualifies as an "enemy combatant" and who decides. How will the line be drawn? Would speech be suspect? Can the government eavesdrop upon those who speak in support of Al Qaeda, or those who criticize government policy in the Middle East? Would such speech "render a US citizen vulnerable to summary arrest and indefinite detention?" Would donations to an Islamic charity suspected of ties to a terrorist organization render one qualified for arrest and detention? (The Monitor, June 12, 2002 - Military Trial for US citizen?)

The question of "who decides?" has been answered by Ashcroft aides who "indicated that a 'high-level committee' [Attorney General, Secretary of Defense, Director of the Central Intelligence Agency] will recommend which citizens are to be stripped of their constitutional rights and sent to Ashcoft's new camps". (CNN.com, Findlaw, A. Ramasastry, 9/4/02) Tim Lynch, Project Director on Criminal Justice at the Cato Institute in Washington states: "The president is asserting the power to take people into custody on US soil outside the judicial process... We have a fourth Amendment, and the president seems to be saying he can set that aside and take into custody anybody he or the FBI thinks are involved in terrorism".

On August 8, the American Bar Association's "Task Force on Treatment of Enemy Combatants" released a preliminary report inquiring "whether the government can-or should-be able to detain American citizens indefinitely without charges and hold them incommunicado without a hearing and without access to counsel." The Report opposes holding detainees without clear standards defining qualifications for detention, due process and judicial review, and access to counsel. The Report finds support in a 1971 law, inspired by the internment of Japanese-Americans during World War II, which provides that "no citizen shall be imprisoned or otherwise detained by the United Sates except pursuant to an Act of Congress." (18 USC 4001 (a)) The 1971 law effectively repealed the 1950 Emergency Detention Act of 1950, "cold war-era statute" that authorized detention camps for "individuals deemed likely to engage in espionage or sabotage." (See ABA Preliminary Report, pgs. 10-11) The ABA Task Force report states that such detentions also violate international law, namely the 1948 Universal Declaration of Human Rights which provides that "everyone has the right to an effective remedy by the competent national tribunals for acts violating ... fundamental rights" and that no one "shall be subjected to arbitrary arrest, detention or exile."

The Justice Department contends that the 1971 law does not apply to the Chief Executive who has sole authority to establish citizen camps for enemy combatants without legislative intervention. The Supreme Court may be unwilling to challenge this use of executive power in light of it holding in Korematsu v. *United States, 321 U.S. 760 (1944),* wherein it held that an executive order for the "civil exclusion" of all persons of "Japanese ancestry" in time of war with Japan was constitutional, regardless that it resulted in the internment of 120,000 Japanese-Americans.

The effectiveness of mass arrests has not been proven to expedite the investigative process. The French and English have utilized such methods as to suspected terrorist in Algeria and Northern Ireland respectively with little success. Although over 1400 persons were detained in the United States and nearly 200 were detained in Europe, very few have been charged in connection with 9/11. Some intelligence experts feel that the mass arrests of suspects "were designed for public consumption" without serving any "real purpose". (Monitor, 3/27/02) Others say that such measures have a deterrent effect, regardless that the traditional law enforcement was unable to make many meaningful arrests. Attorney General Ashcroft made a similar comment regarding Justice's program of voluntary interrogations. (Monitor, 3/27/02)

f. Military Tribunals for Enemy Combatants:

On November 14, 2001 President Bush promulgated a military order allowing for the trial of "non-citizens" suspected of terrorism before special military commissions. At first many believed that this process would likely be "swift and largely secret":

> The release of information might be limited to the barest facts, like the defendant's name and sentence. (Washington Post, "Liberty and the Pursuit of Terrorists, C.Lane, 11/25/01)

In the past, military tribunals were convened in secret before military officers (selected by the Defense Department) who could convict by a two- third's majority. (See Reuters, Anton Ferreira, November 23, 2001). Traditionally, non-citizen suspects would be denied a public trial, the requirement of proof beyond a reasonable doubt, the right of counsel of choice (lawyers are appointed by the military), the right of the unanimous verdict by a jury of peers, the right of cross examination, and the right of appeal.

Public criticism of Bush's initial announcement of tribunals last November was widespread. Spain refused to extradite eight suspected al-Qaeda terrorists who are believed to have been involved in the September 11, 2001 bombings from Spain without guarantees from the United States that they will not face a trial in a military court, saying that such a process falls below "judicial norms" established by the 15-nation European Union. (See New York Times, "Bush's New Rules", Matthew Purdy, November 25, 2001 & Associated Press, "Spain Seeks Extradition Promise", J. Socolovsky, 11/25/01)

New York Times columnist William Safire commented that the President had assumed "what amounts to dictatorial power to jail or execute aliens suspected of terrorism" through the proposed use of a "kangaroo court [which] can conceal evidence, make up its own rules, find defendant guilty even if a third of officers disagree, and execute alien with no review by any civilian court". (See NY Times, "Seizing Dictatorial Power" 11/15/01) Richard Goldstone, chief prosecutor for the United Nations War Crimes Tribunal dubbed the President's plan as "second-or third-class justice". (See Reuters, Legal Expert Attacks Plan, A. Ferreira, 11/23/01)

The American Bar Association Task Force on Terrorism and the Law, Report and Recommendations on Military Commissions, January 4, 2002 questioned the President's authority to utilized military commissions so expansively; and the ABA added that "persons lawfully present in the United States" are protected from such tribunals absent an express act of Congress. (See ABA Task Force on Military Commissions, 1/4/02)

Public attention and legal concerns were thought to have prompted the Bush Administration to modify its original plan with its March 21, 2002 announcement that noncitizen enemy combatants appearing before military tribunals would have certain rights: (1) court-appointed military lawyers or privately retain counsel of choice, (2) public trials in that journalists are allowed to observe except where there is discussion of classified material, (3) conviction requires proof beyond a reasonable doubt by a two-thirds vote of the court, but the invocation of the death penalty requires a unanimous verdict, and (4) appeals would be heard by panels of military and/or civilian specialists. (Chicago Tribune, Bush Sets Rules, John Diamond, March 21, 2002)

However, there was yet another modification by the Attorney General last month (August, 2002) when he announced the detention of two Muslim U.S. citizens deemed "enemy combatants", and then indicated that other U.S. citizens may be detained in "citizen camps"---thus abandoning the idea of confining the military tribunals to "non-citizens" and allowing them access to counsel of choice.

g. Racial/Ethnic Profiling and Discrimination:

Shortly after 9/11, the American-Arab Anti-Discrimination Committee reported that racial profiling of Arab and Muslims in the United States had resulted in 500 alleged hate crimes. (Chicago Tribune, "Americans on Alert for Terror", Karen Brandon and Dahleen Glanton, November 25, 2001)

Negative connotations associated with "profiling" have not always been the case. Law enforcement agencies have historically succeeded in utilizing legally acceptable scientific profiles to identify suspected drug smugglers and hijackers. In private industry, employers have successfully reduced workplace violence through the use of objective, scientific psychological profiling and testing to identify potential violent employees. However, after 9/11 some overzealous private security and law enforcement officers abandoned the use of scientific "identifiers", but instead employed subjective, arbitrary profiling. Shortly after 9/11 many airline passengers who merely appeared Middle Eastern were summarily ejected from domestic and international flights as "a security risk". This includes some Jews found praying in Hebrew on board an international flight from the United States.

Last December an Arab-American secret service agent assigned to fly to Texas to protect the President was refused passage on an American Airlines flight because his credentials were suspicious. The Federal Aviation Administration had acknowledged that airport security screeners at one time were profiling Arab-Americans based upon religion, accent or ethnic appearance: "There appears to have been a rash of improper and insensitive searches," (New York Times, "Directive on Searches", Laurie Goldstein, 11/25/01)

Another perception of governmental "profiling" surfaced when the State Department announced a halt to immigration of young, male immigrants from the Middle East and then proceeded to expel 6000 illegal Arab and Muslim aliens, notwithstanding the millions of other illegal immigrants presently residing in the United States. At the same time, in November of 2001 and again in March of 2002, the Justice Department directed local law enforcement to conduct "voluntary" interrogations of 8000 foreigners residing in the United States, namely Arab and Muslim males between ages 18 and 33. (Chicago Tribune, US to Interview Arab Nationals, N. Bendavid, 3/21/02) The Associated Press reported that some police chiefs were "in open revolt against" the Justice Department's plan because they were hesitant to appear to be engaging in ethnic profiling. Chicago's Police Superintendent Terry Hillard withheld the support of his Department. The Portland, Oregon Police Chief, Andrew Kirkland, refused to follow the directive, saying that the law does not permit the police to "go out and arbitrarily interview people whose only offense is immigration" to the United States. (See AP, "Portland Cops Jilt Feds", 11/22/01; Ashcroft to Testify, J. Salant, 11/26/01; NY Times, Wait Until Dark, F. Rich, 11/24/01)

In May of 2002 federal officials again directed local law enforcement to help with the enforcement of the *1996 Anti-Terrorism Act* as to illegal aliens with emphasis upon Arabs and Muslims. Some believe that this expanded enforcement scheme through local police will present "a grave risk of racial profiling and civil rights abuses, not just against non-citizens but also against citizens deemed not to look "American." (Chicago Daily Law Bulletin, Lawyer's Forum J Lindsay &A Singer, 5/8/02)

h. Freezing Assets:

In still another exercise of executive authority, on December 4, 2001 the President announced that the Treasury Department was freezing the assets of two overseas banks and the Holy Land Foundation [to be distinguished from the "United Holy Land Fund"]. The Foundation and the banks were accused of providing funds to a listed "terrorist organization" under the *1996 Anti-Terrorism Act*; i.e. the Hams. Although Foundation attorneys claimed that the government's motives were political in an attempt to smear the Foundation, an FBI memo published in the Dallas News revealed surveillance evidence that the Hams leaders met with key officials in the Holy Land Foundation in 1993 to discuss collecting funds to help the Hams and defeat a self-rule government in Palestine by waging a "holy war". Attendees agreed that the United States provided a good venue for raising funds, providing a perfect legal atmosphere to obtain financial and political support for the Hams (referred to as "amah") The FBI reported that Hams initially funded the Holy Land Foundation with over $200,000. (N.Y. Times, The Money Trail, David Firestone, 12/6/01).

6. A Community "At-Risk"

The backlash against Arabs and Muslims in American society is serious. Some compare it to the early treatment of German Jews in the 1930s, or the internment of Japanese-Americans in the 1940s, or the Congressional investigations on "Un-American Activities" under Joseph McCarthy in the 1950s. Unfortunately, there is a perception in the community that governmental agencies charged with rights enforcement, such as the EEOC and Justice's Civil Rights Division, cannot be trusted as they appear undistinguishable from their sister agencies, such as the F.B.I and INS, who are charged with law enforcement duties including investigations, interrogations, detentions, and at times deportations.

Consequently, there are clear signs that the Arab-American community has somewhat withdrawn from the political, social and professional process in the United States since 9/11. Attendance at religious, social and professional gatherings is significantly down, as seen, for example, at an annual "professional networking" reception in Chicago last February, or the meeting of a local "Arab-American Democratic Club" on candidates night in March. At a sparsely attended dinner for Arab-American journalists recently a medical doctor commented that "my referrals are down 50%" since 9/11. For a time Muslim women were afraid to leave their home to shop, and they forbid their children from attending school. At a recent public forum sponsored by the United States Commission on Civil Rights, only a handful of persons from the community attended.

However, the most compelling evidence of a community in seclusion is demonstrated by advisory statement issued to "At-Risk Communities" by the Arab-American Anti-Discrimination Committee. Excerpted below are precautions to take "in the event of an attack":

* In the event of an attack, avoid unfamiliar crowds...and consider alternatives to public transportation, avoid "political discussions" with unfamiliar persons, consider maintaining a "low public profile"

* If endangered due to ethnicity or religion, call the police, contact the FBI, "go to a safe location such as; a police station or a church" [note: omits mosque]

* If your business is identified as Arab or Muslim, "know all exits", go home "with at least one friend or colleague", pre-set police protection.

* If child identified as or confused with Arab or Muslim, arrange with school not to let children travel home on school bus or otherwise without two responsible adults, or if child stays on school grounds that they stay in safe location.

*At home, discuss actions to take with your family to keep safe, check locks on doors and windows, and consider home security service and installing cameras over entranceways.

7. Conclusion

When the Arab-American Bar Association issued a warning in its "Preliminary Report on Hate Crimes" a year ago, it was concerned about the protection of life and property in the event of another terrorist attack. This concern has not abated, but rather multiplied into variable threats, all revolving about the bedrock of our democracy, the Constitution. Many fear that measures enacted after 9/11 have empowered the government to: (1) indiscriminately choose foreign or domestic organizations suspected of supporting terrorism and then jail or deport anyone who gives them "material support's on the basis of "secret evidence"; (2) jail those who commit minor criminal offenses that it deems as "dangerous to human life" where the perpetrators intend to "intimidate" society or influence government policy, (3) detain U.S. citizens and non citizens suspected of being "enemy combatants" without bail, *in communicado*, without access to an attorney; (4) prepare "citizen camps" to incarcerate U.S. citizens, and (5) avoid the justice process by trying such individuals before military tribunals.

Many jurists, local police, foreign governments, and even the Foreign Intelligence Surveillance Court have openly voiced opposition to some of these measures such as indefinite, *in communicado* detentions of non citizens, and the use of military tribunals to try foreign and U.S. citizens. Let no one forget that the purpose of the terrorist attacks was not so much to murder innocent people, but rather to stir an over reaction both here and abroad.

Appendix III
AMERICAN MUSLIMS: ONE YEAR AFTER 9-11

By
Council on American-Islamic Relations
CAIR Research Center
Dr. Mohamed Nimer,
Director of Research

EXECUTIVE SUMMARY
- Condemning attacks
- National Muslim leadership takes the lead
- Scholars and imams: Islam demands we stand for justice
- From national to local
- Supporting law enforcement
- National organizations urge support
- Average American Muslim supports anti-terror efforts
- Muslims join in the healing
- Muslims assist relief effort
- Together in mourning
- Honoring heroes

MUSLIMS REACH OUT TO FELLOW AMERICANS
- Opening mosques to neighbors
- Education: getting to know one another

AMERICANS UPHOLD TRADITION OF TOLERANCE
- Opinion polls: Americans not anti-Muslim
- Americans lend hands to their Muslim neighbors
- Minority and faith communities extend support

MUSLIMS TARGETED BY EXTREMISM
- Anti-Muslim rhetoric
- Southern Baptist Convention
- Televangelist Pat Robertson
- Attorney General John Ashcroft
- Senator Gordon Smith
- Conservative commentator Ann Coulter
- Rep. C. Saxby Chambliss
- Free Congress Foundation President Paul Weyrich
- Franklin Graham

- Local churches
- Simon Wiesenthal Center Dean Marvin Hier
- Toward Tradition President Daniel Lapin
- Hate crimes wound a community
- Murders
- Attacks on mosques
- Attacks on Muslim women
- Bombs and arson attacks
- Physical assaults
- Workplace discrimination

GOVERNMENT EFFORTS ON BEHALF OF MUSLIMS
- Law enforcement agencies battle hate

CIVIL LIBERTIES: A VICTIM OF 9/11
- Civil liberty violations

THE USA PATRIOT ACT OF 2001
- Detentions
- Security interviews
- Closing charities
- Raids on businesses
- Passenger profiling
- Guarding America's tradition of liberty
- Ethnic minorities
- The civil liberties coalition
- Congressional action
- Media promotion of tolerance

APPENDIX
- CAIR Full Page Advertisement
- ISNA joins AMPCC in condemning terrorist attacks
- U.S. Muslim Scholars Condemn Attacks
- Scholars of Islam speak out against terrorism; clarify position of Islam
- Statement of California Muslim Organizations
- Muslim Religious figures condemn terrorism
- Participants in the National Day of Unity and Prayer

Executive Summary

Viewed through the American Muslim experience, here are the facts of 9-11 and its aftermath:

1   Muslims have taken a decisive stand against the senseless violence of extremists. They have unequivocally and repeatedly condemned the attacks on the nation. They have communicated their convictions in many forums at various levels. They have met their responsibilities as citizens of this country, participating the nation's healing after the attacks and lending support to government efforts to thwart and punish terrorists.

2   To many Muslims, 9-11 also represented a turning point in how America is struggling to accept them as a community with a distinct religious identity. In that regard, Muslims have witnessed the good, the bad and the ugly. Not only did Muslims die in the attacks, but they also had to cope immediately with a violent backlash and lingering anti-Muslim agitation. Islamaphobes came out strongly in favor of placing the guilt on the religion of Islam and the worldwide community of Muslims. Racist elements exacted vengeance on anyone who looked Muslim (or Arab). Politically influential anti-Muslim elements have worked relentlessly to push this country in favor of a policy of confrontation with the Muslim world.

3   Attacks against Muslims tapered off eight weeks after 9-11, but generally anti-Muslim incidents remained higher throughout the year than in previous years.

4   Despite the fear and stress that Muslims suffered in the wake of the attacks, many things have changed for the better in the life of Muslims as a community. As this report details, interfaith communication has now become part and parcel of ordinary Muslim activity, even in communities where such functions had not even been considered in the past.

5   Public opinion polls varied in their assessment, but overall they indicated that the majority of Americans appreciated the strong stance of Muslims, and showed tolerance and kindness toward them in the wake of anti-Muslim hate crimes.

6   Local and federal authorities have taken a decisive position against hate crimes. However, anti-Muslim sentiment continues to be harbored and tolerated even within sensitive governmental bodies.

7   The U.S. government has hardly found the right balance between security and civil liberty. The hysteria, and perhaps the lack of Muslim political clout, led Congress to acquiesce to government moves sacrificing the civil rights of Arabs and Muslims in the name of fighting terrorism.

8   The wave of anti-Muslim hate crimes after 9-11 was the worst in the nation's history. Although it has tapered off since the early weeks of the crisis, anti-Muslim agitation in television and radio has contributed to unprecedented acts of hate crimes.

9   Islam and Muslims became a matter of public discourse in America. Along with major media organizations, mainline Protestants and Catholics, as well as members from the Black, Latino, Asian and Jewish communities have favored a position that distinguishes between extremists and mainstream Muslims. On the other hand, some Christian conservatives and pro-Israel zealots have actively sought to drive a wedge between Muslims and the nation. Members of these groups revived the defunct "clash of civilizations" thesis and have actively worked for the exclusion of Muslims from public forums, while continuing to argue for anti-Muslim public policies.

Introduction

It is not clear yet how 9-11 will go down in history. Several things, however, are quite clear. The gruesome crime of terror impacted every segment of American society (and a good deal of the international community), so much so, that people followed and reflected on its aftermath and many Americans took action based upon their understanding of the world after the event. One major issue that came to the forefront was the Muslims of America-their status and, in some situations, their presence-became a matter of public debate.

Muslims have had to deal with those who thought Muslims had to choose between commitment to their faith and allegiance to their nation and, on the other end, those who argued for a better understanding of Islam and Muslims. Luckily, the intolerant crowd is in the minority.

This report documents the mixed responses of Muslims and others in the aftermath of the terrorist attacks and reviews actions and policies taken by the government to safeguard security and civil liberty. It is fortified with an appendix containing further illustrations and documentation of Muslim responses to 9-11.

American Muslims: Exercising Civic Duty

The moment that Muslims in America turned on their televisions and were confronted with the horrible reality of 9-11's terrorist attacks, the paths they would need to take in the following months became crystal clear. Muslims realized their responsibilities as a community whose faith has been linked to the worst terrorist attack in U.S. history. Some Americans who succumbed to bigotry and intolerance tried to question their loyalty; some even committed violence against them. At the same time, Muslims felt the anguish of being part and parcel of a nation that had been the target of an inhuman attack. As a result, Muslims in America doubled their efforts to establish themselves as an integral part of the American mosaic, and they seized the opportunity to fulfill their obligations as citizens and residents of the freest country on Earth.

Condemning attacks

The response to the events of 9-11 from American Muslims of every walk of life-leaders, scholars, and laymen-was swift, loud and unambiguous: this act was abhorred by Islam, and must be denounced in the strongest of terms. Muslims set out to make sure their fellow Americans were aware of this sentiment.

National Muslim leadership takes the lead

Within hours of the first plane hitting the World Trade Center on 9-11, American Muslim organizations issued a joint statement condemning the terrorist attacks. The statement was endorsed by major Islamic organization in the United States, including the Islamic Society of North America (ISNA), Islamic Circle of North America (ICNA), Imam Warith Deen Muhammad's Muslim American Society (MAS), the American Muslim Political Coordination Council (an umbrella group for major American Muslim public affairs organizations), and numerous others. The statement read in part:

> "American Muslims utterly condemn what are vicious and cowardly acts of terrorism against innocent civilians. We join with all Americans in calling for the swift apprehension and punishment of the perpetrators. No political cause could ever be assisted by such immoral acts."

CAIR went on to sponsor a full-page advertisement in the *Washington Post* on September 16, 2001, condemning the attacks, calling for the punishment of the perpetrators, and expressing gratitude to the rescue workers and condolences to the families of the victims. The ad read,

> We at the Council on American-Islamic Relations (CAIR) along with the American Muslim community are deeply saddened by the immense loss of human life from Tuesday's tragic events. Our thoughts and prayers are with the families, friends and loved ones of those who have been injured and those who have died. We applaud the heroes from all Fire Departments, Police Departments and Emergency Medical Services and extend our gratitude to all participating in the ongoing rescue and relief efforts. American Muslims wholly condemn the vicious and cowardly acts of terrorism. We join with all Americans in calling for the swift apprehension and punishment of the perpetrators of these crimes against humanity. May we all stand together through these hard times to promote peace and love over violence and hate.

Islamic organizations and leaders then reached out to other faith communities to condemn terrorism in solidarity with one another. Together with other major Christian groups, such as the National Conference of Catholic Bishops, national and regional Muslim umbrella groups issued this statement:

> We believe that the one God calls us to be peoples of peace. Nothing in our Holy Scriptures, nothing in our understanding of God's revelation, nothing that is Christian or Islamic justifies terrorist acts and disruption of millions of lives.

The immediate and unequivocal condemnation of the attacks by national American Muslim leaders was acknowledged and praised by political and community leaders and opinion makers. In a news conference following his visit to a Washington, DC, mosque on September 17, President George Bush praised the national Muslim leaders standing at his side as "good folks who were appalled and outraged at the terrorist attacks. It is my honor to be meeting with leaders who feel just the same way I do. They're outraged, they're sad. They love America just as much as I do…. Americans and Muslim friends and citizens, tax-paying citizens…were just appalled and could not believe what we saw on our TV screens." (www.whitehouse.gov/news/releases/2001/09/print/20010917-11.html). Observed *Boston Globe* columnist James Carroll on October 9, 2001, "Islamic religious leaders have been forthright in condemning the murderous assaults against America."

American Muslim leaders made a special effort to appear in the media of the Muslim world, and in particular, the Arab media. These leaders aired their emphatic condemnation of the terrorist attacks in popular outlets like the satellite television network al-Jazeerah. CAIR's research director published a refutation of al-Qaeda and its worldview in the high-circulation, London-based Arabic language newspaper *al-Hayat* on January 9, 2002. The piece responded to Osama Bin Laden's attempt to draw a parallel between his cause and that of the Palestinians:

"Bin Laden exaggerated in blaming the United States for the woes of the Muslim world. The U.S. is not party to many of the transgressions committed against Muslims, although it could play a greater role in conflict resolution.

It is of particular benefit to highlight the vision of the Muslims of America, who look at American state and society in factual terms. [Here] the American is a neighbor, a classmate, or a coworker. Americans are fellow citizens who have spouses, children, homes, and elderly persons...

Moreover, striking against American economic interests [like Bin Laden instructed his followers] is a threat to the interests of the whole world, including Arab and Muslim regions. This is because Arab and Muslim labor and their economic production are only part of a global, interdependent economy."

Scholars and imams: Islam demands we stand for justice

Nationally known and respected Islamic religious leaders took to the airwaves and print media to communicate the position that the 9-11 attacks violate Islamic teachings. Only days after the attack, Imam Hamza Yusuf, an Islamic scholar and director of the Zaytouna Institute in Santa Clara, California, consulted with President Bush and sat by his side in solidarity when he addressed a joint session of Congress in the week after the attacks. Imam Yusuf appeared with Imam Siraj Wahaj of Brooklyn on CBS's "60 Minutes" to unconditionally condemn the attacks, and went on to make the rounds of print and broadcast media to present Islam's prohibition of terrorism from a scholar's point of view. "No one can grant these attackers any legitimacy," Imam Yusuf told the *San Jose Mercury News* on September 16, 2001. "It was evil."

On September 17, dozens of scholars of Islam at major colleges and universities throughout the country issued a lengthy joint statement, speaking against terrorism, clarifying the Islamic position on the attacks, and expressing their compassion for grieving family members. "We are grief-stricken at these horrifying events," they wrote; "the murder of innocents can never be justified and must not be tolerated." (http://groups.colgate.edu/aarislam/response.htm)

Ingrid Mattson, a professor of Islamic studies and Muslim-Christian relations at Hartford Seminary, told *The New York Times* on October 8, 2001 that there was no basis in Islamic law for the terrorist attacks. "The basic theological distortion is that any means are permitted to achieve the end of protesting against perceived oppression," said Dr. Mattson, a practicing Muslim. "Islamic law is very clear."

Imams repeated this message during Muslim gatherings throughout the year. President of ISNA, Muhammad Nur Abdullah, standing on a stage flanked by U.S. flags on August 30, 2002, said in his opening address to the 30,000 participants in the 39th ISNA convention that Islam condemns the 9-11 violence. Summarizing the prevailing sentiment among America's Muslims, he said, "We're for justice.... This is our country. American Muslims, we care for the betterment of this country and for every human being."

From national to local

The message of condemnation of the terrorist attacks from national Islamic groups and scholars was intended not only for the general public, but for local American Muslim communities as well. National Muslim groups and religious leaders exercised their leadership and responsibility by playing an instrumental role in steering local communities into a united stance against terror in the wake of the 9-11 attacks. The groups that were signatory to the joint condemnation of the terrorist attacks took the message to their constituents, urging them at the grassroots to proclaim this uncompromising stance. CAIR, for example, distributed a response kit, including a sample press release, to local communities in order to help them quickly and unequivocally denounce the attacks as an affront to Islam and humanity.

Local communities responded. Across the nation and in virtually every major American city, community mosques and associations followed the lead of the national organizations. For example, using the national leaders' statement as a foundation, a coalition of ten New Orleans-area mosques issued a joint condemnation of the attacks (*The Times-Picayune*, September 12, 2001). The Islamic Society of Central Jersey (ISCJ) published a full-page open letter on September 23, 2001 in the *New Jersey Star-Ledger* "condemning the vicious and cowardly acts of terrorism." In San Diego, Mohamad Nasser, San Diego chapter president of the Muslim American Society (MAS), told his local paper that the attacks were "absolutely cowardly, absolutely appalling.... There is nothing justifying what happened today. It is just unbelievable." (*San Diego Union-Tribune*, 9-11, 2001) At a Buffalo, New York interfaith meeting the day after 9-11, leaders from the local Islamic community condemned the attacks as an "utter violation of all the principles of Islam," the Rev. Stan Bratton, a meeting participant, told *The Buffalo News* on September 12, 2001. Dr. Khalid J. Qazi, president of the Western New York chapter of the American Muslim Council, also told that paper he condemned "this cowardly act of terrorism" and expressed hope that those responsible are quickly brought to justice. And Arsalan Tariq Iftikhar, executive director of the St. Louis chapter of CAIR, published several op-ed pieces expounding on the difference between extremists and mainstream Muslims. In one article in the *St. Louis Post-Dispatch* on September 16, 2001, he declared, "As a Muslim and as a St. Louisan, I stand in the strongest conviction and say that the terrorists' acts were no more Islamic than Tim McVeigh's actions were Christian."

Supporting law enforcement

American Muslims endorsed the need for a military campaign overseas as well as a domestic law enforcement effort to bring the perpetrators of the 9-11 attacks to justice. But the support went beyond mere endorsement, to include active assistance and cooperation with the military and law enforcement. This cooperation and support flowed across the board: from national Islamic organizations and from individual Muslims.

National organizations urge support

As the U.S. began the military campaign in Afghanistan, American Muslim groups issued statements in support of bringing the perpetrators of 9-11 to justice. For example, the American Muslim Council issued a statement on October 8, 2001 that read,

> "The American Muslim Council supports our government's action against world terrorism and reaffirms its condemnation of the terrorist attacks of 9-11th against our country. The AMC appreciates the President's leadership in reaffirming that this is a war against terrorism and not against the Afghan people, Muslims or Islam. The AMC commends our President for his statement that our military campaign will take measures to protect the civilian population of Afghanistan.
>
> The AMC is particularly grateful for the President's compassion and humanitarian efforts for the Afghani people along with other initiatives, and fully supports his efforts to deal with the causes of terrorism."

National Muslim organizations urged the American Muslim community to be vigilant in sharing any information about suspected terrorists, and to serve in law enforcement. When the FBI announced its need for Arabic and Farsi translators, community organizations publicly encouraged members of the community to apply for such jobs.

These efforts were deeply appreciated by law enforcement authorities as they investigated the 9-11 attacks. In remarks to the American Muslim Council's annual convention in June, FBI Director Robert Mueller said:

> "The active work of many in the American Muslim community in cities nationwide has merited public thanks and praise.
>
> I'll tell you one of the greatest acts of support has been the way the Muslim and Arab communities have responded to our urgent need for translators…for which we are grateful, extraordinarily grateful.…
>
> And again, I want to thank the many Muslim-Americans who have provided help to the FBI over the past nine months in a variety of ways. It has truly been invaluable."

Aslam Abdullah, editor-in-chief of *Minaret*, an American Muslim publication, published a piece in the *Los Angles Times* on July 3, 2002 in support of law enforcement. He wrote,

> "This year, the Fourth of July is more than a holiday and celebration for me. It is going to be a tense day. I will be watching the news closely, praying that the day ends peacefully…I will be praying for those law enforcement officers who will be keeping a close watch on everything that appears to be suspicious. I will be praying for my people, my American people."

Average American Muslim supports anti-terror efforts:

Even as the American Muslim leadership felt a responsibility to speak out strongly on the events of 9-11, polls indicated that the vast majority of Muslims around the country instinctively reacted in revulsion to the terrorist attacks. This was true even though, like many of their fellow Americans, a significant percentage expressed reservations about the possible consequences of war. Still, according to a poll commissioned in early December by the Muslims in the American Public Square (MAPS) Project, most Muslims said they supported the US response.

Nearly 60 percent approved of President Bush's handling of terrorist attacks, 66 percent agreed that the war was being fought against terrorism, not Islam, and more than half said they supported the military action. (The study, conducted by Zoghby International, queried 1,781 American Muslims between Nov. 8 and Nov. 19.)

Acting on their own, individual Muslims reached out to the press to make their fellow Americans aware of their views. One of many such pieces, a letter to the editor in *The New York Times* by Basil Abdelkarim of Torrance, Cal., reads:

"As an American Muslim, I have no doubt that Osama bin Laden sponsored the horrific attacks of 9-11...We have entered a frightening era, and genuine reconciliation between the West and the Muslim world assumes an even greater urgency."

Muslims join in the healing:

Beyond condemning the events of 9-11, disassociating Islam from terror, and urging support for the apprehension of those responsible, Muslims had a need, just as their fellow Americans did, to heal the psychological wounds of the attack. And so, just as their neighbors did, Muslims rushed to help in the rescue and recovery operations, they crowded memorials for the victims, and they honored those who risked and gave their lives to help the survivors.

Muslims assist relief effort:

Immediately following the attacks, Islamic organizations urged their constituents to take specific steps to assist in the relief efforts. They called on Muslim doctors to travel to the scene (a Muslim medical technician died in the rescue operations), they urged donations of goods and money to the Red Cross, and they set up special funds to collect money for relief.

To encourage Muslims to donate blood, leaders of the four organizations that make up the American Muslim Political Coordination Council (AMPCC) waited for hours alongside their fellow Americans lined up to donate blood at the Red Cross building in downtown Washington, DC. As far away as Los Angeles, Muslims responded to the call, with about 250 people giving blood the city's University Muslim Medical Association Free Clinic, as reported by the *Los Angeles Times* on September 30, 2001. Several other blood drives at local Islamic centers were reported as well, especially in the New York, New Jersey and Washington, DC metropolitan regions.

The New York-based ICNA was among the most active Muslim groups in the relief effort, compiling a list of dozens of missing, dead, and injured Muslims as a means of serving the community and demonstrating the universality of grief Americans felt as a result of the attack. ICNA advised its members to donate blood to the victims and suggested that local leaders establish active contacts with local authorities in order to be available to assist when needed. Local centers and associations pitched in as well; for example, the Turkish American Muslim Cultural Association raised $1,000 for the Red Cross 9-11 Fund. All Dulles Area Muslim Society in Sterling, Virginia announced that the mosque had raised $6,000 for the American Red Cross and organized a blood drive.

Another Muslim charity, Mercy-USA for Aid and Development, reported in its September 2002 newsletter the disbursement of $65,000 in cash grants to six major relief organizations involved in the provision of assistance to the victims of the attacks. The groups include the American Red Cross and the Salvation Army, funds set up by New York Governor George Pataki and New York Mayor Rudolph Giuliani, and two firefighter associations.

Together in mourning:

At innumerable events around the country, Muslims participated in events to promote mutual healing after the trauma of the terrorist attacks. Muslims were invited to join fellow Americans in the National Day of Prayer and Remembrance ceremony on September 14 at the National Cathedral in Washington, DC. The nationally televised service emphasized healing and unity and was attended by President George W. Bush, former presidential candidate Al Gore, former Presidents Bill Clinton, Jimmy Carter, George Bush and Gerald Ford, as well as Washington diplomats and members of Congress. In his opening prayer, Dr. Muzammil H. Siddiqi, then president of the Islamic Society of North America (ISNA), read verses from the Qur'an and expressed grief on behalf of all Muslims for those who were killed or injured in the 9-11 terrorist attacks in New York, Pennsylvania, and Washington, DC.

At an emotional interfaith service held at New York's Yankee Stadium for the families and colleagues of the victims of the World Trade Center terrorist attacks, 30,000 people came together to hear words of hope from religious leaders of all faiths. *USA Today* reported that many were moved to tears by the recitation of prayers by Muslim leaders. Addressing the crowd, Imam Izak-El M. Pasha, a New York Police Department chaplain, said: "They (the terrorists) are no believers at all. We condemn them and their acts, their cowardly acts, and we stand with our country. This must stop." (*USA Today*, September 24, 2001).

Local communities helped contribute to the healing in creative and touching ways. The Western New York Chapter of the American Muslim Council presented a check to help buy trees for the Amherst Memorial Hill Grove in honor of the 9-11 terrorist victims. Dr. Khalid J. Qazi, president the chapter, told *The Buffalo News* on November 17, 2001, "The contribution to the Hill Grove fund was a way for the Muslim community to help create a living memorial to the victims and express its horror at the events of 9-11." Imams participated in interfaith memorial services across the country, and Muslims initiated or participated in candlelight vigils in Washington, DC and other cities.

Honoring heroes:

Not only did Muslims condemn the terrorist attacks and grieve over their victims, they were deeply appreciative of the firefighters, police officers, and other emergency response personnel and their grueling efforts to save lives. Muslims expressed this gratitude in local events honoring these heroes. For example, in Chicago, Muslims joined with the National Conference for Community and Justice and city officials in a ceremony to honor Chicago area law enforcement officers, firefighters, and paramedics who had volunteered to assist in the recovery efforts at the World Trade Center (*Chicago Sun-Times*, Nov. 16, 2001).

The American Muslim Council (AMC) established the Salman Hamdani Award to honor the heroism of the award's namesake, a medical technician who died while helping in the relief effort at the World Trade Center on 9-11. Hamdani had left his Queens home in the morning and apparently saw the disaster in Lower Manhattan unfold from the subway train on the elevated tracks. He immediately headed toward the scene. Hamdani, a Pakistani-born laboratory research assistant, was missing for more than six months after the terrorist attacks. His remains-along with his medical bag containing an ID-were finally recovered near the north tower.

The following eulogy by New York Police Commissioner Raymond Kelly was published in the *Washington Post*: "We don't know how many people he helped, how many lives he saved.... But if you look at his life, you know he was determined to make a difference, and he did. He was indeed a hero." At AMC's convention held in Washington, DC on May 16, 2002, Mrs. Talat Hamdani, mother of Salman

Hamdani, received AMC's first Salman Hamdani Award. She also received a similar award from CAIR-New York.

Muslims reach out to fellow Americans

The events of 9-11 were followed by a surge of public interest in Islam and Muslims. Ordinary people wanted to know what Muslims thought of the attacks; others began wondering about the intentions of Muslims in their midst. American Muslims quickly realized that the best way to allay fears, prevent further damage to America's well being, and preserve the society's unity was to reach out to their neighbors to an unprecedented degree. "The American Muslims' outreach to the rest of the country has been noteworthy for its unusual degree of openness," observed the *Los Angeles Times* on September 30, 2001. Mosques opened their doors, Muslims conducted educational programs and teach-ins, and Islamic organizations and centers launched media and advertising campaigns to communicate with their fellow Americans.

Opening mosques to neighbors

Muslim community organizations resolved that their communities should use the national spotlight focused on them to educate others about Islam. Islamic centers, even those where interfaith activities were not particularly encouraged in the past, have begun holding "open mosque" activities, and the practice has spread, especially since CAIR issued an action alert encouraging every mosque to plan an open house for non-Muslims. The response from the public has been quite phenomenal. To the surprise of Muslims, virtually all who attended were amiable, spoke candidly, asked sincere questions about Islam, or expressed sympathy to Muslims at time of crisis.

It is impossible to list or even track all of the hundreds of open house and interfaith events Muslims have held since the attacks, but some examples will demonstrate the widespread nature of this trend. The December 2001 issue of *American Muslim*, published by the Muslim American Society (MAS), featured a report on 140 such exchanges involving MAS members in Texas, California, Maryland, Virginia, Michigan, North Carolina, Florida, Ohio, Oklahoma, Washington, DC, Massachusetts, Illinois, Pennsylvania, and Alabama. In several centers, such events marked the first time mosques welcomed visitors from other faith groups.

1   The Islamic Center of Central Jersey hosted a standing room only Interfaith Prayer Program attended by 1,500 members of the Central

New Jersey Muslim, Christian and Jewish communities as well as local political leaders on September 30.

2   About 90 people attended the October 28, 2001 open mosque event at Darul Islah in Teaneck, New Jersey.

3   In an unprecedented act, the leader of Long Island's Catholic Church visited the Island's largest mosque, Islamic Center of Long Island, attending a multifaith service aimed at fostering religious unity in the wake of the attacks. Bishop William Murphy, of the Diocese of Rockville Center, was joined by Protestant ministers, a rabbi and about 150 others at the Islamic Center in Westbury.

4   The Islamic Center of Fort Collins, Colorado held open-mosque events every week for a month after the terrorist attacks. Turnout ranged between 15 and 250, mostly neighbors. These events marked the first time the mosque received members of other faith groups.

5   For the first time, San Diego's twelve mosques began to invite Christians, Jews and anyone else who was interested to attend Ramadan observances to satisfy their curiosity about Islam and to allay their fears about the religion. The Islamic centers came together under a newly formed coordination council called American Muslim Coalition, and, in addition to the open houses, planned town hall meetings and other events.

6   The Muslim Community of Knoxville, Tennessee invited the public to attend a lecture by Imam Hamza Yusuf on March 23, 2002. The event emphasized the need for mutual understanding between Muslims and others. More than 100 people turned out for the event, including State Sen. Tim Burchett and Knoxville Director of Community Relations, Thomas "Tank" Strickland. More than 100 people attended an open house event at Salahadeen Center of Nashville, which was held on November 27, 2001. Participants asked many questions and one reportedly converted to Islam after the event.

7   In Metairie, Louisiana, Masjid Abu Bakr held an open house in September (attended by 25 people) and October (attended by 100 individuals). The mosque had never held such events before.

8   The first-ever open mosque event at the Birmingham Islamic Society in Alabama, held on September 29, 2001, was attended by 400 people. The

second such event was held on October 12, 2001 when 250 people turned out.

9   On November 12, 2001, the Islamic Center at Auburn, Alabama opened for the first time to visits by neighbors. Nearly 300 people came, including law enforcement and other local officials. This was the first time this center held such an event.

10   On November 11, 2001, about 300 people responded to a public invitation to visit the Islamic Center of Tallahassee, Florida, marking the first time the Islamic center had opened its doors to the public.

11   About 500 people turned out for a first-ever public event at the Islamic Community of South West Florida in Port Charlotte, Florida on December 2, 2001. Some participants wrote letters to the editor of their local paper praising the event and the organization.

12   In Jacksonville, Florida, the open mosque event of the Islamic Center of Northeast Florida was attended by 100 individuals, mostly members of neighboring places of worship.

13   About 100 people turned out for the open house event organized by the Islamic Society of Greater Houston on November 4, 2001. Participants listened to presentations about Islam and Muslims. About 1,500 people showed up at the Islamic Association of Colin County in Plano, Texas on December 9, 2001. The turnout astounded organizers of the open house event, the first time a public event had been held there since the center opened in the city.

Through their interactions with others, Muslims became overtly conscious that the American public is for the most part fundamentally decent, open-minded and good-hearted, sophisticated in its thinking and able to distinguish between the acts of an extreme minority and an entire faith community.

Education: getting to know one another

After the terrorist attacks, many Muslim leaders found themselves in demand as sensitivity trainers for companies and institutions interested in exercising good corporate citizenship by reducing the possibility of bias in their workplace. Also, in some universities, Muslim academics and students hit upon the idea of reviving the old 1960's institution, the "teach-in," an impromptu, interactive educational lecture designed to enlighten attendees about the issues of the day.

Several hundred Ford Motor workers of many faiths and jobs attended a program entitled "An Islamic Perspective on the Events of 9-11." The program was sponsored by the automaker. A Muslim engineer addressed the audience, explaining the tenets of Islam and telling them that the faith repudiates the terrorist attacks.

Federal and local government agencies also hosted educational seminars on Islam and the American Muslim community. For example, in January 2002, CAIR conducted sensitivity training workshops for the National Aeronautics and Space Administration (NASA) and the Department of Transportation. In February, a CAIR team presented a briefing to Congressional staffers on the status of American Muslims after 9-11.

A dozen students from Scripps and Pomona colleges attended a "teach-in" held at the Islamic Center of Claremont, California, two weeks after the attacks. It was a last-minute gathering, arranged the day before, at the students' request (*Los Angeles Times*, September 30, 2001). The University of Wisconsin-Madison and members of the Madison Muslim community held a "teach-in" in the days after the events to increase understanding of Islam. The event, according to the September 18, 2001 issue of the *Milwaukee Journal Sentinel*, focused on Islam's fundamental beliefs, how Islam is practiced, and how that practice affects society and politics throughout the world. In Tennessee, 200 people enrolled in the 9-11 class on the Middle East at Vanderbilt University (www.vanderbilt.edu/News/register/Mar18_02/story7.html).

To reach out to a wider public audience, the Independent Writers Syndicate was established out of the CAIR network to offer a Muslim perspective on current issues. The service distributes original commentaries to newspapers and web sites throughout North America. Commentaries are offered free-of-charge to one media outlet in each market area. Although the idea of the syndicate was conceived in 2000, it materialized after 9-11, with newspapers becoming hungry for input from Muslims. In the few months after the attacks syndicate writers were published in more than 100 newspapers-mainly in the U.S., but also in Europe and the Middle East.

Just as CAIR and other national groups did, several local communities reported taking out newspaper advertisements to explain Islam and reach out to non-Muslims. For example, twelve San Diego mosques that had been organizing open mosques events and town hall meetings under the rubric of the American Muslim Coalition have also taken out informational ads in their local newspaper.

California Muslims spearheaded the effort to erect billboards at three high-traffic Orange County and Los Angeles locations to communicate neighborly messages from Muslims. As part of the campaign, two billboards in Los Angeles County and one in Orange County show seven smiling people, including a young woman holding a U.S. flag, above the caption: "Even a smile is Charity--a message from your Muslim neighbor." The message is drawn from a quote attributed to the Prophet Muhammad: "Your smile for your brother is charity."

Americans uphold tradition of tolerance

As America struggled to come to grips with what happened on 9-11, many American leaders emphasized that the nation must not lose sight of the fact that America's pluralism includes Muslims. While many still did not know much about Islam and Muslims, they were willing to withhold their judgment and to give their fellow Muslim citizens the benefit of the doubt. Evidence shows that despite the terrorist attacks; America's favorable perception of Muslims has improved markedly.

Opinion polls: Americans are not anti-Muslim

Shortly after the attacks, almost equal percentages of Americans felt positive, negative, and neutral about Islam as a religion. A September 15th poll by Reuters and Zoghby International found that 38 percent believed Islam is a religion that encourages fanaticism, 42 percent believed it does not, and 20 percent were not sure. (The survey was conducted September 15 - 16, 2001.) Most were able to distinguish between Islam as a religion and the actions of some Muslims: 84 percent of those surveyed considered the U.S. to be at war with a small group of terrorists who may be Muslim, compared to eight percent who say the U.S. is at war with Islam.

Most of the American public professed generally a negative impression of Muslims and Arabs in America shortly after the attacks. Astonishingly, however, this attitude was no different from months before 9-11. In March 2001, only 45 percent of Americans had a positive opinion of Muslim Americans. Similarly, in a September 15, 2001 poll by the University of Michigan Institute for Social Research, 43 percent of poll respondents rated Muslim Americans and Arab-Americans favorably. It is important to note that even this minority's charitable view was reserved for Muslims and Arabs in America. Muslims and Arabs living in the Middle East were viewed positively by only 22 percent of Americans following the attacks (*USA Today*, October 9, 2001).

Despite this negative impression, just two days after the attacks, a majority-65 percent-reported they felt no different toward Arab Americans than they had before, according to a Time/CNN poll conducted on September 13, 2001. Also, balancing this mixed review of Muslims was the fact that the American public was surprisingly confident that Muslims in America sympathized with the rest of the country about the bombings. Seventy-six percent thought American Muslims' sympathies were with Americans, while only 11 percent thought they sympathized with the attackers (Harris Interactive, Inc., *Harris Study No. 15003*, September 27, 2001).

A week after the attacks, a full 90 percent of Americans felt that "Arab Americans, Muslims, and immigrants from the Middle East" would likely be singled out unfairly by their fellow Americans (*CBS News/New York Times* poll, September 20-23, 2001). Fifty percent thought discrimination would be very likely, 40 percent said it was somewhat likely). About 24 percent admitted to negative feelings about Arab-Americans-far from a majority, but potentially more than enough to cause concern. Several questions demonstrated the public's fear and frustration, with 58 percent saying Arabs should undergo special security checks before boarding planes and 49 percent saying they should carry special identification.

Yet other polls suggested this might have been an initial reaction after the shocking tragedy. A *Newsweek* question that specifically mentioned the internment of Japanese Americans during World War II, found 62 percent who said it would be a mistake to target any national group. A Pew Research Center survey found 57 percent who opposed the idea of internment camps to round up immigrants from "hostile nations." When deeply held values are tested by terrifying events, it takes time for people to work through their fear and let their better judgment temper any rash response.

Still, in a September 14, 2001 poll conducted by CNN and the national daily *USA Today*, only 31 percent said that since the attacks they had personally heard any of their friends, neighbors, fellow workers or acquaintances make negative comments about Arabs living in America.

The most extensive post-9-11 poll on American's views on Islam, jointly sponsored by the ABC television network and the Beliefnet religion news website, was conducted on January 6, 2002. The poll revealed that the percentage of Americans with a favorable view of Islam had dropped slightly, while the percentage with an unfavorable view of Islam had also dropped. In an October 9th poll, 47 percent had a favorable view, 39 percent said unfavorable and 13 percent said they didn't know. (The October survey was apparently conducted by ABC and not reported at the time.) In January, 41 percent said favorable, 24 percent said unfavorable and 35 percent said they didn't know.

Contrary to predictions of increased aversion toward Arabs and Muslims after 9-11, the General Social Survey of the National Organization for Research at the University of Chicago, which measures a wide variety of long-term public attitudes, found otherwise (*Associated Press*, March 8, 2002). Two months after the 9-11 attacks, the number of Americans with a favorable opinion of Muslims jumped by nearly 15 percent to its highest recorded level, providing a major counterweight to the majority's distrust of Muslims in the days immediately after the incidents (Pew Research Center for the People & the Press, *Post 9-11 Attitudes: Religion more prominent; Muslim-Americans more accepted*, December 6, 2001). The trend has held up, with favorability ratings for US Muslims in March 2002 having dropped off only slightly since the surge in favorability documented in November 2001. Obviously the public mood is not constant, but it has overall remained tolerant toward American Muslims.

Americans lend hands to their Muslim neighbors

There were several instances of Americans from various faith communities coming to the aid of Muslims in the wake of the violent post 9-11 backlash. Jennifer Schock, 31, a Web designer from Fairfax, Virginia, sprang into action upon learning that some American Muslim women started leaving their head scarves at home out of fear for their safety. Schock and other non-Muslim women around the USA began donning scarves themselves as a sign of solidarity with their Muslim sisters. Through the Internet (Website: www.interfaithpeace.org), they established a global network called Scarves for Solidarity to support the right of Muslim women to choose their headwear without fearing retaliation.

Muslim community centers reported many spontaneous acts of kindness from members of the public. Within a week after the attacks, Islamic centers in San Diego received bouquets of flower and cards of support and sympathy from members of other faith groups-especially after reports of Muslim women being afraid to leave home.

One week after 9-11, a Muslim in San Francisco, whose store was vandalized, reported that neighbors tried to offer him money toward the $1,500 repair of the damage.

On October 6, 2001, the *Washington Post* reported several similar stories. The article included the following anecdotes:

> "The Islamic Center in Athens, Ohio, reported being mailed a $100 check from a non-Muslim couple who wrote that 'we are all one people.' In San Diego, the Islamic Center said it was 'flooded with letters and cards of support.' And Olga Benedetto, a 27-year-old student at Chicago's Moody Bible Institute, e-mailed an offer of 'help for those in the Chicago area needing groceries or other needs.... I understand that some of you are afraid to leave your homes.'
>
> Similar sentiments have been evident around the Washington metropolitan area. Egyptian-born Ahmed Heshmat, a doctor who lives near Rockville, said that his wife, Jenane, was shopping recently with their two young daughters when 'the manager came running up to her and gave the girls a gift. It turned out to be pencils and papers. He said it was just to show support.'
>
> In Manassas, Virginia a local interfaith group contacted Prince William County's Muslim Association of Virginia with an offer to guard its mosque, said Association President Yaqub Zargarpur, a businessman who came from Afghanistan 20 years ago."

On December 1, 2001, nearly 850 people jam-packed the Muslim Community Association in Santa Clara, California. Some of the participants asked if the center would consider offering classes to give more detailed presentations on Islam.

One measure of this support is surveys targeting Muslim community members. In an August 2002 CAIR survey, about 80 percent of 945 respondents said they have experienced kindness or support from friends or colleagues of other faiths. (In contrast, 57 percent said they have experienced anti-Muslim bias or discrimination). When they were asked about the way in which they received the support answers varied, with many saying they received best wishes for their safety verbally and in writing. Some reported neighbors and coworkers saying they realized that the attackers do not represent the Islamic faith. A large segment reported specific actions members of other faith groups took to express their support. Neighbors visited Muslims in their homes and volunteered to help do grocery shopping or to accompany them on shopping trips. Members of other faith groups showed up at Friday prayer services at their mosque to express solidarity. Colleagues at work challenged rude and negative remarks about Muslims. Supervisors told Muslim employees to report any offensive behavior, as it would not be tolerated.

Minority and faith communities extend support

The events of 9-11 prompted an unprecedented number of interfaith services nationwide, featuring leaders of different religions praying for peace and remembering the attack victims. Almost immediately after 9-11, the National Council of Churches (NCC) issued joint communiqués with Muslim groups condemning the terrorist attack. The NCC board began a series of consultations with Muslim leaders aiming at a better understanding and cooperation. The group was apparently heartened by the outreach initiative from Muslims and reciprocated by issuing a support statement on Ramadan, the Muslim month of fasting. NCC members took similar measures. For example, the United Methodist Commission on Christian Unity and Interreligious Concerns decided in October 2001 to adjust the agenda of its meeting to focus on improving relations with Muslims.

On May 14, 2002, the NCC board issued a statement acknowledging Muslim outreach efforts. The statement read,

"After 9-11, hundreds of Islamic centers and mosques across the United States held open houses, inviting their neighbors of other faiths in to grieve together and build bridges of understanding.... For many Christians, it was their first occasion to enter a mosque and talk with a Muslim.... Muslims for their part wanted their neighbors of other faiths to understand who they really were - not terrorists, but peace-loving, PTA-going, regular Americans who came here from all parts of the world."

The NCC urged Christian congregations to hold interfaith open houses on or around 9-11, 2002, thus commemorating the first anniversary of the attacks by extending hospitality to their Muslim neighbors. This effort, called "Open Doors Project," is aimed at assisting local congregations through printed materials and advice to organize educational activities involving Muslims and Christians.

Pope John Paul II called on Catholics to join in the last day of the Muslim Ramadan fast in 2001. The event was designed to pray for world peace and promote understanding between Islam and Christianity. American Catholics heeded the call by publicizing the event as an ecumenical effort.

California Catholics in particular, appeared to be the most receptive to the idea. Of course, relations between Catholics and Muslims in California have been growing for more than a decade. The U.S. Conference of Catholic Bishops, in an initiative headed by Bishop Todd D. Brown of the Diocese of Orange, has for some time been holding regional conversations with Muslim leaders in three parts of the country. Muslims were part of the Interfaith Coalition to Heal Los Angeles, an effort to improve communication between faith communities and shore up deteriorating neighborhoods after the 1992 riots.

Local Christian congregations sought to publicize their outreach efforts through the Internet. On October 17, 2001, Dr. Arthur Caliandro, senior pastor of Marble Collegiate Church interviewed three New York City Muslim religious leaders: Imam Al-Hajj Talib W. Abdur-Rashid, of the Mosque of Islamic Brotherhood; Shaykh Abd'Allah Latif Ali, of Admiral Family Circle; and Shaykh Ahmed Dewidar, Imam of the Mid-Manhattan Masjid.

Also, local Jewish and Muslim congregations in various parts of the country held joint meetings. In the West Coast, on *Eid al-Fitr*, one of Islam's most important holidays, a day dedicated to the remembrance of Abraham, Los Angeles Muslims and Jews met to remind themselves of their common patriarch. In the East Coast, the Jewish Council of Baltimore visited the Islamic Society of Baltimore on January 23, 2002 during an interfaith exchange evening.

Muslims targeted by extremism

Unfortunately, the spirit of tolerance was clouded at times with intolerant speech directed at Muslims and, in the immediate aftermath of the terrorist attacks, Muslims experienced their worst wave of hate crimes in U.S. history.

Anti-Muslim rhetoric

American Muslims, moving to the national spotlight after the deadly attacks, have grown to appreciate the full diversity of this nation. While many local communities have witnessed a dramatic increase in interfaith exchanges, Muslims were disheartened by the vitriol from the far right wing and anti-Muslim elements.

Southern Baptist Convention

At the June 2002 annual gathering of the Southern Baptist Convention (SBC) in St. Louis, the Rev. Jerry Vines, pastor of First Baptist Church of Jacksonville, Fla., told SBC conventioneers that the Prophet Muhammad was a "demon-possessed pedophile." (Vines is a former SBC president.) Vines added that, "Allah is not

Jehovah either. Jehovah's not going to turn you into a terrorist that'll try to bomb people and take the lives of thousands and thousands of people." When asked by reporters if they would condemn those bigoted remarks, both the outgoing and incoming SBC presidents said they supported Vines and his statements.

Some Southern Baptists do not condone interfaith prayers even with other Christian denominations. But according to numerous reports, not all congregations of the 16 million strong Baptists share Vines' anti-Muslim sentiment. There are hundreds of tolerant congregations across the South and Midwest that no longer send delegates to the annual Southern Baptist Convention or to statewide gatherings such as the one held in Missouri. Many of these congregations do not agree with the national denomination's position on interfaith issues.

There is also American Baptists, which is a separate church organization that has publicly denounced the anti-Muslim remarks by SBC leaders. In a statement issued on June 14, 2002, American Baptist Churches USA General Secretary A. Roy Medley remarked:

> "As General Secretary of the American Baptist Churches, USA, I am deeply saddened by remarks made by some Baptist leaders and other Christians that have maligned the Islamic faith and religion. Historically American Baptists, while deeply committed to the unique truth of the Christian Gospel, have stood for freedom of religious expression and practice. As Baptists we respect the faiths of others and have benefited from dialog and cooperative work with people of other faiths, especially on such issues of common concern as peace and justice."

In November 2001, the General Board of American Baptist Churches USA issued a declaration on anti-Islam, anti-Muslim and anti-Arab prejudice in the U.S. That declaration called on American Baptists:

> "(1) To pursue a better understanding of Islam, Muslims and Arabs (including Arab Christians) by including in their churches' educational programs a study of Islam, of the Muslim world and the Christian minorities within that world, and of the issues that have united and divided us by inviting Muslims and Arabs to be a part of the leadership and fellowship of such programs;
>
> (2) To encourage local and regional ecumenical and interfaith agencies to seek conversation and cooperation with Muslim religious organizations;

(3) To advocate and defend the civil rights of Arabs and Muslims living in the U.S. by such means as monitoring organizations and agencies which exercise responsibility for the peace, welfare and security of the community;

(4) To reject the religious and political demagoguery and manipulation manifest in the reporting of events related to the Middle East, to seek an understanding of the underlying causes of the events, and to condemn violence as a means of enforcing national will or achieving peace;

(5) To challenge and rebut statements made about Islam, Muslims, and Arabs that embody religious stereotyping, prejudice and bigotry."

Also, there is the National Baptist Convention, an African American denomination that does not harbor anti-Muslim views. In fact, the National Baptist Convention issued a media advisory reflecting on the tragedy by warning against divisiveness. The press release asked people

"to respond with all of our capacities of love to meet the needs of those who administer and receive aid;

to encourage individuals to gather at appropriate times and places of worship throughout the weeks ahead to seek the solace and guidance of The Divine;

to pray for calm and rational thought and behavior;

to pray that our shock and anger do not turn to hatred or fear;

to pray that our passions do not goad us into cries for vengeance;

to pray that our energies be mobilized to seek a just peace wherever wars exist and people lift up sword against people;

to pray that the finest character of America will emerge from the chaos of this experience."

Televangelist Pat Robertson

In contrast, televangelist Pat Robertson, speaking on his Christian Broadcasting Network's '700 Club' (www.cbn.com) program in February 2002, described a veritable infestation of America with violent, subversive Muslims. He chose to blast President George W. Bush's position on Islam as well. He said, "I have taken issue with our esteemed president in regard to his stand in saying Islam is a peaceful religion.... It's just not. And the Quran makes it very clear, if you see an infidel, you are to kill him."

He said, "Our immigration policies are now so skewed towards the Middle East and away from Europe that we have introduced these people into our midst and undoubtedly there are terrorist cells all over them...They want to coexist until they can control, dominate, and then if need be destroy."

Various Muslim groups and scholars responded to the Robertson's assertions in his widely watched network. Muslims exposed Robertson's distortion of the Quran, which permits defensive struggles but calls for peace when aggression ends. The Quran teaches, "Let there be no compulsion in religion" (2:256) Several other verses of the Quran calling for peace once oppression ends were cited, including "God does not forbid you to be kind and equitable to those who had neither fought against your faith nor driven you out of your homes. In fact God loves the equitable." (60:8) and "Fight in the cause of God with those who fight against you, but do not exceed the limits...If they desist, let there be no hostility except against the oppressors." (2:190-193)

On the issue of a Muslim's friendship with people of other faiths, Muslims reminded the public that a number of verses support cordial relations with anyone who does not attack their faith. These include "O ye who believe! Take not for friends and protectors those who take your religion for a mockery or sport..." (5: 57); "God only forbids you to make friendship with those who fought you on account of your faith and drove you out of your homes and backed up others in your expulsion." (60:9); and "And dispute ye not with the People of the Book [Christians and Jews] except with means better (than mere disputation) unless it be with those of them who inflict wrong (and injury): but say, 'We believe in the Revelation which has come down to us and in that which came down to you.'" (29:46) As a call to religious tolerance, the Quran states: "Those who believe (in the Quran) and those who follow the Jewish (scriptures) and the Christians and the Sabians and who believe in God and the last day and work righteousness shall have their reward with their Lord; on them shall be no fear nor shall they grieve." (2:62)

Attorney General John Ashcroft

In February 2002, Muslim and Arab-American groups called on Attorney General John Ashcroft to clarify offensive remarks he allegedly made in December about the faith of Islam. According to an interview with syndicated columnist Cal Thomas published on the internet site, crosswalk.com, Ashcroft said: "Islam is a religion in which God requires you to send your son to die for him. Christianity is a faith in which God sends his son to die for you." Despite several requests from Muslim and Arab-American groups, Ashcroft did not responded publicly. Eventually, under increasing public pressure he said that the reported remarks "do not accurately reflect what I believe I said."

Senator Gordon Smith

In January, Senator Gordon Smith (R-OR) made a public statement that Oregon has been a hub of terrorist fund-raising activities. Smith, citing unclassified information he learned in confidential security briefings, said terrorism-related fund raising has occurred in Corvallis and at Portland State University. University officials said they knew nothing about Smith's claims. Oregon Muslims have responded to the baseless allegation from the senator. A statement by a coalition of Muslim groups read,

> "We believe that Senator Smith, who is up for reelection, is attempting to curry favor with the electorate by engaging in Muslim-bashing. While such a tactic to exploit the 9-11 tragedy and the current war on terrorism may improve his visibility with the electorate, it comes at a very high price to many already-marginalized citizens"

Conservative commentator Ann Coulter

In an address at Michigan University conservative commentator Ann Coulter referred to Native Americans as "peyote smoking Indians" and Middle Easterners as "camel riding nomads." In her online column responding to the 9-11 terrorist attacks, she wrote of the terrorists, "We should invade their countries, kill their leaders, and convert them to Christianity."

Rep. C. Saxby Chambliss

While speaking to Georgia law enforcement personnel, Rep. C. Saxby Chambliss (R-GA), chairman of the House Subcommittee on Terrorism and Homeland Security and a candidate for the Senate, said "just turn [the sheriff] loose and have him arrest every Muslim that crosses the state line." Under pressure, he sent a letter to the *Valdosta Daily Times*, contending that his comments were taken "out of context" and "should in no way be interpreted as my view of what should happen...If my remarks were offensive in any way, I apologize."

Free Congress Foundation President Paul Weyrich

Paul Weyrich, president of the Free Congress Foundation, called for the U.S. Postal Service's year-old "Eid Greetings" stamp to be rescinded and "overprinted with the image of the twin towers," because "America's most notable experience with Islam was the attacks on 9-11."

Franklin Graham

After 9-11 evangelist Franklin Graham, son of the renowned Reverend Billy Graham, repeatedly called the Islamic religion "wicked, violent and not of the same God." He also said "I don't believe this is a wonderful, peaceful religion.... When you read the Koran and you read the verses from the Koran, it instructs the killing of the infidel, for those that are non-Muslim." In a report aired on *NBC Nightly News*, Graham stood by remarks he made about Islam last month at the dedication of a chapel in North Carolina. At that event, Graham said: "We're not attacking Islam but Islam has attacked us. The God of Islam is not the same God. He's not the son of God of the Christian or Judeo-Christian faith. It's a different God, and I believe it is a very evil and wicked religion." Later Graham issued a statement in which he said: "It is not my calling to analyze Islam or any other religions, though I recognize that all religions have differences. In the past, I have expressed my concerns about the teachings of Islam regarding the treatment of women and the killing of non-Muslims or infidels." Mr. Graham publicly dismissed invitations of Muslims to meet to clear his misconceptions about the faith.

Local churches

A sign outside the Crossroads Assembly of God Church in the town of Wilder, Idaho equates Islam with evil. The sign, posted in block capital letters, reads: "The spirit of Islam is the spirit of the Antichrist." The church's pastor, Geoff Cole, who put up the sign said the message reflects not hatred, but the Gospel. He said he drew the sign's statements from the Bible: 1 John, 4:2-3. The quotation reads, in part, "...every spirit that does not acknowledge Jesus is not from God."

Local leaders criticized the sign but stressed that it was a form of protected speech. Wilder Mayor Steve Rhodes said he finds the sign offensive, but the city cannot censor the opinion reflected on the sign. He told a local newspaper, "It is inappropriate. It doesn't reflect the community, and it sure doesn't reflect myself or my council." Muslims in Idaho were dismayed by this cold reaction to what they believed a clear case of hate. While Muslims did not contest that hateful speech is not prosecutable, they felt that other Christians should have been more vocal in their opposition to bigotry and ignorance.

Simon Wiesenthal Center Dean Marvin Hier

Rabbi Marvin Hier, Dean of the Simon Wiesenthal Center Museum of Tolerance in Los Angeles, made the accusation that the Quran holds "extremist" views. Hier made this claim during a discussion of the possibility of peaceful coexistence between Judaism, Christianity and Islam on CNN's Larry King on December 1, 2001. The following is part of the interview:

"Rabbi Hier: There are direct references in the Quran to violence. I'll read one from the Quran: 'O you who believe, take not the Jews and Christians for friends. He among you who taketh them for friends is one of them.' And that's a quote from the Quran.

Larry King: It doesn't say kill them.

Rabbi Hier: No, but it infers, of course, that there is a difference. And there are other quotes, as well. So if someone asks me straight: Are there any extremist views in the Quran? I would say yes."

A Muslim guest on the program, Dr. Maysam Al-Faruqi of Georgetown University, corrected Hier's mistranslation of the Qur'anic text. She said,

"The verse that the Rabbi actually quoted is not at all what he says. It is: 'Do not take Christians and Jews as auwliya,' which does mean friends, it means as overlords. In other words, people who will dictate to you your behavior. In fact, the verse that deals with friendship is that one that says: 'As for such as those who do not fight you on account of your faith and neither drive you forth from your homeland, God does not forbid you to show them kindness and equity, he only forbids you to turn in friendship to those who fight you because of your faith.'"

Toward Tradition President Daniel Lapin

Rabbi Daniel Lapin, President of Toward Tradition, which works to build an alliance between Jews and the right wing, recently proclaimed, "Conservative Christians are the natural allies of the Jewish community." Lapin does not believe that Christians, Jews and Muslims form one great 'Abrahamic' civilization. In his opinion "today we are witnessing two distinct religious civilizations in conflict: that of the Koran, allied with the believers in no God, violently challenging the civilization of the Bible, of Christianity and Judaism."

Hate crimes wound a community

The 9-11 attacks were followed by a dramatic rise in anti-Muslim hate crimes. CAIR received 1717 reports of harassment, violence and other discriminatory acts in the first six months. Although violent attacks have dropped sharply, CAIR has logged more than 325 complaints in the second six-month period after the attacks-a 30 percent increase over the same period prior to 9-11. And most recently, on August 30, 2002, an anti-Muslim hate-rape took place in California, perhaps the first such attack on record in U.S. history. An 18 year-old man raped a 15-year old girl inside Palo Alto Longs Drugs store while making anti-Muslim comments, according to the Palo Alto Police Department.

Murders

A dozen murders have been reported, including a handful of incidents in which the victims were simply mistaken for Muslims and Arabs because of their appearance.

1   In Dallas, Hassan Waqar, a 46-year-old Muslim owner of a convenience store was shot to death on September 15, 2001.

2   In Mesa, Arizona, Balbir Sodhi, a 49-year-old Sikh Indian man, was killed in front of his business on September 15.

3   In San Gabriel, California, Adel Karas, a 48-year-old Egyptian Christian Copt, was murdered in his import shop by two men on September 15.

4   In Lincoln Park, Michigan, Ali al-Mansoop, an American citizen of Yemeni descent was shot to death in anger over 9-11 by the ex-boyfriend of the woman he was dating.

5 The *New York Times* reported on January 24, 2002 that the death of an immigrant might have been a hate crime. The victim's lawyer alleged that the Queens man charged with murdering the Afghan-born filmmaker and then freezing his head was motivated in part by misguided patriotism.

6 In Minneapolis, in October 2001, a 66-year-old Somali immigrant, Ali W. Ali, died a few days after he was found injured and unconscious at a bus stop. He had been punched in the head by a Caucasian male. The coroner ruled that Ali died of natural causes. Members of the Somali community in Minneapolis contend he was a victim of a hate crime and that a white man struck Ali in the face.

7 In Chattanooga, Tennessee, a Palestinian business owner was shot four times in the back and killed in front of his grocery store. The store was open and unattended and there was cash in the victim's wallet, but nothing was stolen.

8 In early October, 2001 Abdullah Mohammed Nimer, a traveling salesman, was murdered on the street in South Central Los Angeles.

9 In Ceres, California, just a week after 9-11, the police found in a canal the body of Surjit Singh Samra, a 69-year old Sikh man with a turban who appeared to have been murdered. On the day of the killing, Mr. Samra had left for his daily walk but never returned to the family's home.

10 On September 29, 2001 in Reedley, California, Abdo Ali Ahmed, a 51-year-old convenience store owner of Arab descent, was shot to death.

11 In April 2002, a Dallas, Texas jury convicted Mark Stroman for the murder of Vasudev Patel last October. Storman thought the Hindu man looked Middle Eastern and killed him to avenge the attacks on New York and Washington.

Attacks on mosques

Many mosques were attacked or threatened. The following incidents, among others, were reported to CAIR:

12 In Detroit, Michigan, the Islamic Center of Detroit was attacked by a group of people who threw rocks and broke the mosque's windows and glass showcase on 9-11.

1 Immediately after the 9-11 attacks, a drive by shooting occurred at the Islamic Center of Greater Toledo.

2 In Irving, Texas, nine shots were fired at the Islamic Center of Irving on September 12, breaking the windows and damaging the furnishings. The community asked the police to investigate it as a hate crime, but the police told them they would record it as a regular crime.

3 In Sparks, Nevada, someone shot at the North Nevada Muslim Community Center on September 12. In addition, a bomb threat was received by the Center.

4 The Islamic Center of Charlotte, North Carolina was forced to close down its full-time school, the Charlotte Islamic School, on September 12 after receiving threatening phone calls. The Islamic Center of Charlotte continued to receive threatening calls for a whole week, during which the school remained closed.

5 In Perrysburg, Ohio, the Islamic Center in Perrysburg Township was vandalized; its windows broken by rocks on September 13.

6 In Princeton, West Virginia, racial slurs were spray-painted in the rear of the Islamic Society of the Appalachian Region on September 15.

7 In San Diego, California, two individuals fired a device that emitted smoke and caused a loud sound near the entrance of the local mosque on September 17. Nobody was hurt. The police arrested two individuals and they treated this case as a hate crime.

8 In Colorado, the Islamic Center of Fort Collins received threatening phone calls on September 18.

9   In Chicago, Illinois, hate messages were left on answering machine of the Islamic Center of Illinois on September 20. Threats were made as well as accusations.

10 In Kingman, Arizona, someone shot over 70 rubber bullets at Masjid Ibrahim. No worshipers were hurt in this September 12 attack.

11 In Seattle, Washington, Idriss Mosque was subject to an attempted arson on September 13. Patrick Michael Cunningham, the suspect in the attack, was caught by two community members who were leaving the mosque at the time of the attack. The man was charged with attempted arson, the obstruction of the free exercise of religious beliefs, and attempted defacement of religious real property.

12 In Canejo Valley, California, evidence of vandalism was found in the parking lot outside the Islamic Center of Canejo Valley two days after the terrorist attacks, which included spray painted comments like, "Jesus is the Lord and Allah is the Devil."

13 In Manassas, Virginia, passersby shouted near Manassas Mosque on September 12: "We hate you f_____ Muslims and we hope you all f_____ die."

14 In Fargo, North Dakota, a couple of incidents were reported. The Islamic Center received crank calls on September 14. Four days later, several men brandishing a shotgun appeared in the Center's parking lot, but they left without incident.

15 In Lynnwood, Washington, a woman left the following message on the phone of Masjid Dar Al-Arqam on September 15: "It's time for you people to get out from here."

16 In New Orleans, Louisiana, Masjid Ar-Rahma received a threatening phone call on September 12.

17 In Raleigh, North Carolina, Al-Iman School and Mosque received a bomb threat on September 12.

18 In Silver Spring, Maryland, the Muslim Community Center received over 15 calls between the day of the terrorist attacks and September 14

threatening to destroy their building and bring harm to the members of the community.

19 In Lubbock, Texas, an unknown person called the Islamic Center of the South Plains on September 16 and left the following message on the answering machine: "You Arabs are all guilty. Go back to your ugly countries."

20 In San Francisco, California, two hate flyers were posted at entrance of the Islamic Center of San Francisco on September 17. They read, "Allah is dead, Rambo killed him." and "Enslave all Arabs... get free gas."

21 In Cleveland, Ohio, 29-year-old Eric Richley of Middleburg Heights rammed his car through the Grand Islamic Mosque of Cleveland with his Ford Mustang on September 17. The front wall collapsed, causing an estimated $100,000 in damage.

22 In Sterling, Virginia, the sign at the entrance of ADAMS Center was vandalized on September 17 with insults to Islam and Muslims. Curses were spray-painted inside the facility.

23 An attack by vandals on the Islamic Center of Columbus on December 29, 2001 caused severe damage to all three floors of the center. The attackers drilled holes in floors at the Islamic Center of Columbus, ripped up copies of the Quran and pulled water pipes from walls, saturating floors and ceilings of the three-story building. The damage was discovered when members arrived for prayer services on Sunday morning.

24 The *San Francisco Chronicle* reported on December 10, 2001 that rock-throwing vandals smashed the front window of an East Bay mosque on December 9, 2001, while 15 worshipers were inside performing the Morning Prayer. Two large river rocks, each twice the size of a fist, crashed through the 10-foot-by-5-foot window at The Islamic Center of Contra Costa on Clayton Road in Concord, showering the interior with broken glass.

25 In Sioux Falls, South Dakota, the Islamic Center of Sioux Falls was vandalized on the night of October 3. The local FBI is investigating the incident as a hate crime.

26 The building of the Islamic Society of Kentucky in Lexington was set on fire on October 24, 2001, and the arson is believed to be hate motivated.

27 The Islamic Center of Greensboro received a death threat on its answering machine on October 25.

28 In Bridgeview, Illinois, a mob of several hundred teenagers waving American flags led by a local evangelical preacher started to march to the Mosque Foundation on October 26, but their path was blocked by the police.

29 In Evansville, Indiana, a Neo-Nazi skinhead vandalized and damaged the local Islamic Center in Evansville on October 26.

30 In Nashville, Tennessee, the front window of the mosque was broken on November 2, causing several thousand dollars worth of damage.

31 A molotov cocktail was thrown at the Islamic Society of Denton, Texas on November 17.

32 On March 25, 2002, Charles Franklin, a 41-year-old carpenter, drove a truck into the Islamic Center of Tallahassee at Florida State University. The man left the scene after the crash, but was caught by the police later. Luckily, no one was injured in the crash, which occurred 30 minutes before evening prayers. A police spokesman said the man had a Bible wrapped in a blue cloth on the front seat of his truck and later he admitted that was motivated by hatred of Muslims.

33 Robert Goldstein, a 37-year-old doctor plotting to bomb mosques in Florida, was arrested on August 23, 2002. Deputies found more than 30 explosive devices, including hand grenades and a 5-gallon gasoline bomb with a timer and a wire attached, and a cache of up to 40 licensed weapons, including .50-caliber machine guns and sniper rifles, inside Goldstein's home. They also found a list of 50 Islamic centers and organizations in the state, mostly in the Tampa Bay area.

Attacks on Muslim women

Many Muslim women became fearful of wearing head cover in public. A few asked religious scholars whether they could take it off in public in fear for their lives.

1   Houda Koussan, 27, of Dearborn Heights said she has been spit at because she wears a headscarf.

2   In Brooklyn, New York, a group of teenagers and adults cursed at two Muslim women and threw rocks at them on 9-11.

3   In Fremont, California, a woman with hijab attempting to attend college on 9-11 was told by a police officer that she should return home because of anti -Muslim sentiment and the possibility of violence.

4   In Alexandria, Virginia, a woman was riding the Metro Rail on September 12, 2001, when several men purposely stepped on her feet several times. She has also been the recipient of taunts and verbal abuse.

5   In Fontana, California, a woman got out of her car to pick her children up from school on September 13, when a Caucasian woman began cursing and verbally harassing her. When the woman walked back to the parking lot, the harasser physically attacked the woman.

6   In Atlanta, Georgia, an unidentified man called the office of the Islamic Circle of North America on September 13 threatening to rape Muslim women and yank off their scarves.

7   In Annandale, Virginia, a woman was on her way to the Dar Al-Hijrah Islamic Center on September 18, when two men assaulted her. They hit her with a stick and said that she should go home.

8   In Clarkston, Georgia, three men attacked a woman as she was leaving her apartment building on September 26. One of them took off her hijab; another put his foot on her neck, while the third kicked her back. As she tried to pick up her hijab, they kicked her while cursing at Arabs. The men also attempted to take off her clothes. She was dragged to a tree, screaming and pleading, while one of them held a knife to her two-year old son. The attackers escaped when they noticed cars were approaching the crime scene.

9   In Laguna Hills, California, on September 27, a woman's car was vandalized. The car had deep cuts with a sharp object and one of the tires had been spray painted red.

10 In Manchester, New York, a woman was attacked on October 15 by her neighbor, who yelled racial slurs and death threats. The neighbor also let her dog loose on the woman and later pushed her down the apartment building stairs when the latter went to do her laundry. The police arrived after each incident but did not arrest the neighbor. The victim filed a 10-day restraining order.

11 In Orlando, Florida, on October 26, a woman was at a shopping mall with her mother who wears a hijab, when a Caucasian man approached them and started yelling, "Get out of our country, you rag head! Go back! Get out of here!"

12 In Alexandria, Virginia, a woman was approached on November 9 by a male in the Metro, who spat on her, threatened to kill her and send her back to her country. The Metro police were notified but they could not track the man down.

13 In Pembroke Pines, Florida, a Pakistani woman with a scarf was attacked and hit at Winn Dixie grocery store on September 13.

Bombs and arson attacks

1 In Bethesda, Maryland, two connecting stores owned by different persons of Middle Eastern descent were burned down on September 12.

2 In Alexandria, Virginia, the owner of an Islamic bookstore found that two bricks had been thrown through his store window when he arrived to work on September 13. The bricks had messages attached to them, one of which read: "Death to Arabs."

3 In Long Island, New York, on September 13, a Muslim-owned restaurant was firebombed.

4 In Tulsa, Oklahoma, a store owner's shop was vandalized on September 14, with damages amounting to $500. The front panels and windows of the shop were smashed.

5 In Springfield, Michigan, the front window of an Arabic store was shattered on September 16.

6   In Buena Park, California, the Islamic Halal Tandoori Restraunt was set on fire on September 27. The police called the owner at 4:00 a.m. to let him know about the fire.

7   In Houston, Texas, Prime Tires, an auto mechanic shop, was gutted by fire on October 26. The Houston Fire Department Arson Unit is reportedly investigating the case as a hate crime.

8   In San Francisco, the owner of a building received 2 bomb threats and on September 13, a fire occurred in the building and was confirmed as an arson attack. The fire had been set in the dental office on the lower floor, near some oxygen tanks.

9   In Bowling Green, Kentucky, a bookstore owner found two bullet holes in the door of his shop in the morning of September 13. He also discovered that glass window had been shattered.

10 In Yonkers, New York, while a store clerk was working at the Madaba Deli on October 26, a rock was thrown through the window, breaking it.

11 In Somerset, Massachusetts, a group of teenagers torched a convenience store owned by a man they mistakenly thought was Arab on November 7.

12 In Anaheim, California, a small bomb went off in front of a man's house on September 15. The police did not take a report after being called to the house but returned several days later, after much complaining by the victim's friend.

Physical assaults

1   The *News-Gazette* reported on December 20, 2001 that a Muslim student was beaten by a Campus town mob in what he described as a racially motivated attack. Saleem Mahjub, a senior in mechanical engineering at the University of Illinois, was attacked shortly before 3 a.m. outside an apartment building near the intersection of Fifth and John streets, in Champaign. Mahjub was taken by ambulance to Carle Foundation Hospital, where he received stitches and was treated for a broken nose.

2   In Santa Barbara, California, the liquor store of a Christian Syrian was vandalized on September 13. The perpetrator was caught on tape.

3   In Santa Barbara, Mr. Passat's Pennywise Market was vandalized on September 19. He is an Indian of the Hindu faith.

4   In Corona, New York, a man was leaving a Halal meat store on September 22, when he was forcefully hit on the back of the head, which caused him to fall. The perpetrators walked away laughing.

5   In Queens, New York, a 66-year old Sikh Indian man was shot with a pellet gun and battered with a baseball bat by three local teens on November 7.

Workplace discrimination

Workplace discrimination complaints with the Equal Employment Opportunity Commission (EEOC) soared after 9-11. Between 9-11 and Dec. 6, officials said the EEOC received 166 complaints of illegal discrimination, mostly involving Muslim workers who were fired from their jobs. During the same period a year ago, only 64 such claims were filed. By early February 2002, the agency has received 260 claims from Muslims since 9-11, an increase of 168% over the same period a year earlier. By early March 2002, the national figure of complaints reached 300. These do not include complaints filed with state and local agencies. The number continued to increase. The *Chicago Tribune* reported on March 15, 2002,

> "Eight months after the attacks on America, the number of workplace bias complaints by Arab, Muslim, Middle Eastern and South Asian employees are increasing rapidly. The EEOC has received 488 complaints since 9-11.... By April 11, 62 new claims had been filed and by May 7, the agency had received another 74, the largest increase to date."

Many such incidents were received by CAIR. The following are a few examples:

1   In Fuquay-Varina, North Carolina, a Muslim employee was called on September 12 and told not to report to work the following day without explaining the decision.

2   In Malden, Massachusetts, two Muslim employees reported that their supervisors harassed them on September 12 and falsely accused them of rejoicing about the 9-11 attacks.

3   In Gaithersburg, Maryland, on September 12, a co-worker said to a fellow Muslim employee, "We need to ship their behinds out of here and they can take their Allah with them." When the Muslim responded with, "I never messed with you during your Bible study," the co-worker went into a rage and the Muslim was sent home.

4   In Dallas, Texas, four Muslim employees were sent home from work on September 16 for no apparent reason.

5   In Roland Heights, California, a Muslim employee reported that his coworker started yelling at him and pushing him around on September 17. The supervisor suspended the complainant with pay, but let the attacker go. Later she was terminated.

6   In Duluth, Georgia, a teacher who refused to remove her hijab on September 18 was told to sign a waiver stating that if she is harmed, the school would not responsible, but if others come to harm then she would be held responsible.

7   In Alexandria, Virginia, a man was beaten by the husband of a co-worker on September 19 and was taken to the emergency room. The attacker shouted, "Let me see how your god and your Islam is going to protect you now!"

8   In McLean, Virginia, a woman reports being terminated without a valid reason on September 24. She believes it was connected to the fact that her supervisor was always making comments about immigrants, including statements like "I don't feel safe in my own country anymore because of all of the foreigners in my building."

Government efforts on behalf of Muslims

Early on in the crisis, national political leaders worked to set the tone of tolerance toward Muslims. Congress strongly supported that sentiment. In fact, the House of Representatives passed a resolution condemning bigotry and violence against Arab Americans, American Muslims and South Asians in the wake of 9-11. Local and federal authorities acted with resolve against the anti-Muslim backlash.

Law enforcement agencies battle hate

Local and federal authorities have been on alert since the beginning of the crisis to the possibility of a violent backlash. Generally, the authorities have taken measures to monitor, investigate, prosecute, and even prevent incidents. Local and federal agencies responded quickly to stem the rise the anti-Muslim hate crimes. Police departments across the country stepped up patrols around Muslim facilities.

Local police departments kept the public apprised of anti-Muslim attacks. The *Washington Post* reported on October 3, 2001 that Montgomery County logged 12 hate crimes reported since 9-11. The police in Dearborn, Michigan reported receiving 22 complaints of intimidation incidents against Arabs and Muslims during the last three weeks of September 2001 (There was only one reported case in the same period of 2000). The Los Angeles Police Department reportedly logged nearly 100 incidents, most targeting Arab-Americans, Muslims, Afghan-Americans, Sikhs, Asians and others mistaken for Arabs or Muslims. On January 11, 2002, the *San Francisco Chronicle* cited California Attorney General Bill Lockyer noting that normally his office logged about five hate crimes a day, but since the terrorist attacks, the number has jumped to 20 per day. He also noted that crimes against Arab Americans, Muslims and those perceived to be in those groups accounted for the large increase.

In mid-October 2001, the government was investigating 170 hate crime reports. By February 2002 the Department of Justice had investigated approximately 300 incidents. In some cases, suspects were apprehended, put on trial and convicted for the crimes they committed. For example, 29-year-old Eric Richley, who smashed his car into an Ohio mosque, was sentenced to a five-year prison term. He pleaded guilty in Cuyahoga County Court to burglary, ethnic intimidation, vandalism and drunk driving in the September 16th incident in which he drove his car at high speed through the glass entrance of the Islamic Center of Greater Cleveland.

Also, the EEOC updated its anti-discrimination guidelines to employers, warning against the increased incidence of workplace discrimination on the basis of religion, ethnicity, and country of origin. On December 11, 2001, the EEOC held a public hearing about workplace discrimination in the wake of 9-11. This came as a response to the finding by the Commission showing that more than 130 charges of employment discrimination directly related to the events of 9-11 have been filed with EEOC since that tragic day.

Also, a federal judge handed down a longer-than-normal sentence for a man who falsely connected his fiancée's Arab-American boss to the 9-11 attacks. Judge

Nina Gershon of U.S. District Court sentenced Jack Barresi, 38, to 21 months in prison for falsely telling the FBI that his fiancée's boss was a potential suspect. Prosecutors requested Barresi be given more than the normal six-month sentence for such violations because of the "heightened anti-Arab sentiment." Barresi told federal authorities right after the attacks that on September 7, his fiancée's boss told him that he could "not wait for you Americans to blow up and die," authorities said. Barresi later admitted that he made the claim up.

Muslim communities around the country expressed gratitude to the law enforcement community. The Islamic Center of Boca Raton, Florida held a reception on January 19, 2002 to thank the police department for extra patrols aimed at protecting Muslim community facilities against threats and vandalism after the terrorist attacks. The center had received a number of anonymous threats by phone, and the center's imam was reportedly threatened at gunpoint at the end of September.

Also, Muslim community groups hailed the vigilance of law enforcement authorities when they foiled a bombing attack by the Jewish Defense League (JDL) in California. JDL chairman Irv Rubin and another member of his group were arrested on December 11, 2001 on suspicion of plotting to blow up a mosque in Culver City, California and the offices of the Muslim Public Affairs Council and Arab American Congressman Darrell Issa (R-CA). Rubin was arrested after the last bomb-making components were allegedly delivered to his co-conspirator's home. Other bomb components were seized at the home as well.

An alarming development took place in November 2001, when Middle East Forum director Daniel Pipes was appointed to a newly formed Special Task Force on Terrorism Technology sponsored by the Defense Advanced Research Projects Agency (DARPA), a division of the Department of Defense. Concerns of Muslims were heightened by the fact that Mr. Pipes has been among the leading personalities agitating the public against Muslims. After September 11, he told a Salon.com reporter that 10 to 15 percent of Muslims in the world are "potential killers."

Also alarming was the silence of President Bush (after his initial leadership in setting a tolerant tone for the country) in the face of repeated bigoted statements from high profile people like Franklin Graham, who swore the President into office.

Civil liberties: a victim of 9/11

As has been noted above, in the first few days after the 9-11 attacks, government officials, including President Bush, made a point to reach out to the Muslim community. He visited the Islamic Center in Washington, D.C. in the company of national Muslim leaders. In the face of hate crimes against Muslims, he warned Americans against "picking on" people because they are different. He also praised Americans who expressed sympathy with Muslim women wearing hijab after they were attacked. Local and federal agencies worked to combat the hysterical anti-Muslim backlash. But since that initial period of support, a number of governmental policies have singled out American Muslim organizations and immigrants from Muslim countries.

Civil liberty violations

THE USA PATRIOT ACT OF 2001

On October 26, 2001, the President signed the Uniting and Strengthening America by Providing Appropriate Tools Required to Intercept and Obstruct Terrorism Act, better known by its acronym, the USA PATRIOT Act. The law, which hurriedly passed with little public debate, has been criticized by constitutional law experts saying it eroded civil liberties Americans take for granted. In particular, critics have charged that the Act gives the executive branch the power to detain immigrant suspects for lengthy periods of time, sometimes indefinitely. Critics have also pointed out that the Act allows the executive branch to circumvent the Fourth Amendment's requirement of probable cause when conducting wiretaps and searches. Under the current law, critics say, persons and organizations searched could be U.S. citizens who are not suspected of any wrongdoing. The law permits personal or business records to be seized for an investigation without prior evidence of connection to terrorism or criminal activity. The government only needs to claim that the seizure is designed to look for such evidence.

Critics also noted that under the USA PATRIOT Act, businesses are required to monitor their customers and report "suspicious transactions" to the Treasury Department. Buried in the more than 300 pages of the new law is a provision that "any person engaged in a trade or business" has to file a government report if a customer spends $10,000 or more in cash. The threshold is cumulative and applies to multiple purchases if they're somehow related-three $3,500 pieces of home or office furniture, for example, might trigger a filing.

Detentions

A year after the 9-11 attacks, a significant number of non-U.S. nationals originally from Arab and Muslim countries still remain in detention. Most of these people are believed to have overstayed their immigration visas, although they have neither been linked to the attacks nor charged with any criminal offenses. There are some 300,000 absconders in the U.S. These are immigrants who entered the country legally but overstayed their visa. Government critics view the selective enforcement of immigration law on absconders from Muslim-majority countries as a form of bias.

Many detainees have been deported since the initial sweep. While the detentions have been surrounded by secrecy, news reports suggest that nearly 1,200 people were taken into custody in the initial stage of the crackdown. There have been charges that detainees have not been informed of the reasons of their detention. Many have not had prompt access to a lawyer and detainees have been treated as if they were guilty until proven innocent.

The lengthy detentions have been criticized in particular for their violation of the Constitution's Sixth Amendment, which states: "...the accused shall enjoy the right to a speedy and public trial, by an impartial jury of the State and district wherein the crime shall have been committed, which district shall have been previously ascertained by law, and to be informed of the nature and cause of the accusation; to be confronted with the witnesses against him."

Many Muslims see the plight of Dr. Al-Najjar as a symbol of the misplaced retaliation against Muslims after the 9-11 attacks. Dr. Mazen Al-Najjar, a stateless Palestinian who had overstayed his immigration visa, was held in solitary confinement on the basis of secret evidence from November 24, 2001 until his deportation in late August 2002. He was only allowed one hour of exercise each day and was reportedly strip-searched twice a day. Al-Najjar had previously been detained for more than three years as the U.S. worked to deport him. A U.S. Appeals Court forced his release only months prior to his 2001 arrest. The court ruled that prosecutors could not try him with secret evidence, but that did not stop the government from jailing him again on the same grounds.

In addition to this group of detainees, there were also an unidentified number of people taken into custody and interrogated for a short period of time, days or hours. Most of these were legal immigrants. Some were interrogated in their homes and places of work or business. Some of the people held for such questioning included two children who are British citizens of Pakistani descent, ages 11 and 13, in

Dumphries, Virginia. They were reportedly taken from their school by local police officers, who were later joined by FBI agents to conduct the interrogation. They were asked if they practiced Islam and what they thought about various religious concepts (particularly jihad). They were also questioned about the mosque they attended and the views of their imams. The detention took place after the teacher of the older boy found out he was a Muslim from Pakistan and had attended Islamic activities.

Among those interrogated by federal government personnel were individuals with pilot licenses, those in pilot training programs, or individuals working in areas classified as sensitive, such as trucking or hazardous material handling. Some of the victims of this type of profiling were legal immigrants; others were American citizens, including members of the military. Interrogators reportedly asked people about their views of what happened on 9-11, what was happening in Afghanistan and whether they sent money to their country of origin.

Even Muslims with record in public service were searched and questioned. More than 30 FBI agents and a hazardous materials team participated in raids at the home of the Pakistan-born Dr. Irshad Shaikh, who has been the health commissioner of Chester, Pennsylvania since 1994. Authorities wouldn't say why the homes were searched. Federal court documents used to obtain search warrants were sealed. No charges have been filed. The man said agents told him he had been seen dumping a cloudy liquid on the ground behind his home and handing a silver canister to someone. The liquid, the man said, was soapy water from a clogged sink and the canister was a food dish.

Security interviews

In November 2001, Attorney General John Ashcroft announced that the government would conduct "voluntary" interviews with 5,000 legal Muslim foreign nationals. When this was completed earlier this year, Mr. Ashcroft announced that an additional 3,000 people of the same category of individuals would next be sought. The attorney general said the government learned a great deal from the initial interviews, but little was known as to how that information related to the investigation of the 9-11 attacks or any suspected terrorists. News reports suggested that fewer than 20 of the initial interviewees were arrested, all on charges unrelated to terrorism.

In November 2001, U.S. Department of State officials announced the introduction of a 20-day waiting period for men from predominately Muslim nations who apply for visas. The new policy reportedly applied to males aged 18 to 45 for the purpose of completing a background check based on answers to a special questionnaire the applicants must fill out. The list of countries where the new policy will take effect includes: Afghanistan, Algeria, Bahrain, Djibouti, Egypt, Eritrea, Indonesia, Iran, Iraq, Jordan, Kuwait, Lebanon, Libya, Malaysia, Morocco, Oman, Pakistan, Qatar, Saudi Arabia, Somalia, Sudan, Syria, Tunisia, Turkey, the United Arab Emirates and Yemen.

Closing charities

Three Muslim charities have been effectively shut down since December 2001 and are now engaged in a legal battle against the federal government. On December 4, 2001, the government designated the Holy Land Foundation for Relief and Development (HLF) a terrorist organization and seized its assets. The government accused HLF of supporting Hamas, a group listed as a terrorist organization by the U.S. Department of State. HLF has insisted that its social and health services have been extended to assist Palestinian orphans, widows and poor persons irrespective of political views. The group stated it did not condone terrorism and that it has never offered any financial support to any party outside its humanitarian mission. Some anti-Palestinian groups have been lobbying for years to shut down the charity.

In addition, Global Relief Foundation (GRF) and Benevolence International Foundation (BIF) were hit with financial sanctions by the Treasury Department without the government having specified any suspicions about the conduct and financial ties of the two groups. No criminal charges have been filed against any of the three charities. These closures have had a wide impact; roughly 50,000 donors were affected by the closures. These foundations had established a track record of effective relief work. They carried out several development projects in high-need areas and served refugees and victims of natural disasters. Donors view such organizations as essential to the ability of Muslims to practice the religious duty of *zakat* (alms giving), a pillar of their faith. Many Muslims believe shutting down religious charities because of suspicion that some of its associates or recipients have extreme political views is a form of profiling that is discriminatory by nature.

Those who oppose the government closure of the charities believe the government violated the Fourth Amendment of the Bill of Rights, which states: "The right of the people to be secure in their persons, houses, papers, and effects, against unreasonable searches and seizures, shall not be violated, and no Warrants shall issue, but upon probable cause."

Prosecution by means of secret evidence has been criticized as inherently unfair. The accused cannot possibly defend himself against evidence he does not know. Critics argued that the use of secret evidence is in violation of the Fifth Amendment, which states that no person shall "be deprived of life, liberty, or property, without due process of law."

Raids on businesses

On March 20, 2002, federal agents raided a number of Muslim offices and homes in Virginia and Georgia. A U.S. magistrate judge signed a search warrant indicating that a U.S. senior special agent had reason to believe that the raided homes and businesses concealed unnamed evidence of "the provision of material support for foreign terrorist organizations...." Targets of the raids included respected leaders and organizations in the American Muslim community such as the International Institute of Islamic Thought, which conducts research on Islamic reform issues, and the Graduate School of Islamic Social Sciences, which has trained chaplains serving in the U.S. military. Those whose homes were targeted said frightened mothers and daughters were handcuffed for hours and, in the case of a woman and her teenage daughter, were refused their request to wear their headscarves. Affidavits that led to the raids were sealed and thus the targeted individuals and organizations do not know what led the government to suspect they had any connection to terrorism. Again, no criminal charges were filed and no evidence was produced to back up the government's actions.

The raids were launched as part of Operation Green Quest, a task force created to track and disrupt the sources of terrorist finances. According to Customs, Operation Green Quest is said to be carrying out more than 300 probes into terrorist finances. In its four months of operation, it has seized about $10.3 million in smuggled US currency and $ 4.3 million in other assets. The government shut down and seized approximately $1 million from Al Barakaat and Al Taqwa, alleging they were funding Osama bin Laden's al Qaeda terrorist network. Offices of the two money transfer businesses were closed down in Northern Virginia, Minneapolis, Boston, Seattle and Columbus, Ohio. Some of the businesses, such as the Minneapolis-based Al Barakaat, were lifted from the terrorist ban in August 2002, when the government cleared them.

Passenger profiling

The U.S. has had in place an extensive passenger-profiling program at the nation's airports since 1996. Muslims have complained in the past of the discriminatory nature of singling people out because of complexion and religious appearance or any other signs of faith and ethnicity. But the experiences of Muslims in the post-9-11 climate have been unmatched by any previous period. Persons of Muslim or Arab appearance were not just pulled out of passenger lines; they were treated rudely.

A few examples can illustrate the point. A Muslim woman from Lincoln, Nebraska was ordered to remove her hijab before boarding an American Airlines flight. She was frightened by the guards with guns, so she complied.

In another incident, Anila Sial wrote the following column in the *St. Louis Post-Dispatch* on November 20, 2001 describing how she was forced to take off her hijab at the airport.

"I prepared myself for some delays when I took my first post-9-11 flight. Like most travelers, I had read about tighter security at airports. Plus, as a 22-year-old, scarf-wearing Muslim woman, I figured I might be targeted for extra scrutiny. But I wasn't prepared for what happened when I left St. Louis to visit my sister in New York City recently. Getting there from St. Louis was no problem. It was the return trip from John F. Kennedy Airport where things became surreal. Following the same procedure as I have on countless other flights, I checked my baggage and proceeded to the first security checkpoint. This is where travelers lay their luggage through the X-ray machine and walk through the metal detector. I laid down my purse, jacket and cell phone to be scanned and walked through the metal detector without setting off the alarm. I stepped ahead to grab my belongings, when one of the airport security women stopped me abruptly. 'I need you to take that off,' she said, pointing towards my scarf. Caught off guard by this unusual request, I stuttered, 'What? Why?' The woman repeated in a much louder voice, 'Take your thing off!' 'I can't,' I started to explain. At this point, she began to yell: 'Yes you can, take that off now!' I had no choice but to follow her directions, especially since everyone was now looking at me. I unpinned my scarf and let it sit on my shoulder. Under the scarf I wore a tight cap to keep my hair in place. The security guard pointed to it and demanded I remove it, as well. I pulled the hat down half way. Finally, she was satisfied and allowed me to go. Completely shocked and humiliated, I felt like crying. I realized that the security agent probably didn't even realize how violated I felt. Imagine if the woman behind me was randomly targeted and asked to remove her blouse in front of everyone. She would probably be stunned."

In another similar incident, a 17-year-old Muslim high school student from Virginia says that she was intimidated into removing her religiously mandated headscarf by a security guard at Baltimore/Washington International Airport (BWI). The teenage traveler told CAIR that after she went through a security checkpoint on her way to a Northwest Airlines flight, a guard shouted, "Hey, you need to take that off," referring to her headscarf. She responded by asking, "Why do I have to take off my head cover?" The girl was then surrounded by military personnel in camouflage uniform with combat rifles. She became terrified and removed her headscarf immediately.

In a number of cases the abuse included the selective removal of Arab and Muslim passengers from the airplane. The case of a Muslim Secret Service agent captured national attention. The agent, who was on his way to his assignment of protecting President Bush, alleged that he was kicked off American Airlines Flight 363 from Baltimore to Dallas on December 25th because the captain had concerns about his identity, even though the agent went through the proper procedures for armed security personnel who are passengers. The agent's identification was subsequently checked several times by American Airlines personnel and by local police. He even offered to have the Secret Service confirm his identity. When the agent asked to go back on the plane to retrieve his jacket, the captain said: "I don't want him back on that plane."

Most cases of similar nature did not receive extensive media coverage. University of Florida newspaper the *Independent Florida Alligator* reported on November 21, 2001 that University of Florida liberal arts and sciences seniors Ismael Khan and Nauman Piracha were removed from Delta Flight 915 to Atlanta. Delta flight attendants reportedly thought they looked suspicious. In another situation, Shaun Ahmad, a passenger who was escorted off a plane wrote the following description of his experience in the *Charlotte Observer* on December 20, 2001:

"I was flying from Charlotte to New York. Soon after I took my seat, a passenger of South Asian descent sat down next to me. Although I am an American, I too have brown skin as my parents are from Pakistan originally. A couple of minutes later a US Airways security agent came to our row and asked my neighbor to leave the plane. Another agent then asked me to take my bags and follow him. When I asked why, he refused to answer. After being escorted off the plane, I was searched. When I asked again why I had been removed from the plane, I was told that I and the passenger I was traveling with had acted erratically. When I asked why the agent thought I was traveling with this other South Asian, he remained silent. I have brown skin and I am a Muslim, but I am also an American. I should not have to put up with harassment because of my ethnic or religious background. And although Attorney General Ashcroft continues to insist that justice in America remains blind to race and religion (I'm not so sure), one thing is for certain: US Airways certainly does not."

The government's profiling system, which includes ethnic and religious criteria, does not actively discourage such abuses. In some cases, the same procedures for scrutinizing Muslims and Arabs have also been applied to American citizens at the country's ports of entry. In February 2002, a man and his three friends, all American citizens, were traveling on business to Houston, Texas and decided to cross the border to Mexico for dinner. Upon returning, they were pulled aside, interrogated, and held for more than two hours. They were allegedly told they looked Middle Eastern and were in the wrong place at the wrong time. While immigration officers at the port may be acting on their own in such cases, there is little effort by the government to prevent such mistreatment.

Still, the Federal Aviation Administration (FAA) released a fact sheet reaffirming anti-discrimination on the basis of race, color, national origin, sex or creed. In part it reads,

"In the aftermath of the terrorist attacks on 9-11, security measures have been heightened for the safety of all. While safety and security are the highest priorities, of equal importance is a smooth, and safe experience for all individuals as their journey takes them through the aviation system.... None of the new security measures decrease the responsibility of airports and airlines to enforce ...Title VI of the Civil Rights Act of 1964 and the implementing regulations... regarding discrimination. Federal civil rights laws prohibit discrimination on the basis of a person's race color, national origin, religion, and sex.... However, everyone may experience some inconveniences and delays while the nation adjusts to the new security reality. You may be asked to exhibit an increased level of cooperation in security searches with today's new security regulations. Please assist the security staff in accomplishing their required tasks. Private security screening requests should be accommodated when possible. Just as there can be no discrimination against people on the basis of race, color, national origin, sex, or creed, there can be no compromise to the commitment and enforcement of safety and security standards in the aviation community."

Despite the official warning, reports of incidents mounted. According to a March 4, 2002 report by the *Washington Post*, the U.S. Department of Transportation has received 98 discrimination complaints from airline passengers, including 26 who said they were kicked off flights since 9-11. Only 10 reports were filed in the same period a year earlier.

Guarding America's tradition of liberty

Ethnic minorities

A November report by the North American Congress on Latin America (NACLA) expressed fear that in the wake of the 9-11 attacks progress on the status of undocumented workers would be reversed due to an increased association between immigration and security threats resulting from the attacks. The report points out that restrictive immigration provisions have been included in new anti-terrorism measures, leaving the immigrant rights community with new sets of civil liberties and civil rights concerns. On the other hand, the war on terrorism has forced the administration to adopt more of a global and regional perspective than it previously had, to secure future collaboration with its partners in other countries and to think about meeting future threats from a multinational position.

The specific impact on immigrant communities is summarized in the NACLA as follows:

Many foreign nationals, immigrants, and first-generation U.S. citizens are included among the numerous victims and heroes of the attacks. Family members of some immigrant workers, however, have been hesitant to report missing loved ones out of fear of the INS; further, many of these immigrants and their family members, due to severe restrictions on eligibility for public services, have been unable to access certain public programs such as disaster relief programs and unemployment insurance. Many more immigrant workers found themselves among the unemployed as a result of cutbacks in travel and other affected industries. And despite strong statements from U.S. officials urging racial and ethnic tolerance, reports of violence, harassment, and hate crimes against Arab Americans, Muslim Americans, and others simply mistaken for "terrorists" have been distressingly common. In the wake of the attacks, some people immediately called for even more severe restrictions on immigrant admissions and a further curtailment of the rights of immigrants already in the country. Issues that previously had low priority such as national ID cards, increased border enforcement and INS restructuring have re-appeared in light of recent events.

The Congressional Black Associates organized a panel discussion on November 16, 2001, hosting representatives of the Hispanic, Sikh and African-American communities in challenging the effectiveness and legality of profiling as a law enforcement tool. Several of the panel participants noted that although profiling is now being directed primarily at Muslims and people who look "Middle Eastern," experience shows that it will also be used against other minorities. Many African Americans oppose profiling Arab and Muslim Americans since the practice has been deployed against blacks.

The civil liberties coalition

The American Civil Liberties Union (ACLU) and eighteen other organizations went to federal court early December 2001 in hopes of obtaining detailed information on detainees. The groups, which include Amnesty International, the Council on American-Islamic Relations, and Human Rights Watch, filed suit in a federal court in Washington under the Freedom of Information Act. They are seeking the names of people detained in connection with the investigation, along with charges filed, length of detention, place where the detainees are jailed, and names of their lawyers.

Also, two federal lawsuits have been filed seeking to open the deportation hearings of Rabih Haddad, founder of Global Relief Foundation, which is accused of funding terrorist activities. The American Civil Liberties Union filed suit on behalf of the *Detroit News*, the weekly *Metro Times* and Rep. John Conyers, (D-MI). The *Detroit Free Press* and the *Ann Arbor News* filed a separate lawsuit for the same purpose.

Fearing the impact of Justice officials' sweeping new powers, national civil rights groups and Arab and Muslim organizations have formed a coalition to defend against practices they say violate people's civil liberties. The coalition, which includes the ACLU, the Arab American Institute and the Black Leadership Forum, called for more congressional oversight, including hearings. It also is demanding that Justice Department officials release more information about the remaining detainees held for immigration violations and stop the questioning of young male foreigners, most of whom are from Middle Eastern and Central Asian countries. The coalition kicked off its campaign with a rally January 19th in Washington in commemoration of Dr. Martin Luther King Jr.'s birthday.

On January 16, 2002, the ACLU, joined by other civil rights groups, filed a lawsuit in a federal district court in Chicago alleging that an Illinois National Guardsman and three private security personnel at O'Hare International Airport engaged in an unnecessary, unjustified, illegal and degrading search of a 22-year-old United States citizen of Pakistani descent last November. In the complaint, the ACLU asserts that Samar Kaukab was pulled out of a group of airline passengers and subjected to repeated and increasingly invasive searches based on her ethnicity and her religion. Ms. Kaukab's religion was evident because she was wearing hijab. The lawsuit names Major General David Harris, Adjutant General for the Illinois National Guard, and Argenbright Security, Inc., as defendants for their personnel's role in the abuses directed toward Ms. Kaukab. The lawsuit stresses that Ms. Kaukab was identified and subjected to a humiliating search not because she posed any security threat, but only because her wearing of a hijab identified her as a Muslim. Security personnel surrounded her, detained her and subjected her to an embarrassing and degrading search simply based on her ethnicity and religion.

In August 2002, a federal judge ruled that the justice department had engaged in unconstitutional behavior by holding the deportation hearing of Rabih Haddad behind closed doors. The man has since filed to attain political asylum in the U.S. The court also ruled that the government has to release the names of detained individuals, unless the detainees wish otherwise or in cases of material witnesses whose identity must remain anonymous.

Congressional action

On November 8, 2001, the Senate blocked the passage of an amendment introduced by Senator Robert C. Smith (R-NH) to the Intelligence Authorization Bill that would have stripped away the requirement that the government present the accused with a summary of any secret evidence-classified information not shown to a defendant-used against him or her during deportation proceedings before the so-called Alien Terrorist Removal Court. The Smith amendment failed after the Senate voted unanimously for substitute language that would require the Attorney General to submit a report on the matter in three months. Civil libertarians regarded the failure of the Smith Amendment a victory in the battle to safeguard the U.S. Constitution. Both Senators Patrick Leahy (D-VT) and Bob Graham (D-FL) spoke against the amendment in its original form, saying Congress should resist "going down the road" of the notorious Alien and Sedition Acts of 1798, the laws passed during the administration of John Adams that allowed the arbitrary and utterly unwarranted deportations of law-abiding non-citizens.

Also, U. S. Representative John Conyers Jr., member of the Black Caucus and House Judiciary Committee, has been among the most outspoken critic of secret evidence and profiling. He took interest in a number of cases involving Muslims detainees after 9-11. His opinion piece in *The Detroit News* on January 22, 2002 read,

> "I recently strongly criticized the Justice Department's decision to change its longstanding practice of holding public immigration hearings behind closed doors ("Muslim man denied bail," Jan. 3) I became concerned after being denied admission to a bond hearing in Detroit involving Rabih Haddad, a well-respected member of Michigan's Muslim community who was being detained for an immigration violation. In this time of heated passions and rhetoric, we must make the critical distinction between our government's detention of suspected terrorists based on specific evidence of illegal behavior and the government's disregard for the constitutional rights to have a fair and public hearing. To be clear, I have firmly supported the need to bring terrorists to justice, while consistently protesting against government abuses of our Constitution... pending a hearing, and hearings before an immigration judge are open to the public. What I find objectionable is the fact that Pastor Haddad continues to be detained without credible evidence being offered regarding the need for his detention and without the benefit of public hearings...I fear the Justice Department, in its zealousness to protect our freedoms by detaining Middle Easterners without disclosing evidence and holding secret hearings, is quickly whittling away the constitutional foundation that has made freedom a beacon for the world."

Media promotion of tolerance

While media coverage of 9-11 and its aftermath is not the focus of this research, it is important to note the stark contrast between the anti-Muslim tone of several conservative media personalities and other reporters who took a more balanced approach in their coverage of 9-11. Among the commentators who engaged in Muslim bashing were Sean Hannity and Bill O'Reilly of Fox, Rich Lowry of the *National Review*, Dr. Laura Shlesinger, Rush Limbough, Cal Thomas, and Allen Keys. However, several media outlets have made an effort to draw a clear distinction between Islam and terrorism. They have also been vigilant on the issue of civil liberties. Here are a few examples.

1   *Oprah Winfrey Show*, October 5, 2001

The one-hour, widely watched NBC program gave a crash course on Islam that was generally balanced. It introduced the main beliefs of Islam and featured an American Muslim couple practicing their faith and going about their daily lives in Chicago. The program also made a distinction between the faith and its adherents, featuring a variety of political hotspots in Muslim countries and discussing matters of religion and politics.

1   *San Jose Mercury News*, November 15, 2001. The newspaper ran the following editorial:

First, the Justice Department rounds up more than a thousand people and holds them without letting anybody know the charges against them, or even who is being held. Then the State Department announces that it will slow the process for granting visas to men from Arab and Muslim countries. But don't stop there. Why not violate the long-held principle that people in custody are entitled to private conversations with their attorneys? And while we're at it, why not just ignore the American criminal justice system for some people and let their cases be handled in secret, by military courts? What next? Summary executions? ...The president has the constitutional authority to do what he's doing. He nonetheless undermines the values America seeks to defend as it battles those for whom civil rights have no meaning.

2   *Seventh Heaven Show*, January 8, 2002.

This Warner Brothers Television Network show featured Ruthie stepping in to protect her Muslim friend Yasmine from bullies who have been terrorizing her because of her ethnic and religious background, and gains the support from the entire Camden family. Eric, Annie and the other kids all work together to defend Yasmine and her family and discover in the process the sad truth that many people in their community share the same fears.

3   *Michigan Daily*, January 9, 2002. The newspaper ran the following editorial:

Rabih Haddad, a leader of the Ann Arbor Muslim community, was arrested on Dec. 14 by the Immigration and Naturalization Service on charges of overstaying his tourist visa. Since then he has been detained and has been denied bond on two separate occasions, the latest reasons proffered by the court being risk of flight and danger to society. Haddad has visited the U.S. off and on for more then a decade and in that time has founded the Global Relief Foundation, taught at a local Islamic school, served as assistant to the leader of Ann Arbor's mosque and applied for permanent residency. While it is within INS jurisdiction to arrest or detain visitors for overstaying visas, the elements of secret evidence, racial profiling and inconsistency indicate justice is not being served in this case.... [I]t should take care to uphold the civil liberties that are fundamental to those values.

4 *Washington Post*, February 7, 2002. The newspaper ran the following editorial:

Ten days after the 9-11 attacks, the administration instructed its immigration judges to keep certain proceedings closed. Not only would hearings be conducted in secret with "no visitors, no family, and no press" present, but the "record of the proceeding [was] not to be released to anyone" either -- including "confirming or denying whether such a case is on the docket or scheduled for a hearing." The Justice Department has since been conducting its 9-11-related immigration cases under these indefensible rules, though the cases thus far have not involved classified evidence. Last week two Detroit newspapers, Rep. John Conyers (D-Mich.) and the American Civil Liberties Union challenged in court both the policy generally and the closure of one immigration case in particular -- that of a man named Rabih Haddad. Mr. Haddad, the co-founder of a Muslim charity suspected of terrorist links, was detained on immigration charges. Whatever the merits of the case against him, he has a lot of supporters, and they -- along with the press -- want to attend his immigration trial. Yet, officially, there is nothing to attend. It doesn't matter that no sensitive or classified information has been discussed at the hearings to date, the plaintiffs claim. Public access has been nonexistent anyway. Immigration cases carry enormous consequences for people's freedom. They should, like criminal trials, be open for public scrutiny and criticism unless there is a compelling reason to the contrary. Holding trials in secret is a tactic unworthy of a great legal system.

5 *A Walk In Your Shoes*, February 10, 2002.

Noggin and Nickelodeon simulcast this episode, which was designed to help children understand the world around them and dispel any myths they may have about Muslims and the Islamic faith. The 30-minute episode of featured Nancy, a 15-year-old Protestant teen from the suburbs of Boston and Mariam, a 13-year-old Muslim teen from northern New Jersey. Nancy spends two days with Mariam to get a better understanding of the life of a Muslim-American teen. Nancy is nervous about terrorism in America and apprehensive about Muslims since her friends lost family members on 9-11. As Nancy explores Mariam's life, she gets the opportunity to attend Mariam's Muslim school, pray at her mosque, wear a hijab and celebrate Ramadan with Mariam's family. During the episode, Mariam teaches Nancy why Muslims fast and that

Islam is a religion that preaches love and kindness to others. The two girls also go ice-skating, shop at the mall and surf the web together.

6   *Kansas City Star*, February 14, 2002

If a report that Attorney General John Ashcroft made a tactless and inaccurate comment about Islam is correct, he should immediately apologize. So far Ashcroft has failed to give this matter the attention it deserves. He simply had a Justice Department spokeswoman issue a statement saying that the words attributed to him by Thomas "do not accurately reflect the attorney general's views." This careful wording implies denial but is actually silent on whether the quote was accurate. Thomas insists that it was. The columnist said he even repeated the quote in Ashcroft's presence to make sure that it was right. The quoted remark amounts to a broad and unfair attack on an entire faith. The attorney general needs to quickly clarify the situation. If Thomas' report is accurate, Ashcroft owes Muslims a sincere apology.

Appendix: 5CAIR Full Page Advertisement, Washington Post, September 16, 2001

ISNA JOINS AMPCC IN CONDEMNING TERRORIST ATTACKS

(Plainfield, IN - 9/11/2001) - The Islamic Society of North America (ISNA), along with other Muslim organizations throughout North America, today condemned the terrorist attacks in New York and Washington and offered condolences to the families of those who were killed or injured.

The AMPCC statement read in part:

"American Muslims utterly condemn what are vicious and cowardly acts of terrorism against innocent civilians. We join with all Americans in calling for the swift apprehension and punishment of the perpetrators. No political cause could ever be assisted by such immoral acts."

- END -

Signatories:

American Muslim Alliance
American Muslim Council

Association of Muslim Scientists and Engineers
Association of Muslim Social Scientists
Council on American-Islamic Relations
Islamic Medical Association of North America
Islamic Circle of North America
Islamic Society of North America
Ministry of Imam W. Deen Mohammed
Muslim American Society
Muslim Public Affairs Council

U.S. Muslim Scholars Condemn Attacks

CHICAGO, Sept 12 (IslamOnline) - Muslim scholars in North America unanimously condemned the attacks on the World Trade Center and Pentagon and expressed their deep sorrow and sympathy for those Americans who were killed and injured.

The Detroit-based Shari'a Scholars Association of North America (SSANA) strongly condemned the attack and said that there is no cause that justifies "this type of an immoral and inhumane act that has affected so many innocent American lives."

Insisting that Islam condemns such despicable attacks, the Association in a statement said, "Certainly, there is no justification for these acts from either an Islamic perspective or, in truth, from the perspective of any other moral and freedom-loving people. These acts diminish the freedom of all Americans, including American Muslims. Our condolences go out to all of the victims of these inhumane acts."

Additionally, the statement added that, "SSANA supports all efforts to investigate and immediately capture the evil persons responsible for these immoral can cowardly acts."

Sheikh Muhammad Hanooti, member of the Fiqh Council of North America and resident scholar at IslamOnline, told Islamonline that Muslims all over the world condemn this heinous act in the strongest of expressions and feelings. He said, "Islam tells us murdering one person is equal to murdering all humanity. We feel that great many innocent lives have been lost in this barbaric attack."

He added, "We pray to God to enable the people of United States of America to have peace, stability, security and prosperity."

Muzammil Siddiqui, director of Islamic Society of Orange County (ISOC) and former president of Islamic Society of North America (ISNA) could not be reached for comment but a statement released by the ISOC, which mentions him as the contact person, said that in each of its prayers yesterday the Society offered a special prayer and supplication for the victims of the tragedy in both New York and Washington DC.

"We encourage Muslim medical professionals and Muslim relief agencies to assist in whatever possible way with humanitarian and relief efforts both locally and nationally. Moreover, we urge people of diverse religious traditions, faith groups and spiritual expressions, including Christians, Jews, Buddhists, Hindus and members of other communities, to share their grief and sorrow together as one family, the human family," the statement read.

"We pray to God Almighty to provide safety and security to those working to alleviate the suffering and pain of the victims and their families of this tragic violence. We pray to God Almighty to instill patience and tranquility to all those involved in the process. Lastly, we pray to God Almighty to continue to bless and protect this land and all of its inhabitants," the statement added.

M. Amir Ali, Director of the Chicago-based Institute of Islamic Information and Education said, "Our condemnation of this terrorist act is unconditional and unequivocal and we support an impartial investigation for bringing perpetrators to full justice. I would like to add that there should be no retaliation against any party or a country without proof, but based on suspicion and prejudice."

"The Muslim leaders of Chicago discussed an action plan to help the victims and survivors of the terrorist attack by sending a team of doctors to New York, donating blood for the victims and sending money to help the needy. Committees were established to implement the resolutions immediately," he said.

Leading Islamic scholar Sheikh Taha Jaber Alwani, president of the School of Islamic and Social Sciences in Leesburg, Virginia, told AP news, "Muslims in this country would think this is unacceptable. I can't accept anything against any American citizen. I'm Muslim. I'm also American. I love America."

All local and national imams and scholars have expressed similar sentiments.

Scholars of Islam speak out against terrorism; clarify position of Islam

Monday, September 17, 2001

Dozens of scholars of Islam issued a statement today, condemning the violent attacks of 9-11th.

"We are grief-stricken at these horrifying events," they wrote; "the murder of innocents can never be justified and must not be tolerated."

In a lengthy statement, professors from major colleges and universities throughout the country expressed their compassion for grieving family members while also decrying the increase in violence against American Muslims this past week. "Anger and frustration are completely understandable and shared by us all," they wrote, "yet that anger must not be directed at individuals utterly innocent of these terrible crimes."

In recent days, verbal and physical attacks against Muslims (and people who were thought to be Muslims) have been reported from California to Vermont. Muslims have been warned to stay home or to avoid wearing traditional dress. "Particularly distressing is the fact that many American Muslims have fled to the United States, seeking a haven from intolerant regimes in Kosovo, Afghanistan or Iraq. For them now to face intolerance and violence here is an abuse of our Nation's most deeply cherished beliefs" they said.

The co-signers of the statement are members of many scholarly societies in the United States and Canada. They include:

Professor Asma Afsaruddin, of Notre Dame University
Professor Vivienne Sm. Angeles, La Salle University
Professor Ghazala Anwar of the University of Canterbury, New Zealand
Professor Jonathan Brockopp, Director of the Religion Program at Bard College
Professor Patrice C. Brodeur of Connecticut College
Professor Arthur Buehler of Louisiana State University
Professor Amila Buturovic of York University
Professor Juan E. Campo of the University of California, Santa Barbara
Professor Vincent J. Cornell of University of Arkansas
Professor Frederick M. Denny Chair of Islamic Studies and the History of Religions, University of Colorado

Professor Abdullahi Gallab of Hiram College
Professor Behrooz Ghamari of Georgia State University
Professor Alan Godlas of University of Georgia
Professor Hugh Talat Halman, of University of Arkansas
Professor Pieternella (Nelly) Harder Vandoorn,, of Valparaiso University
Professor Marcia Hermansen of Loyola University, Chicago
Professor Valerie J. Hoffman, of University of Illinois at Urbana-Champaign
Professor Qamar ul-Huda, of Boston College
Professor Aaron Hughes of the University of Calgary
Professor Amir Hussain of California State University, Northridge
Professor John Iskander of Georgia State Univeristy
Professor Ahmet Karamustafa of Washington University in St. Louis
Professor Tazim Kassam of Syracuse University
Professor Zayn Kassam of Pomona College
Professor Ruqayya Khan of University of California at Santa Barbara
Professor Kathryn Kueny, of Lawrence College
Professor Jane Dammen McAuliffe, Dean of the College, Georgetown University
Professor Richard C. Martin, Emory University
Professor J.W. Morris, Chair of Islamic Studies at the University of Exeter
Professor Gordon D. Newby, Executive Director, Institute for Comparative and International Studies at Emory University
Professor James Pavlin of Rutgers University
Professor Jack Renard of St. Louis University
Professor Omid Safi of Colgate University
Professor Walid Saleh of Middlebury College
Professor Zeki Saritoprak of Berry College
Professor Michael Sells, Haverford College
Professor Laury Silvers-Alario of Holy Cross University
Professor Alfons Teipen of Furman University

Statement of California Muslim Organizations

Released September 21, 2001

We, the undersigned Muslim organizations, support the President and Congress of the U.S. in the struggle against terrorism. Holding to the ideals of both our religion and our country, we condemn all forms of terrorism, and confirm the need for perpetrators of any such acts of violence to be brought to justice, including those who carried out the attacks of Tuesday, 9-11, 2001.

At the same time, in the planning of this "war against terrorism," we call upon the President and Congress to reaffirm the values and principles that make this country great, namely that one is innocent until proven guilty, that all accused have the right to a fair trial, that no one be punished for the acts of another, and that respect for human life is supreme, regardless of race or religion. To this end, we urge the U.S. government not to abandon the due process of law in determining responsibility for the attacks and punishing the guilty parties.

We are saddened by the possibility of military action, as we do not believe that terrorism can be eliminated solely or even effectively through military force. Rather we call upon our leaders to recognize that in order to rid the world of the ugliness of terrorism, our nation must understand its root causes. We hold out the hope that these root causes can be addressed through non-violent means, in a way that promotes peace and harmony between the nations of the world.

Signed:

Afghan Muslim Association (Fremont, CA)
American Muslims for Global Peace and Justice (AMGPJ)
American Muslims for Jerusalem (Northern California)
American Muslims Intent on Learning and Activism (AMILA)
Arab-American Congre
Council on American-Islamic Relations (Northern California)
Islamic Circle of North America (ICNA) Bay Area
Islamic Networks Group (ING)
Islamic Society of the East Bay (Union City, CA)
Islamic Society of San Francisco
Islamic Society of North America (ISNA) West Zone
Muslim American Society
Muslim Community Association (MCA)
Muslim Peace Fellowship (Nyack, NY)
South Bay Islamic Association (San Jose, CA)
Zaytuna Institute (Hayward, CA)

Rallying to make a difference

By Katherine Morales, *Dallas Morning News*, October 21, 2001

Imad Ismail stood on a sidewalk in downtown Dallas, telling strangers the same things he has told his friends at school for the last six weeks.

The 14-year-old didn't commit the Sept. 11 terrorist attacks.

Nobody he knew was involved.

His religious beliefs don't condone them, and he was appalled by them.

"I'm here because I think I can try to make a difference - to inform the public about what's going on," he said.

Imad joined hundreds of other families and community leaders, Muslim and non-Muslim, on Saturday for a rally against terrorism sponsored by the Council on American-Islamic Relations-DFW.

He stood with his siblings and cousins holding banners and American flags.

"Most people have been pretty cool - they've waved and smiled," Imad said, referring to passers-by.

The Duncanville teen said the reception hasn't always been as friendly.

"People would yell things at me on the street, and people at school would ask me if I was a terrorist," he said. "I don't take it seriously. They don't know me."

Behind Imad, speakers at the rally walked onto a small stage and denounced the attacks.

"The last six weeks have been difficult for our nation as a whole," said Mohamed Elmougy, president of the council. "We are here to reclaim our faith from those who have hijacked it from us. We cannot allow the few to ruin it for the many."

Mr. Elmougy also said it was unfair of people to think of Osama bin Laden as a true representative of Islam.

That statement brought rounds of applause from the audience. Some people waved handmade signs above their heads with messages of patriotism and peace.

Shamshad Haider Murtazawi, a Muslim cleric, gave those who gathered a perspective from the Quran on terrorism and murder.

"We do not kill, and it is absolutely forbidden in the Quran unless it is for self-defense," he said. "Human conscience does not allow terrorism, and Muslims will fight against it."

Melissa Walker drove from Sulphur Springs with her husband and two children to attend the rally after reading about it on a local website.

"I'm glad they have a variety of speakers with different perspectives," she said. "They speak for all of us and say the things we want to say. I wish there were more outlets for this."

A few non-Muslims also attended the event to show support for the Islamic community and to learn more about the tenets of Islam.

"I'm opposed to the violence that has been exhibited toward some of these people, although they had nothing to do with the attacks," said Norma Bell of Garland. "I'm Catholic, but we're all just trying to get to the same place."

Muslim Religious figures condemn terrorism

* "Hijacking Planes, terrorizing innocent people and shedding blood constitute a form of injustice that can not be tolerated by Islam, which views them as gross crimes and sinful acts."

Shaykh Abdul Aziz al-Ashaikh (Grand Mufti of Saudi Arabia and Chairman of the Senior Ulama, on September 15th, 2001)

*The terrorists acts, from the perspective of Islamic law, constitute the crime of hirabah (waging war against society)."

Sept. 27, 2001 fatwa, signed by:

Shaykh Yusuf al-Qaradawi (Grand Islamic Scholar and Chairman of the Sunna and Sira Countil, Qatar)

Judge Tariq al-Bishri, First Deputy President of the Council d'etat, Egypt

Dr. Muhammad s. al-Awa, Professor of Islamic Law and Shari'a, Egypt

Dr. Haytham al-Khayyat, Islamic scholar, Syria

Fahmi Houaydi, Islamic scholar, Syria

Shaykh Taha Jabir al-Alwani, Chairman, North America High Council

*"Neither the law of Islam nor its ethical system justify such a crime."

Zaki Badawi, Principal of the Muslim College in London. Cited in Arab News, Sept. 28, 2001.

*"It is wrong to kill innocent people. It is also wrong to Praise those who kill innocent people."

Mufti Nizamuddin Shamzai, Pakistan. Cited in NY Times, Sept. 28, 2001.

*"What these people stand for is completely against all the principles that Arab Muslims believe in."

King Abdullah II, of Jordan; cited in Middle East Times, Sept. 28, 2001.

*Ingrid Mattson, a professor of Islamic studies and Muslim-Christian relations at Hartford Seminary in Hartford, said there was no basis in Islamic law or sacred text for Mr. bin Laden's remarks. "The basic theological distortion is that any means are permitted to achieve the end of protesting against perceived oppression."

Dr. Ingrid Mattson, a practicing Muslim.

Participants in the National Day of Unity and Prayer

Organizations participating in the 9-11, 2002 Day of Unity and Prayer (as of September 2, 2002

AK	ICNA North-West Region
	Unitarian Universalist Society of
	Chicago Islamic Center
AR	Almobarak Cultural Center
	Immaculate Conception Church
CA	Islamic Society of Orange County & CAIR - LA
	Basileia, an Open Door Community of Christ
	Islamic Center of Conejo Valley
	Coachella Valley Islamic Socity
	Orange County Islamic Foundation
	Muslim Community Center of Greater San Diego
	Islamic Society of San Francisco
	Atonement Lutheran Church & Islamic Society of San Diego
	Unity Network
	Islamic Center of Claremont
	First Congregational Church of Escondido
	Masjid Al Islam
	Islamic Center of Fremont
	Muslim Women In Action
	Islamic Center Woodland California
	Muslim Student Union (USC)
CO	Islamic Center of Fort Collins
FL	Islamic Center of Northeast Florida
	Unitarian Universalist Fellowship of Bay County
	Nur Ul Islam of South Florida
GA	Masjid Al-Hedaya

IA	Islamic Center of Cedar Rapids
IL	Islamic Center of Macomb
	Unitarian Universalist Society of Geneva
	Islamic Center of the Quad Cities
	Central Illinois Masjid and Islamic Center
	Evanston Friends Meeting
	Chicago Islamic Center
KS	Islamic Center of Topeka
MA	Duxbury Interfaith Council
	Islamic Society of Western Massachusetts
	United Muslim Mothers
	Islamic Center of New England
	Islamic Society of Greater Worcester
MD	Islamic Society of Baltimore

APPENDIX IV
Urban terrorism, homegrown violence and hate crimes: The enemy within

Compiled
by
Aladdin Elaasar

CONYERS RENEWS CALL FOR PASSAGE OF HATE CRIMES LAW

"New Figures on Muslim Bias Make Need for Passage Compelling "

Representative John Conyers, Jr., the Ranking Democrat on the House Judiciary Committee, and lead author of hate crimes legislation in the last three Congresses issued the following statement In light of the FBI's annual hate crimes report finding that incidents targeting people, institutions and businesses identified with the Islamic faith increased from 28 in 2000 to 481 in 2001:

"These new statistics clearly make the case for passage of hate crimes legislation. If our nation is going to battle terrorism abroad, we must be willing to confront the domestic terrorism of hate crimes, and that means a willingness to make it a federal crime to harm or kill someone because of their race, religion or other factors. I am confident that we have bipartisan majorities in both the House and the Senate to pass such a law, but we need leadership from the White House to make this happen. I will reintroduce this bill when Congress returns early next year, and plan on making this a principal priority for the next Congress...

The increase in hate crimes against Muslims seen in the FBI report of 1,600 percent is truly shocking. Muslims previously had been among the least targeted religious group...

This increase is a direct consequence of the fear and suspicion that followed the Sept. 11 terror attacks. Sadly, the policies promulgated by the Administration and the Department of Justice may have contributed to the climate of distrust of Arab-Americans that is reflected in hate crimes data. Recently disclosed intelligence programs, such as the questioning and monitoring of thousands of Iraqi citizens and Iraqi-Americans, sends the message that these are untrustworthy people, not worthy of basic Constitutional protections...

Hate Crimes Against Arabs Surge, FBI Finds *

"Arabs and others who appeared to be Muslim were threatened, beaten and generally discriminated against more last year than at any other time in the past, according to the FBI's annual survey of hate crimes released yesterday. Largely in the aftermath of the terror attacks of Sept. 11, 2001, the FBI counted 481 attacks against people of Middle Eastern descent, Muslims and South Asian Sikhs, who are often mistaken as Muslim. That number was up from 28 in 2000, an increase of more than 1,500 percent. Directors of Arab and Asian groups said the report validated surveys they had taken after the attacks, including a report titled "Backlash: When America Turned on its Own," by the Washington-based Asian-Pacific American Legal Consortium. "

"This absolutely validates what we were saying," said Hussein Ibish, spokesman for the American-Arab Anti-Discrimination Committee. "This data corresponds to our data, to Human Rights Watch, to all the available data."

The committees found more than 700 hate crimes but said it used different means to define and verify such crimes.

The FBI's annual report defines hate crimes as acts motivated by prejudice, racial and otherwise. Hate crimes against African Americans held steady from the preceding year at 2,900. Crimes against Jews totaled 1,043, down slightly. Gay people were the victims in 1,393 incidents, and white people, 891, according to the FBI.

One of the attacks recorded against Arabs and Asians was a phone call from Boston to James Zogby, director of the Arab American Institute in Washington. The caller called Zogby a "towel head" and threatened to kill members of his family.

Zogby said the threats against Arab Americans after Sept. 11 were similar to what befell Arabs immediately after the 1995 bombing of the Alfred P. Murrah Federal Building in Oklahoma City.

"The difference this time is that the president intervened quickly," Zogby said, "and the entertainment community provided public service ads that brought it down to a trickle. People were prosecuted, and there were investigations."

Zogby said he watched his attacker receive a two-month jail sentence. He supported the FBI report's findings that serious crimes have tapered off into what he called job and housing discrimination.

Ibish agreed with Zogby that considering the devastation of Sept. 11, the problem could have been worse.

"This doesn't mean the people of this country acted badly," Ibish said. "It means there's a particular problem facing an exposed and vulnerable community that comes from people who didn't know how to control their emotions."

Hate Crimes in the United States, 2001, FBI's Annual Report **

Final data released by the FBI's Uniform Crime Reporting (UCR) Program in the annual publication Crime in the United States, 2001 indicate that:

The estimated 11.8 million Crime Index offenses (murder, rape, robbery, aggravated assault, burglary, larceny-theft, and motor vehicle theft) in the Nation in 2001 represented a 2.1-percent increase over the 2000 estimate, the first year-to-year increase since 1991.

Estimated violent crime in 2001 rose 0.8 percent over 2000 estimates. Estimated aggravated assault volumes decreased 0.5-percent from 2000 data. Robberies increased 3.7 percent, murders rose 2.5 percent, and forcible rapes increased 0.3 percent in volume.

Estimated property crimes were up 2.3 percent over 2000 estimates. Motor vehicle thefts increased 5.7 percent, burglaries rose 2.9 percent, and larceny-thefts increased 1.5 percent.

Hate crime data were provided by 11,987 law enforcement agencies. The 9,726 hate crime incidents reported in 2001 involved 11,447 separate offenses, 12,016 victims, and 9,231 known offenders.

Law enforcement made an estimated 13.7 million arrests for criminal offenses (excluding traffic violations) in 2001.

Most data associated with the events of September 11, 2001, are included only in a special report in Section V of Crime in the United States, 2001. The book and press release are available electronically at the FBI's Internet site at http://www.fbi.gov/ucr/ucr.htm.

Hate Crime Statistics and Offenses, 2001

A total of 11,987 law enforcement agencies in 49 states and the District of Columbia collectively reported 9,730 bias-motivated incidents during 2001.The majority of these were single-bias incidents, meaning that all offenses involved in the incident resulted from the same bias motivation. Multiple bias incidents are those in which two or more offenses were committed as a result of two or more bias motivations. For 2001, participating agencies reported 9,721 single-bias and 9 multiple-bias incidents.

An examination of data from the single-bias incidents showed that 44.9 percent were motivated by racial prejudice, 21.6 percent were driven by a bias toward an ethnicity/national origin, 18.8 percent were motivated by religious intolerance, 14.3 percent by sexual-orientation bias, and 0.4 percent by disability bias. (Based on Table 1.)

The Hate Crime Data Collection Program codes all of the offenses that occur within hate crime incidents as belonging to one of three scoring categories-crimes against persons, crimes against property, or crimes against society. Of the 11,451 offenses reported, 67.8 percent were crimes against persons, 31.5 percent were crimes against property, and the remaining 0.7 percent were crimes against society. Within these offense types, intimidation was the most frequently reported of the crimes against persons at 55.9 percent. Destruction/damage/vandalism accounted for 83.7 percent of reported crimes against property. (Based on Table 2.)

A review of the total offenses (11,451) demonstrated that intimidation was the most frequently reported hate crime, accounting for 37.9 percent of the total. Destruction/damage/vandalism made up 26.4 percent; simple assault, 18.8 percent; aggravated assault, 10.8 percent. The remaining offenses accounted for 6.1 percent of the total. (Based on Table 2.)

Of the 11,430 offenses that occurred within the single-bias incidents, 46.3 percent were motivated by racial bias. Within those 5,290 offenses, investigators determined that 66.7 percent resulted from anti-black bias, 19.5 percent resulted from anti-white bias, 6.6 percent reflected an anti-Asian or anti-Pacific Islander bias, 5.3 percent resulted from bias directed against groups comprised of individuals of varying races (anti-multiracial group), and 1.8 percent were anti-American Indian or anti-Alaskan Native bias. (Based on Table 1.)

Among the 2,004 offenses motivated by religious prejudice (17.5 percent of the single-bias offense total), anti-Jewish bias made up 55.7 percent; anti-Islamic bias accounted for 27.2 percent; anti-Catholic bias, 1.9 percent; and anti-Protestant bias, 1.8 percent. Bias against other religious groups accounted for 10.5 percent.

The remaining percent of offenses were motivated by a bias against groups of individuals of varying religious beliefs and anti-atheism/anti-agnosticism/etc. bias.

Sexual-orientation bias (1,592 offenses) made up 13.9 percent of all offenses within the single bias incidents. Within this bias category, anti-male homosexual bias motivated 69.3 percent of offenses, anti-female homosexual bias accounted for 15.4 percent, and bias against homosexuals as a group, 13.0 percent. Anti-heterosexual and anti-bisexual bias accounted for the remainder. (Based on Table 1.)

An analysis of the data from those offenses resulting from bias against a particular ethnicity or national origin showed that anti-Hispanic bias accounted for 30.1 percent of the total. The remaining percent (69.9) of offenses were classified as bias against various other ethnicities or national origins. (Based on Table 1.)

Thirty-seven of the total offenses associated with single-bias incidents were motivated by anti-disability bias of which 25 were attributed to an anti-mental disability bias. (Based on Table 1.) A review of the data by offense type and bias motivation revealed that there were 10 hate-motivated murders during 2001. Of these, 5 were the result of an ethnicity or national-origin bias, 4 were driven by racism, and 1 was attributed to a sexual-orientation bias. Law enforcement attributed 2 forcible rapes to racial prejudice, 1 to sexual-orientation bias, 6 and 1 to an anti-ethnicity or national-origin bias. Concerning the offense of robbery, investigators determined that 66 robberies were racially motivated and 48 were motivated by a bias against a sexual orientation. Thirty-four arson offenses were traced to the offenders' religious intolerance, 26 to racial prejudice, and 22 to bias against an ethnicity or national origin. (See Table 4.)

The term victim throughout this publication refers to a person, business, institution, or society as a whole, unless otherwise specified. In 2001, there were 12,020 victims of 11,451 hate crime offenses. Victims of racial bias accounted for 46.2 percent of the 11,998 victims of single bias hate crime incidents. Victims of ethnicity or national-origin bias accounted for 22.0 percent, victims of religious bias comprised 17.7 percent, victims of sexual-orientation bias made up 13.9 percent, and victims of disability bias 0.3 percent. There were 22 victims of multiple-bias incidents in 2001. (Based on Table 1.)

An examination of data from single-bias incidents showed that of the 5,545 victims of racial bias, 66.7 percent were victims of anti-black bias, 19.2 percent of anti-white bias, 6.5 percent anti-Asian or anti-Pacific Islander bias, 1.8 percent anti-American Indian or anti-Alaskan Native bias, and 5.7 percent were victims of bias directed at groups composed of individuals of different races. (Based on Table 1.)

A breakdown of the 2,118 victims of hate crimes motivated by religious bias showed that the majority of victims were Jewish, 56.5 percent. Anti-Islamic bias accounted for 26.2 percent of victims of hate crimes motivated by religious bias, anti-Catholic bias accounted for 1.9 percent, anti-Protestant 1.7 percent, and anti-atheism or anti-agnosticism 0.2 percent. Biases directed at members of other religious groups and those directed at groups made up of individuals from various religious faiths accounted for 11.1 percent and 2.5 percent of the victims, respectively. (Based on Table 1.)

Male homosexuals accounted for the majority of the 1,664 victims of sexual-orientation bias, 69.2 percent. Anti-female homosexual bias accounted for 15.4 percent, anti-homosexual bias 13.0 percent, anti-heterosexual bias 1.3 percent, and anti-bisexual bias 1.0 percent. (Based on Table 1.)

Victims of anti-Hispanic bias accounted for 30.8 percent of the total 2,634 victims of anti-ethnicity or anti-national origin bias hate crimes. The remaining 69.2 percent of victims were of other ethnicities or national origins. (Based on Table 1.)

In 2001, within single-bias incidents, there were 37 victims of disability bias. The majority of those, 67.6 percent, were victims of anti-mental disability bias, and 32.4 percent were victims of anti-physical disability bias. (Based on Table 1.) A review of the data concerning the types of victims showed that of the 12,020 hate crime victims, 7,768 victims or 64.6 percent were of crimes against persons in 2001. Of the 7,768 victims of crimes against persons, 55.9 percent were victims of intimidation. (Based on Table 2.) Nearly 35 percent (34.7) of the 12,020 total were victims of crimes against property. Within this category, 83.4 percent were victims of destruction, damage, or vandalism. (Based on Table 2.) Among the 3,607 crimes against property offenses, 52.5 percent were directed at individuals, and 10.4 percent were directed at business or financial institutions. Property hate crimes directed against religious organizations accounted for 7.6 percent; against society or the public, 6.2 percent; and at government, 5.9 percent.

The remainder was directed toward other, unknown, or multiple victim types. (Based on Table 6.)

Additionally, agencies contributing NIBRS data reported 76 hate crime offenses against society in 2001. These offenses accounted for 0.6 percent of the total victims. (Based on Table 2.)

Offenders

As defined by the Hate Crime Data Collection Program, the term known offender does not imply that the suspect's identity is known, but that an attribute of the suspect is identified which distinguishes him or her from an unknown offender. In the hate crime program, the offender's suspected race is the identifying attribute. In 2001, law enforcement agencies reported a total of 9,239 known offenders associated with 9,730 bias-motivated incidents. (See Table 1.) Of these known offenders, 65.5 percent were white, 20.4 percent were black, 0.9 percent were Asian/Pacific Islander, and 0.6 percent were American Indian/Alaskan Native. Groups of individuals representing various races accounted for 4.4 percent of all known offenders. The remaining 8.2 percent of offenders were of unknown race. (See Table 9.)

The 11,451 reported hate crime offenses in 2001 were committed by 9,239 known offenders; 349 of these offenders were involved in more than one offense. (Based on Table 2.) A review of the 7,649 known offenders involved in hate crimes against persons demonstrated that most (40.6 percent) committed the offense of intimidation. There were 3,607 hate crime offenses committed against property in 2001. Of the 1,851 known offenders for crimes against property, 59.9 percent were involved in destruction, damage, or vandalism. (See Table 2.)

Locations

Residences and homes were the scenes of 30.9 percent of the total 9,730 hate crime incidents in 2001. Incidents perpetrated on highways, roads, alleys, or streets accounted for 18.3 percent of hate crime incidents, and 10.1 percent occurred at school or colleges. Other or unknown locations accounted for 9.6 percent of incidents. Of the 4,367 incidents motivated by racial bias in 2001, 32.3 percent occurred at residences or homes; 21.7 percent on highways, roads, alleys, or streets; and 11.1 percent at schools or colleges. A breakdown of the total incidents by bias motivation showed that the majority of the 1,828 incidents motivated by religious bias (28.8 percent) occurred at residences or homes; 17.0 percent were committed in religious settings such as churches, synagogues, or temples; and 11.2 percent took place in schools or colleges. The data indicated that of the 1,393 hate crime incidents motivated by sexual-orientation bias, 33.4 percent of the incidents occurred at residences or homes; 22.6 percent, on highways, roads, alleys, or streets; and 11.7 percent, at schools or colleges.

Of the 2,098 hate crime incidents based on an ethnicity/national-origin bias, 27.8 percent occurred at residences or homes; 17.0 percent occurred on highways, roads, alleys, or streets; and 7.7 percent took place at parking lots or garages. In regard to the 35 hate crime offenses motivated by a physical or mental disability bias, 42.9 percent occurred at residences or homes; 14.3 percent took place on highways, roads, alleys, or streets; and 8.6 percent happened at schools or colleges. (See Table 10.)

* Darryl Fears, Washington Post Staff Writer, November 26, 2002

** FBI National Press Office, October 28, 2002

APPENDIX V
"WE ARE NOT THE ENEMY" Hate Crimes Against Arabs, Muslims, and Those Perceived to be Arab or Muslim after September

PREPARED
BY

Amardeep Singh, Hate Crimes Researcher, U.S. Program of Human Rights Watch,
New York City.

> Those who feel like they can intimidate our fellow citizens to take out their anger don't represent the best of America, they represent the worst of humankind, and they should be ashamed of that kind of behavior.
> -- George W. Bush

> I stand for America all the way! I'm an American. Go ahead. Arrest me and let those terrorists run wild!
> -- Frank Roque, after being arrested for the murder of Balbir Singh Sodhi

I. SUMMARY
II. RECOMMENDATIONS
1 Policing
2 Prosecution
3 Bias Crime Tracking
4 Affected Community

III. U.S. LAW AND INTERNATIONAL HUMAN RIGHTS STANDARDS
1 Hate Crimes Legislation
2 State and Local Agencies Responsible for Addressing Hate Crimes
3 Federal Agencies Responsible for Addressing Hate Crimes
4 International Law

IV. A HISTORY OF BACKLASH ATTACKS AGAINST ARABS AND MUSLIMS IN AMERICA.

1 Middle East Tensions in the 1970s and1980s
2 Persian Gulf War
3 Oklahoma City Bombing and TWA Flight 800
4 September 11: Expectations of Backlash Violence

V. THE SEPTEMBER 11 BACKLASH

1 Murder
2 Assaults
3 Place of Worship Attacks ...
4 Arson

VI. FEDERAL, STATE, AND LOCAL HATE CRIME PREVENTION EFFORTS BEFORE AND AFTER SEPTEMBER 11

1 Public Condemnation
2 Mixed Messages
3 Policing
4 Backlash Planning
5 Police Deployment
6 Initial Classification of C 28
7 Hate Crime Units and In 29
8 Support for Hate Crimes Training
9 Prosecution
10 Publicizing Prosecutions
11 Hate Crime Prosecutor
12 Crimes with Mixed Motive
13 Affected Community
14 Relationship With Affected Communities Before September11
15 Outreach after September 11: Barriers to Trust
16 Cultural Competency
17 Language Barriers
18 Community Liaisons
19 Creation of Hotlines on Hate Crimes
20 Bias Crime Tracking
21 Federal Hate Crime Statistics
22 City and State Hate Crime Tracking

APPENDIX
I. SUMMARY

In the aftermath of the September 11, 2001 terrorist attacks, Arabs and Muslims in the United States, and those perceived to be Arab or Muslim, such as Sikhs and South Asians, became victims of a severe wave of backlash violence. The hate crimes included murder, beatings, arson, attacks on mosques, shootings, vehicular assaults and verbal threats. This violence was directed at people solely because they shared or were perceived as sharing the national background or religion of the hijackers and al-Qaeda members deemed responsible for attacking the World Trade Center and the Pentagon. The post-September 11 violence against Arabs and Muslims was not unprecedented.

Over the past twenty years backlash hate crimes against Arabs and Muslims in the United States have become predictable, triggered by conflict in the Middle East and acts of terrorism associated with Arabs or Muslims. The hate crimes that followed the September 11 attacks nonetheless were unique in their severity and extent. While comprehensive and reliable national statistics are not available, Arab and Muslim groups report more than two thousand September 11-related backlash incidents. The Federal Bureau of Investigation reported a seventeen-fold increase in anti-Muslim crimes nationwide during 2001. In Los Angeles County and Chicago, officials reported fifteen times the number of anti-Arab and anti-Muslim crimes in 2001 compared to the preceding year.

In many cases, government officials responded quickly and vigorously to the backlash violence. President George W. Bush and numerous state and city officials publicly condemned anti-Arab and anti-Muslim hate crimes. In addition, as this report documents, state and local government across the nation undertook a series of steps seeking to contain acts of violence and bring perpetrators to justice. Nevertheless, aspects of the U.S. government's anti-terrorism Campaign ?the detention of twelve hundred mostly Middle Eastern and South Asians because of possible links to terrorism, the effort to question over five thousand young Middle Eastern men, and the decision to fingerprint visitors from certain Middle Eastern and Muslim countries reinforced a public perception that Arab and Muslim communities as a whole were suspect and linked to the "enemy" in the U.S. war against terrorism.

In this report, Human Rights Watch documents the nature of the September 11 backlash violence and the local, state, and federal government responses to it. Drawing on research in six large cities, Human Rights Watch identified public practices used to protect individuals and communities from hate crimes. The report focuses particularly on four areas of response: police deployment, prosecutions, bias crime monitoring, and outreach to affected communities. Our research demonstrates that action in advance of potential outbreaks of hate crimes can help mitigate the harm to individuals and property from backlash crimes.

The success in combating backlash violence in Dearborn, Michigan, for example, where only two violent September 11-related assaults occurred in a city with 30,000 Arab-Americans, reflected steps taken by local and state officials long before September 11. In particular, Dearborn police had already identified high-risk communities and were ready to deploy officers where needed within hours of the attacks on the World Trade Center and Pentagon; pre-existing relationships between community leaders and officials facilitated communications. In cities such as Los Angeles and New York City, where police departments did not have strong pre-existing relationships with Arab and Muslims, police quickly deployed officers in vulnerable areas once backlash incidents began.

Although various systems existed to track bias crimes in the United States, flaws in those systems limited complete and accurate reporting of the nature and extent of September 11 backlash violence. The effective allocation of public resources to prevent and respond to hate crimes requires better, complete, accurate and timely monitoring of such crime.

None of the cities researched developed backlash mitigation plans. Yet recent U.S. history, as described in this report, had clearly shown that backlash violence usually followed acts of terrorism attributed to Arabs or Muslims. Given that future acts of terrorism in the United States or conflict in the Middle East can be expected to generate new outbreaks of violence against members of Arab and Muslim communities, Human Rights Watch believes that federal, state and local government should develop plans to prevent and mitigate backlash violence. Ultimately, prevention of anti-Arab violence will require an ongoing national commitment to tolerance, respect for multicultural diversity, and recognition that "guilt by association" has no place in the United States. In the meantime, public officials face the challenge and the responsibility under U.S. and international law of combating backlash violence undertaken by private individuals.

The September 11 backlash against Arabs and Muslims is part of a larger, long-standing problem of hate crimes in the United States. Over the past ten years, the Rodney King beating, the 1993 Yusef Hawkins racial murder in Bensonhurst, New York, the 1993 shooting spree on the Long Island Railroad, the summer of 1996 African American church burnings, the 1998 murder of James Byrd, and the

1999 murder of Mathew Shepard have strengthened calls in the U.S. for increased attention to violent bigotry and crimes motivated by bias against distinctive communities identified by race, religion, ethnicity, gender or sexual orientation. While the focus of this report is on violence against Arabs and Muslims, the strengths and weaknesses of official responses to the September 11 backlash reflect the strengths and weaknesses of the official response to all hate crimes.

II. RECOMMENDATIONS

Our research confirmed that local, state, and federal governments in the United States are committed to meet their obligation to protect Arab and Muslim communities from backlash violence but vary in the extent to which they have succeeded in doing so. While no government can wholly prevent hate crimes against Arabs and Muslims or any other vulnerable community ?after September 11 public officials took steps to minimize such violence, to ensure its successful investigation and prosecution, and to reassure communities that the government is committed to their protection. We provide recommendations below drawn from our research. Because Human Rights Watch believes that some government entities have developed measures or practices that may serve as useful examples to others we have provided their contact information in the Appendix.

Policing

1. Law enforcement authorities should prepare a "backlash emergency mitigation plan" that may be implemented immediately following any event that might trigger backlash violence.

2. Following any event that might trigger backlash violence, public officials, as well as civic and social leaders, should make unequivocal statements that bias-motivated violence will not be tolerated and that those who engage in it will be prosecuted.

3. When the possibilities of backlash crimes arise, police should heighten their presence in vulnerable communities. Police should also insure open channels of communication with affected
communities during these periods.

4. Every law enforcement agency should have one or more officers trained to identify and investigate bias-motivated crimes.

5. All police reports which indicate that a responding officer or a victim believes that a crime may be bias-motivated should be given for review and guidance to a law enforcement officer trained to detect and investigate bias motivated crimes.

6. Law enforcement agencies should ensure that residents in their jurisdictions know where and to whom and how to report hate crimes. Literature summarizing how victims may report bias-motivated crimes should be produced, translated into foreign languages as necessary, and distributed widely.

Prosecution

1. Every county and city should provide specialized training to least one, if not more, prosecutors in identifying and prosecuting criminal acts that may constitute a bias motivated crime and should assign all hate crime prosecution to prosecutors who have received such training.

2. State attorney general offices should create hate crime prosecution units that provide assistance to county prosecutors.

3. Prosecutors should prominently publicize prosecution of bias-motivated crimes to the general public and to the targeted community, and should do so regardless of whether a bias motivated act is prosecuted under hate crimes legislation

Bias Crime Tracking

1. All local, county, state and federal law enforcement agencies should cooperate with the Federal Bureau of Investigation's National Incident-Based Reporting System (NIBRS) program to report all bias-motivated crimes.

2. Law enforcement agencies should regularly publish and make public comprehensive statistics on bias-motivated crimes in their jurisdictions regardless of whether the crimes are prosecuted under special hate crime legislation. Published statistics on bias-motivated crimes should include: the number of hate crimes committed in the jurisdiction for the specified period; whether the crime was based on the victim's race, ethnicity, religion, national origin, gender, disability, or sexual orientation; the victim's race, ethnicity, religion, national origin, gender, disability, or sexual orientation; the type of crime committed; the setting in which the crime was committed; whether the perpetrator was apprehended and how many of the reported bias-motivated crimes are being prosecuted.

Affected Community Outreach

1. Government agencies should ensure that communities affected by backlash violence are aware of the agencies within their jurisdiction that combat bias-motivated violence and know whom to contact within their jurisdiction in case they are a victim of a hate crime.

2. Where significant numbers of members of a community affected by bias-motivated violence live in a particular jurisdiction, government agencies should establish ongoing channels of communication and interaction with community leaders. They should also consider appointing a community liaison or an advisory council to facilitate interaction between government and the community.

III. U.S. LAW AND INTERNATIONAL HUMAN RIGHTS STANDARDS

The violent acts against Arabs and Muslims after September 11 violate U.S. criminal law regardless of their motivation. U.S. officials recognize their responsibility to prevent, investigate, and prosecute crime in general and to ensure that all U.S. residents, without regard to their race, national origin, or religion, are protected. While flaws exist with the U.S. system of law enforcement and criminal justice, no one doubts that all levels of the U.S. government federal, state, and local take crime control seriously.

Hate crimes are a uniquely important and socially devastating kind of crime, however, that warrant enhanced public attention and action. What distinguishes a bias or hate crime1 from others is not the act itself-e.g. murder or assault -but the racial, ethnic, religious, gender, or sexual orientation animus that propels its commission. While typically directed at a particular individual often randomly chosen hate crimes are motivated by anger toward an entire community distinguished by specific shared characteristics. While the bias that motivates a hate crime may be unusual in its ferocity, it is rooted in a wider public climate of discrimination, fear, and intolerance against targeted communities,

1 We use the terms bias-motivated crime and hate crime interchangeably in this report.

Intolerance against targeted communities can also be echoed in or enhanced by public policy. U.S. law as well as international human rights law single out hate crimes for particular attention precisely because of their broad social impact and their roots in discrimination and intolerance.

Hate Crimes Legislation

Over the past several decades, the persistent problem of bias-motivated violence in the United States has spurred the enactment of hate crimes legislation. This legislation either enhances the penalties for a crime when it is motivated by bias or make a bias-motivated criminal act a distinct crime in the criminal code. The first law uniquely criminalizing bias motivated conduct in the United States was the federal hate crimes statute.2 Originally created to protect civil rights workers in the 1960s, the law criminalizes bias-motivated conduct where the perpetrator attempts to stop the victim from engaging in one of six designated activities: (1) enrolling in or attending a public school; (2) participating in a service or facility provided by a state; (3) engaging in employment by any private or state employer; (4) serving as a juror; (5) traveling in or using a facility of interstate commerce; and (6) enjoying the services of certain public establishments. The federal hate crimes law only addresses racial, ethnic, national origin, or religious bias and does not protect persons who are attacked because of their gender or sexual orientation.

The limited scope of the federal hate crimes law and the continuing problem of bias motivated crime led to the creation of broader state hate crime laws during the 1980s and 1990s. All but five of the fifty U.S. states now have hate crimes legislation.3 Supporters of hate crimes legislation marshaled a number of arguments to support such laws, including: (1) Because hate crimes cause additional harms over and above the injury caused by crimes not motivated by hate, their unique nature should be recognized in the criminal law and receive greater punishment. For example, a swastika scrawled on a synagogue offends the entire Jewish community, not just the congregants of the affected temple; (2) Legislative recognition of bias motivated crime encourages increased efforts by public officials to prevent, investigate, and prosecute such crimes; and (3) Hate crimes legislation is an important public affirmation of societal values against bias as well as bias motivated violence, reinforcing society's commitment to equality among residents. State hate crime laws typically either make a bias-motivated criminal act a distinct crime or enhance the punishment during sentencing for a

2 18 U.S.C. § 245 (1994).

3 The states that do not have a law uniquely punishing bias motivated crimes or enhancing punishment for bias motivated crimes are: South Carolina, Indiana, Arkansas, New Mexico, and Wyoming. *See*, Anti-Defamation League, "State Hate Crime Statutory Provisions," retrieved on September 10, 2002, from http://www.adl.org/99hatecrime/intro.html.

4 For example, Washington State makes bias motivated crime a distinct crime called "malicious harassment." *See,* § 9A.36.080, Revised Code of Washington (2001). Arizona state law, on the other

crime shown to be motivated by bias.4 At present, all state hate crime laws include crimes motivated by racial, religious, or ethnic animus.

Twenty-six states include crimes motivated by animus against sexual orientation in their hate crime laws,5 and twenty-four states include crimes motivated by gender animus.6 In addition to the federal hate crimes law, the U.S. Congress passed the Hate Crimes Statistics Act (HCSA) in 1990.7 HCSA requires the U.S. Department of Justice to acquire data from law enforcement agencies across the country on crimes that "manifest prejudice based on race, religion, sexual orientation, or ethnicity" and to publish an annual summary of the findings. In1996, Congress enacted the Church Arson Prevention Act of 1996.8 The act criminalizes any intentional destruction, defacement or damage to religious property "because of the religious character" of the property.9 The Act also criminalizes acts that interfere "with the enjoyment" of a person's "free exercise of religious beliefs."10

State and Local Agencies Responsible for Addressing Hate Crimes

In the United States, the prevention, investigation, and prosecution of crimes against persons or property? whether or not bias motivated is primarily the responsibility of local authorities. The federal role is limited but nonetheless crucial, with federal authorities serving most often as a backstop when local efforts to address bias crimes issues fail.11 Local police are the front line in preventing and investigating hate crimes. The mandate of most police forces is similar to that contained in the New York City Charter: "the police department and force shall have the power and it shall be their duty to preserve the public peace, prevent crime, detect and arrest offenders, suppress riots, mobs and insurrections... protect

---

hand, calls for an enhanced penalty during sentencing where the prosecutor can demonstrate that a criminal act was motivated by bias. *See* § 13- 702, Arizona Revised Statutes (2001). The model for most state legislation enhancing penalties was developed in 1981 by the Anti-Defamation League (ADL), a Jewish civil rights organization. The ADL's model hate crimes legislation, however, also required hate crime data collection and police hate crimes investigatory training, features which are not typically included in state hate crime laws. Lu-in Wang, *Recognizing Opportunistic Bias Crimes*, 80 B.U.L. Rev. 1399, 1411 (December 2000).

5 See Human Rights Campaign, "Does Your State's Hate Crimes Law Include Sexual Orientation and Gender Identity?" retrieved on September 19,2002, from http://www.hrc.org/issues/hate_crimes/background/statelaws.asp.

6 See Anti-Defamation League, "State Hate Crime Statutory Provisions," retrieved on September 10, 2002, from http://www.adl.org/99hatecrime/intro.html.

7 28 U.S.C. § 534.

8 18 U.S.C. § 247.

9 Ibid.

10 Ibid.

11 Human Rights Watch telephone interview with Ralph Boyd, assistant attorney general for civil

the rights of persons and property... and for these purposes to arrest all person guilty of violating any law or ordinance...."12 Police departments are also another source of statistics on hate crimes. County prosecutors are primarily responsible for prosecuting crimes covered by state legislation, including hate crimes. In some counties, county officials have created ties, county officials have created specialized hate crime prosecution units staffed by prosecutors who receive specialized hate crime prosecution training. Hate crimes also often fall within the mandate of local and state civil rights agencies. In recent years, some cities and states have created agencies that specifically address bias-motivated crime. For example, the California Civil Rights Commission on Hate Crimes, created in 1998, advises California's attorney general on methods to improve hate crime prevention, tolerance and appreciation for diversity, law enforcement training, and the monitoring and suppression of organized, extremist groups. Similarly, the Michigan Alliance Against Hate Crimes is a statewide coalition of federal, state, and local law enforcement agencies, civil rights organizations, and community-based groups who meet periodically to exchange ideas on ensuring that responses to hate crimes are complete and effective.

In addition, a few entities have been created with a specific focus on issues affecting the Arab and Muslim communities. For example, the Chicago mayor's office has an Advisory Council on Arab Affairs which provides guidance and direction on issues affecting the Arab community in Chicago, including hate crimes.

Federal Agencies Responsible for Addressing Hate Crimes

Federal officials complement and supplement the efforts of state and local agencies to prevent, investigate, monitor, and prosecute hate crimes. The Civil Rights Division of the U.S. Department of Justice is charged with enforcing and prosecuting federal hate crimes laws. Federal hate crime prosecutions are relatively few in number, however, both because of the narrow scope of the federal hate crimes law and because of federal reluctance to preempt or disrupt local prosecution. On average, there are less than six federal hate crimes prosecutions annually.13

Numerous federal agencies assist in addressing bias-motivated violence. Established by the 1964 Civil Rights Act, the Community Relations Service

---

rights, United States Department of Justice, August 25, 2002.
12 New York City Charter § 435 (2001).
13 "The Hate Crimes Prevention Act of 1998," Senate Hearing on Senate Bill 1529 before the Senate Committee on the Judiciary, 105th Congress 4-19 (1999) (statement of Eric Holder, deputy attorney general).

(CRS), an agency within the U.S. Department of Justice, assists communities in addressing inter-group disputes. CRS mediators, working with police officials and civil rights organizations, have often acted to defuse community tensions that might otherwise escalate into racial or ethnic violence. CRS also has played a leading role in the implementation of the HCSA, organizing HCSA training sessions for law enforcement officials from dozens of police agencies across the country. Also established by the 1964 Civil Rights Act, the U.S. Commission on Civil Rights (UCCR) holds hearings and briefings on race relations and hate violence. It presents its findings on civil rights issues, such as hate violence, in reports submitted to the U.S. Congress and relevant federal agencies. UCCR has branch offices in each of the fifty states in the United States.

The Federal Bureau of Investigation (FBI) is the primary domestic law enforcement agency of the federal government. It conducts investigations into crimes covered by federal hate crimes legislation and can assist local police with hate crime investigations. The results of its investigations are used by the Civil Rights Division and the United States attorneys to initiate federal hate crime prosecution. In conjunction with CRS, the FBI also trains local law enforcement agencies in federal standards of data collection contained in the HCSA and publishes hate crime data collection guidelines for local police agencies.

The Bureau of Justice Statistics (BJS), an office within the U.S. Department of Justice, collects, analyzes, publishes, and disseminates information on crime, including hate crimes, criminal offenders, victims of crime, and the operation of justice systems at all levels of government. BJS is responsible for publishing an annual nationwide hate crimes report that provides the most comprehensive national statistical overview of hate crimes.

The Bureau of Justice Assistance (BJA), another arm of the Justice Department, provides grants to support local police and government agency efforts to build safe communities. BJA has funded numerous local initiatives to prevent and address hate crimes.

International Law

The condemnation and prohibition of racial or ethnic discrimination plays a pivotal role in international human right law. Both the International Covenant on Civil and Political Rights (ICCPR) and the International Convention on the Elimination of All Forms of Racial Discrimination (CERD), enjoin state parties from race discrimination (including discrimination based on ethnicity or national origin) and require them to provide their residents with equal protection of all laws.14 The United States is a party to both treaties. In addition, article four of the United Nations Declaration on the Elimination of All Forms of Intolerance and of Discrimination Based on Religion or Belief requires states to "prevent and eliminate discrimination on the grounds of religions" and to "take all appropriate measures to combat intolerance on the grounds of religion...."15 CERD requires governments to punish by law all acts of violence motivated by racial, ethnic, or national origin animus. Specifically, CERD article 4(a) obliges governments to declare "all acts of violence or incitement to such acts against any race or group of persons of another color or ethnic origin" as offenses punishable by law.16 Nevertheless, a question remains under international law of whether bias motivated violence must be penalized by special legislation or whether it can simply be punished through ordinary criminal laws. Some countries have adopted the position that bias-motivated violence must be uniquely criminalized through the creation of hate crimes legislation.17 The plain text of CERD, however, is silent on this question. It simply calls for bias-motivated violence to be punished without prescribing a means for doing so.18

The *Programme of Action of the World Conference Against Racism, Racial Discrimination, Xenophobia and Related Intolerance*, published on January 25, 2002, did not call on governments to pass specific hate crime laws. Instead, it recommended that bias motivation be considered by judges during sentencing as an aggravating factor. In particular, the report urged governments to: "take measures so that such motivations are considered an aggravating factor for the purposes of sentencing, to prevent these crimes from going unpunished and to ensure the rule of law." 19

14 International Covenant on Civil and Political Rights (ICCPR), article 26; International Convention on the Elimination of All Forms of Racial Discrimination (CERD), article 2(1).
15 Declaration on the Elimination of All Forms of Intolerance and of Discrimination Based on Religion or Belief, article 4, General Assembly resolution 36/55, November 25, 1981.
16 The Committee on the Elimination of Racial Discrimination, a treaty monitoring committee created pursuant to CERD, similarly calls on states parties to penalize "acts of violence against any race or group of persons of another color or ethnic origin. Committee on the Elimination of Racial Discrimination, "General Recommendation XV," paras. 3 and 4, retrieved on September 19, 2002, from
17 The Canadian Department of Justice (CDOC) concluded that "the creation of special criminal legislation to combat hate-motivated violence more forthrightly satisfies Canada's obligations under international law." Glenn A. Gilmour, Hate-Motivated Violence, Canadian Department of Justice, WD1994-6e (1994), retrieved on September 19, 2002, from http://canada.justice.gc.ca/en/dept/pub/hmv/hate_42.html.
18 CERD, article 4(a).
19 Report of the World Conference Against Racism, Racial Discrimination, Xenophobia, and Related Intolerance, Programme of Action (WCAR Report), para. 84, retrieved on September 19, 2002, from http://www.unhchr.ch/huridocda/huridoca.nsf/(Symbol)/A.Conf.189.12.En? Opendocument.

The program of action also enumerates a range of other measures that governments should take to address and remedy biasmotivated violence. Taken together, these measures provide a useful list of actions that http://www.unhchr.ch/tbs/doc.nsf/ (Symbol)/e51277010496 eb2cc12563ee004b9768?Opendocument.

The Law Reform Commission of Australia, citing Article 4(a) also concluded CERD requires the creation of specific hate crimes legislation, The Law Reform Commission of Australia, Multiculturalism and the Law, p. 153, 155, Report 57 (1992) retrieved on September 19, 2002, from http://www.austlii.edu.au/au/ other/alrc/publications/reports/57.states parties to CERD, including the United States, may employ to combat bias-motivated violence. The measures include: establishing working groups of community leaders and national and local law enforcement officials to coordinate efforts to address bias motivated violence; 20 enhancing data collection on bias motivated violence; 21 ensuring that civil rights laws prohibiting bias-motivated violence are rigorously enforced; 22 training law enforcement on how to investigate bias motivated crimes;23 developing educational materials to teach young persons the importance of tolerance and respect;24 and recognizing the need of all states parties to CERD to counter the present rise of "anti-Arabism and Islamophobia world-wide."25 Many of these measures are discussed below in our assessment of the government response to September 11-related hate crimes in the United States.

IV. A HISTORY OF BACKLASH ATTACKS AGAINST ARABS AND MUSLIMS IN AMERICA

Long before September 11, the stereotype of the Arab or Muslim as a "terrorist" had taken hold in the American imagination and fueled anti-Arab and anti-Muslim prejudice. That prejudice sometimes led to hate crimes, particularly after acts of violence ascribed rightly or wrongly to Arab or Muslim terrorists. In light of the history of backlash violence against Arabs and Muslims in the United States before September 11 2001, the hate crimes that followed September 11 were all too predictable. Government officials should be aware that there is a danger of an anti-Arab or anti-Muslim backlash anytime terrorism is linked to these communities.

20 WCAR Report, *Programme of Action*, para. 74(b).
21 Ibid.
22 Ibid.
23 Ibid.
24 Ibid.
25 Ibid., para. 150.

The victims of this violence have not been limited to one nationality or religion. Those who have been attacked include persons who only appear? at least to some Americans to be Middle Eastern, Arab, or Muslim. South Asians, for example, have regularly been attacked. So have people who "appear" Muslim even though Muslims are found among all races, ethnic groups, and nationalities. In the context of U.S. hate-violence, however, "Muslim" has been equated with Middle Eastern or Arab. Sikh men who wear turbans have also been lumped with "Arab" terrorists and victimized. In short, a confluence of events in U.S. history has led to the construction of a new racial stereotype and target for bias, fear, and hate crimes: persons who are or appear to be "Middle Eastern, Arab or Muslim." For brevity's sake, in this report we refer to this violence as anti-Arab and anti- Muslim, while fully cognizant of the heterogeneous composition of the victims.26

Middle East Tensions in the 1970s and 1980s

Though neither government agencies nor Arab or Muslim nongovernmental organizations (26 See Leti Volpp, "The Citizen and the Terrorist," 49 UCLA Law Review 1575 (2002) tracked incidents of bias-motivated crime in the 1970s,27 Arab and Muslim activists point to the 1973 Arab-Israeli war and oil embargo as a starting point for increased prejudice and hostility against their communities in the United States.28 An Arab-American from Dearborn, Michigan described the change in public attitudes towards Arab-Americans after 1973 in the following way: "suddenly we were being held responsible for things we had nothing to do with and no control over and maybe didn't even support in the first place."29 Activists contend that hostility increased during the Iran hostage crisis in 1979.

According to Albert Mokhiber, former President of the American Arab Anti-Discrimination Committee (ADC), the oldest Arab-American civil rights organization, "Iranians were being targeted for hate crimes at that point... so were Arab-Americans, and Arabs and Iranians aren't the same...."30 Arab-American activists also believe the ABSCAM scandal of 1980 heightened negative stereotypes of Arabs. 31 ABSCAM, short for "Arab Scam," was a federal political

27 The federal government began tracking hate crimes data with the passage of the Hate Crime Statistics Act in 1990.
28 David Lamb, "Loyalty Questioned; U.S. Arabs Close Ranks Over Bias," *Los Angeles Times*, March 13, 1987.
29 David Lamb, "Loyalty Questioned; U.S. Arabs Close Ranks Over Bias," *Los Angeles Times*, March 13, 1987.
30 Albert Mokhiber, "American Arab Anti-Discrimination Committee News Conference," National Press Club, Washington, D.C., Federal News Service, February 20, 1992.
31 Patrick Cooper, "Daschle's Proud Mentor Looks Back," *Roll Call*, July 19, 2001; "Human

corruption sting operation in which federal agents posed as wealthy sheiks and offered bribes to politicians.

As one Arab-American noted, after ABSCAM: "[A]ll Arabs were bad. Everybody was lumped together. You became that horrible, hook-nosed, terrorizing murderer. You were not to be trusted."32 The founders of the ADC credit the negative publicity surrounding the ABSCAM scandal as the impetus for the group's creation.33

The hijacking of TWA Flight 847 by Shiite militants on June 14, 1985 and the hijacking of the Italian cruise liner the Achille Lauro on October 7, 1985 by the Palestinian Liberation. Organization were followed by a spate of violent crimes against Arab and Muslims in the United States. On October 11, 1985, the regional director of the ADC Southern California office, Alex Odeh, was killed when a bomb exploded outside the front door of his office.34 The day before, Odeh had been on local television denying PLO involvement in the hijacking.35 The ADC office in Washington, D.C., was firebombed two months after Odeh's death.36 Two months before Odeh's murder, a bomb outside the ADC's Boston office injured a policeman when it detonated while the officer was trying to defuse it.37 In the same time period, a Houston mosque was pipebombed (causing $50,000 in damage), 38 the windows of the Islamic Institute in Dearborn, Michigan were broken,39 and a mosque in Potomac, Maryland was vandalized.40

Rights: American-Arab Committee Fights Discrimination," *Inter Press Service*, August 20, 1985; Alan Achkar and Michele Fuetsch, "Taking Pride In Their Heritage; Arab-Americans Battle The Sting Of Stereotypes As They Work To Open Others' Eyes To Reality Of Their Culture," *Plain Dealer*, November 26, 1995.
32 Alan Achkar and Michele Fuetsch, "Taking Pride In Their Heritage; Arab-Americans Battle The Sting Of Stereotypes As They Work To Open Others' Eyes To Reality Of Their Culture," *Plain Dealer*, November 26, 1995.
33 Chris Tricarico and Marison Mull, "The Arab: No More Mister Bad Guy?" *Los Angeles Times*, September 14, 1986.
34 Steve Lerner, "Terror Against Arabs in America: No More Looking the Other Way," *New Republic*, July 28, 1986.
35 Steve Lerner, "Terror Against Arabs in America: No More Looking the Other Way," *New Republic*, July 28, 1986.
36 Thomas Lerner, "Cover Story Language, incidents increasingly [sic]," *United Press International*, December 15, 1985.
37 Thomas Lerner, "Cover Story Language, incidents increasingly [sic]," *United Press International*, December 15, 1985.
38 "Terror Against Arabs in America: No More Looking the Other Way," *New Republic*, July 28, 1986.
39 "Human Rights: American-Arab Committee Fights Discrimination," *Inter Press Service*, August 20, 1985.

In 1986, the day the United States attacked Libya, five Arab students at Syracuse University were beaten while their attackers yelled anti-Arab epithets.41 Arab-American businesses in Dearborn, Michigan were also vandalized soon after the attack on Libya.42

Persian Gulf War

The beginning of the Persian Gulf crisis in August 1990 led to a major wave of hate crimes nationwide against Arabs and Muslims in the United States. The ADC recorded four anti-Arab hate crimes, from January to August 1990, before the crisis began43; between August and the start of the war on January 16, 1991 it recorded forty hate crimes. During the first week of the war, it recorded another forty-four.44 In Los Angeles, fires destroyed the businesses of a Lebanese-American and an Iranian Jew.45 In Cincinnati, a store owned by an Arab-American was firebombed.46 In New York, ten men with a bottle beat a man who looked Arab on the subway.47 In Baltimore, four or five men yelling "filthy Arab" attacked and broke the car window of a Polynesian Jew.48

In San Francisco, vandals smashed the windows of four Arab-American businesses.49 In Tulsa, Oklahoma, the house of an Iraqi native was burned

---

40 Ibid.

41 "Arab-Americans Are Targets Of Terrorism In U.S.," *Seattle Times*, September 7, 1986.

42 Murray Dubin, "'Hate acts' against minorities are on the rise, experts say," *Houston Chronicle*, December 7, 1986.

43 "American Arab Anti-Discrimination Committee News Conference," Federal News Service, February 20, 1992. The ADC data is based on reports of hate crimes filed by victims with its national office. Unlike a law enforcement agency, the ADC does not conduct an investigation to confirm whether a report of a bias incident is true. In classifying a criminal act and as a hate crime, the ADC used the federal definition of a hate crime.

44 Albert Mokhiber, "American Arab Anti-Discrimination Committee News Conference," National Press Club, Washington, D.C., Federal News Service, February 20, 1992.

45 Kenneth Reich and Richard A. Serrano, "Suspicious Fires Probed for Ties to Gulf Tension Crime: An Arson Unit studies a West Los Angeles Market Blaze and Police Label the Torching of a Sherman Oaks Store Likely Hate Crime. Owners of Both Businesses are of Mideast Descent," *Los Angeles Times*, January 24, 1991.

46 Adam Gelb, "War's Backlash: Two Communities Torn by Conflict; Arabs Emerge as New Target of Prejudice," *Atlanta Journal and Constitution*, January 19, 1991.

47 Cynthia Ducanin, "Crisis in the Middle East: American Sentiment: Threats Against Arab-Americans Rise, Hotline Set up for Victims; Savannah Station Stirs Outcry," *Atlanta Journal and Constitution*, September 1, 1990.

48 Adam Gelb, "War's Backlash: Two Communities Torn by Conflict. Arabs Emerge as New Target of Prejudice," *Atlanta Journal and Constitution*, January 19, 1991.

49 "Vandals Strike at Arabs in The City," *San Francisco Examiner*, January 25, 1991.

down.50 Threats against Arab and Muslim Americans were so numerous in Detroit that a criminal act and as a hate crime, the ADC used the federal definition of a hate crime.

Mayor Coleman Young asked Michigan's Governor to assign National Guard troops to protect the city's Arab and Muslim population.51 The severe nature and extent of the crimes prompted the first efforts by public officials to address violence against Arab and Muslim Americans. President George H.W. Bush strongly called for an end to hate attacks against Arab-Americans, insisting on September 24, 1990 that "death threats, physical attacks, vandalism, religious violence and discrimination against Arab-Americans must end." 52 In California, noting that the current "wave of hate crimes is greater than we have seen since the brutal heyday of the Klu Klux Klan," Lieutenant Governor Leo McCarthy introduced hate crimes legislation that proposed to increase civil and criminal penalties for those who commit bias motivated crime.53 In Los Angeles, the district attorney's office released a public service announcement asking viewers to call the Los Angeles County district attorney's office if they had any knowledge of crimes against Arabs, Muslims or Jews.54 In Chicago, the Human Relations Commission helped Arab and Muslim shopkeepers post signs warning against committing hate crimes.55

Oklahoma City Bombing and TWA, Flight 800

On April 19, 1985, a bomb destroyed the Alfred P. Murrah Federal Building in Oklahoma City, Oklahoma, killing 168 people. In the two days before federal authorities stated that foreign terrorists were not responsible, many Americans assumed Arab terrorists were behind the attack.

---

50 Ted Bridis, "Suspected 'Hate Crime' Yields to Flood of Support," Associated Press, February 23, 1991.
51 Rick Hampson, "Arab-Americans: Dual Loyalties and Nagging Worries," Associated Press, January 20, 1991.
52 "Home-Grown Hatemongers," *New York Times*, February 27, 1991.
53 "McCarthy, Lockyer Announce Legislation to Battle Hate Crimes," *Business Wire*, February 6, 1991. The California
State Legislature enacted the legislation that year.
54 "Southland: Briefly TV Ads to Fight Hate Crimes," *Los Angeles Daily News*, February 1991.
55 Frank Burgos and Zay N. Smith, "Shops Asked to Help Fight Hate Crimes," *Chicago Sun-Times*, January 30, 1991.
56 The Council on Islamic Relations
56 Bonnie Miller Rubin, "U.S. Muslims Are Looking For Apology," *Chicago Tribune,* April 22, 1995. Timothy McVeigh, a U.S. citizen who was neither Arab nor Muslim, was eventually tried and executed for the bombing.

(CAIR), a Muslim civil rights organization, recorded over two hundred incidents of anti- Muslim harassment, assault, or property damage in the days immediately following the bombing. 57 In Oklahoma City, a Muslim woman who was seven months pregnant suffered a miscarriage after a brick thrown through her window traumatized her the morning after the bombing.58

At a Muslim day care center in Texas, a teacher and sixty young students were frightened when a passing driver shouted to the teacher, "Here's a bomb for you lady," and then threw a bag of soda cans at her.59 In New York City, callers threatened to bomb Arab-owned business and attack the families of the owners.60 In Richardson, Texas, a mosque received ten threatening phone calls.61 Just one day after the bombing, as reports of backlash attacks began to surface, President Bill Clinton called on Americans not to rush to any judgments or blame any religion for the attack.62

On July 17, 1996, TWA Flight 800 exploded soon after leaving New York, killing all its passengers. As with the Oklahoma City bombing, there was public speculation in the media that Muslim or Arab terrorists were responsible for the explosion.63 Ultimately, the downing of TWA Flight 800 was blamed on a mechanical failure.64 Nevertheless, CAIR received ten reports of anti-Muslim verbal harassment and threats of violence prompted by anger against Muslims after the plane exploded. 65

57 Farhan Haq, "United States: Terrorism Fears Put Muslims on the Alert," *Inter Press Service*, August 17, 1995. CAIR data is based on reports of bias incidents filed by victims with its national office. These incidents include everything from verbal harassment to discrimination to bias-motivated criminal acts. CAIR accepts the facts reported to it as true.
58 Charles M. Sennott, "After the bombings, America Faces up to Prejudice," *Boston Globe*, June 21, 1995.
59 Hamzi Moghradi, "A Rush to Judgment - Again," *Plain Dealer*, April 23, 1995.
60 Laura Outerbridge, "American Muslims Articulate Fear
of Backlash," *Washington Times*, April 21, 1995.
61 Hamzi Moghradi, "A Rush to Judgment - Again," *Plain Dealer*, April 23, 1995.
62 John Nichols, "Bumbling Analysis Of Bombing Promoted Ethnic Stereotypes," *Capital Times*, April 24, 1995.
63 David Johnston; "Terror In Oklahoma City: The Investigation; At Least 31 Are Dead, Scores Are Missing After Car Bomb Attack In Oklahoma City Wrecks 9-Story Federal Office Building," *New York Times,* April 20, 1995; Stewart M. Powell and Holly Yeager, "FBI Issues Bulletin for 3 Suspects," *Seattle Post-Intelligencer*, April 20, 1995.
64 Rick Hampson, "Another Grim Task," *USA Today*, November 1, 1999.
65 Suzanne Cassidy, "Muslim Report Validates Local, National Aura of Bias: Pervasive Bigotry Alleged to Arise from Unjust, Constant Media Pairing of Islam with Terrorism," The Harrisburg Patriot, August 5, 1997.

September 11: Expectations of Backlash Violence

The past history of backlash violence left many of Arabs, Muslims, and those perceived to be Arab or Muslim, apprehensive that they would be targets of backlash violence whenever a terrorist incident was blamed on Arabs or Muslims. This fear was vividly expressed in messages sent by Muslims, Arabs, and Sikhs to community e-mail groups in the hours immediately after the September 11 attacks. A few of the messages are excerpted below: "Both towers of the World Trade Center are burning. In the coming hours (minutes?), the finger pointing will start just as it did after Oklahoma City."66?

??"I apologize for this haphazard email. I am shocked beyond belief as our great country is going through crisis as none before. At this time we stand with our hands folded in Ardas (Sikh prayer) to all victims of this dastardly attack. However...it is critical that we as Sikh-Americans do not become victims of this terror...What I am saying is very simple, "though we are peace loving people with no connections whatsoever to... (Osama bin Laden etal[sic]), there are individuals which may not see the difference"... Everyone's work or school situation is different but no one [sic] should go under any bullying or even be made uncomfortable by fellow colleagues."67 "I'm sure we've all heard of the tragedy this morning... Needless to say, we all realize that no Muslim in their right mind would condone such an action. I'm only writing to be sure you are all aware of the unavoidable atmosphere that will rise as a result of this attack: we're non-white, we're Arab... we're Muslims... There will be some 'serious' anti-Arab, anti-Muslim sentiment running rampant through this country...So be careful, stay with your families, stay off the streets unnecessarily, and watch your fellow sisters and brothers."68 "During this period of time in which events unfold in NY and Washington, we urge Arabs and Muslims to be watchful and proactive in handling what may result in backlash against our communities, property and persons."69

66 Alex Khalil, September 11, 2001, written to Global Network of Arab Activists Yahoogroup at 9: 49 a.m.
67 "Sikh-Americans: we need to be proactive During this Crisis!!!!!!," retrieved on September 11, 2001, from http://groups.yahoo.com/group/sikh-sewa/. Accessed by subscribing to Sikh-Sewa Yahoogroup and viewing archives.
68 "Bismillah," retrieved on September 11, 2001, from http://groups.yahoo.com/group/ymaonline. Accessed by subscribing to Young Muslim Association Yahoogroup and viewing archives.
69 "Action Alert: Report Hate Crimes and Contact Media Outlets," from http://groups.yahoo.com/group/adcsf. Accessed by subscribing to American Arab Anti-Discrimination Committee Yahoogroup and viewing archives.

V. THE SEPTEMBER 11 BACKLASH

The September 11 hate crime backlash confirmed the fears of Arabs and Muslims in the United States: a major terrorist attack gave rise to a nationwide wave of hate crimes against persons and institutions perceived to be Arab or Muslim. Unlike previous hate crime waves, however, the September 11 backlash distinguished itself by its ferocity and extent. The violence included murder, physical assaults, arson, vandalism of places of worship and other property damage, death threats, and public harassment. Most incidents occurred in the first months after September 11, with the violence tapering off by December. Both official and community-based organization tabulations derived from self-reported incidents and newspaper accounts? clearly demonstrate the severity of the September 11 backlash. The FBI reported that the number of anti-Muslim hate crimes rose from twenty-eight in 2000 to 481 in 2001, a seventeen-fold increase. 70 The ADC reported over six hundred September 11-related hate crimes committed against Arabs, Muslims, and those perceived to be Arab or Muslim, such as Sikhs and South Asians.71 Tabulating backlash incidents ranging from verbal taunts to employment discrimination to airport profiling to hate crimes, CAIR reported one thousand seven hundred and seventeen incidents of backlash discrimination against Muslims from September 11 through February 2002.72

State and local agency data provide additional perspective on the extent of the violence. In Chicago, the police department reported only four anti-Muslim or anti-Arab hate crimes during the year 2000; in the three months of September through November 2001, the number was fifty-one.73 In Los Angeles County, California, there were twelve hate crimes against persons of Middle Eastern descent in the year 2000, compared to 188 such hate crimes in 2001.74 In Florida, the attorney general directly attributed the 24.5 percent increase in the total number of hate crimes registered for the year 2001 to September 11-related bias.75

70 "Crime in the United States - 2001," Federal Bureau of Investigation, retrieved on October 30, 2002, from http://www.fbi.gov/ucr/01cius.htm.
71 "ADC Fact Sheet: The Condition of Arab Americans Post-September 11," American Arab Anti-Discrimination Committee, retrieved on September 24, 2002, from http://www.adc.org/index.php?Ibid.=282&no_cache=1&sword_list[]=hate&sword_list[]=crime.
72 "Anti-Muslim incidents," retrieved on September 8, 2002, from http://www.cair-net.org.
73 "Hate Crimes in Chicago: 2001," Chicago Police Department, p. 13, retrieved on September 24, 2002, from http://www.ci.chi.il.us/CommunityPolicing/Statistics/Reports/HateCrimes/HateCrimes01.pdf.
74 "Compounding Tragedy: The Other Victims of September 11," Los Angeles County Commission on Human Relations, p. 12, 14, retrieved on September 24, 2002, from http://humanrelations.co.la.ca.us/Our_publications/pdf/200 1HCR.pdf.
75 "Hate Crimes in Florida: January 1, 2001-December 31, 2001," Office of Attorney General, p. 6, retrieved on September 24, 2002, from http://legal.firn.edu/justice/01hate.pdf.

Not surprisingly, the persons most vulnerable to September 11-related hate crimes were those easily identified as Arabs or Muslims, including Muslim women who wear hijabs.76 Sikhs who wear turbans also appear to have been disproportionately targeted, presumably because of the erroneous assumption by many Americans that men wearing turbans are Arab or Muslim. Similarly, bias-motivated property attacks were often directed at property that could easily be identified with Muslims or Arabs, such as mosques. Many Arabs and South Asians who have come to the United States seem to have clustered in certain jobs, including driving taxis, or have become small business owners, running gas stations, convenience stores, and motels. This may account for the prevalence of backlash victims among persons with these occupations. Two of the three September 11-related murders for which charges have been brought were of convenience store workers.77 The other September 11-related murder for which charges have been brought was of a gas station owner.78 In Tulsa, Oklahoma and Seattle, Washington, taxi dispatch services noted that after September 11 they had received threatening calls saying that their Muslim and Arab taxi workers would be killed.79

In addition to bias-motivated criminal acts, the September 11 attacks spurred complaints of non-criminal acts of discrimination and racial profiling. As of May 2002, the U.S. Equal Employment Opportunity Commission (EEOC), the federal agency charged with enforcing federal employment discrimination laws, had received 488 complaints of September 11-related employment discrimination. Of these, 301 involved persons who were fired from their jobs.80 Similarly, as of June 2002, the U.S. Department of Transportation (DOT) reported, that it had investigated 111 September 11-related complaints from airline passengers who claimed that they were singled out at security screenings because of their ethnic or religious appearance.81 The DOT reported that it was also investigating an additional thirty-one complaints of persons who alleged they were barred altogether from boarding airplanes because of their ethnic or religious appearance.82 The overwhelming number of September 11-related discrimination complaints compelled the DOT and EEOC to specially track and report the backlash incidents. 83

76 Hijab is the practice among Muslim women of covering the head and body.
77 Vasudev Patel and Waquar Hassan were killed while working in convenience stores.
78 Balbir Singh Sodhi was killed while working at his gas station.
79 Curtis Killman, "Tulsa-area Muslims feel fear," *Tulsa World,* September 16, 2001; "Bush Appeals For Calm
81 William Wan, "Four Airlines Sued For Alleged Post-Sept. 11 Discrimination," Cox News Service, June 4, 2002.
82 Ibid.
83 William Wan, "Four Airlines Sued For Alleged Post-Sept. 11 Discrimination," Cox News Service, June 4, 2002; "EEOC Provides Answers About the Workplace Rights of Muslims, Arabs, South Asians and Sikhs," Press Release, Equal Employment Opportunity Commission, May 15, 2002, retrieved on September 23, 2002, from http://www.eeoc.gov/press/5-15-02.html. 11.

Polls conducted by national Arab and Muslim advocacy groups measured the cumulative perceptions created by September 11-related criminal and non-criminal bias incidents in the Arab and Muslim communities. In July 2002, CAIR polled 945 Muslim Americans on how September 11 and its aftermath affected them. The poll found that 48 percent believed their lives had changed for the worse since September Amid Incidents Of Hate; Threats And Attacks Have Targeted Mosques, Arab Americans," *Seattle Post-Intelligencer,* September 14, 2001. 80 "EEOC Provides Answers About the Workplace Rights of Muslims, Arabs, South Asians and Sikhs," Press Release, Equal Employment Opportunity Commission, May 15, 2002, retrieved on September 23, 2002, from http://www.eeoc.gov/press/5-15-02.html. of Bias Crime Data Collection," The Center for Criminal Justice Policy Research College of Criminal Justice, p. 61

Anti-Arab or Anti-Muslim Hate Crimes
During The Years 2000 and 2001

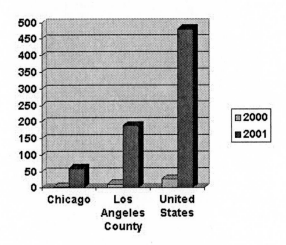

84 While 79 percent said they experienced an act of kindness or support from friends or colleagues of other faiths since September 11, 57 percent experienced an act of bias or discrimination, ranging from a disparaging remark to employment discrimination to a hate crime.85 A poll of Arab-Americans conducted in May 2002 found that that 20 percent had personally experienced discrimination since September 11. The full dimensions of the backlash may, never be known. As discussed in section V, there are two reasons for what amounts to a systemic gap in public knowledge about the extent of hate crimes in the United States. First, the federal hate crimes reporting system contains significant limitations, including the voluntary nature of the reporting system and the failure of some local law enforcement agencies that ostensibly participate in the federal reporting system to furnish information on hate crimes to federal authorities. These gaps

Anti-Arab and Muslim Hate Crimes During 2001
Before and After September 11, 2001

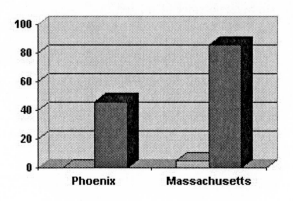

Murder

I stand for America all the way! I'm an American. Go ahead. Arrest me and let those terrorists run wild!89

?Frank Roque, after being arrested for the murder of Balbir Singh Sodhi

At least three people were murdered as a result of the September 11 backlash. There is reason to suspect four other people may also have been murdered because of anti-Arab and anti-Muslim hatred. *Balbir Singh Sodhi* Balbir Singh Sodhi, a forty-nine-year-old turbaned Sikh and father of three, was shot and killed while planting flowers at his gas station on September 15, 2002. Police officials told Human Rights Watch that hours before the crime, Sodhi's alleged killer, Frank Roque, had bragged at a local bar of his intention to "kill the ragheads responsible for September 11."90 In addition to shooting Sodhi three times before driving

---

in the federal hate crimes reporting system were detailed in a September2000 U.S. Department of Justice-funded study, which estimated that almost six thousand law enforcement agencies in the United States likely experience at least one hate crime that goes unreported each year.86 Second, the racial or ethnic identity of a crime victim without more is an insufficient basis on which to determine whether a crime is hate-related. Absent specific indicia of bias? e.g, statements made by the perpetrator ?hate-based crimes may not be recorded as such.
84 "Poll: Majority of U.S. Muslims suffered post September 11 bias," Council on American-Islamic Relation, August 21, 2002, retrieved on August 28, 2002, from http://www.cairnet.org/asp/article.as p?articleid=895&articletype=3.
85 Ibid.
86 "Improving The Quality And Accuracy Of Bias Crime Statistics Nationally: An Assessment of the First Ten Years of Bias Crime Data Collection," The Center for Criminal Justice Policy Research College of Criminal Justice, p. 61 (2000).

away, Roque also allegedly shot into thehome of an Afghani American and at two Lebanese gas station clerks.91 The Maricopa County prosecutor's office was due to try Roque for Sodhi's murder on November 12, 2002.

Vasudev Patel

On October 4, 2001, Mark Stroman shot and killed Vasudev Patel, a forty-nine-year old Indian and father of two, while Patel was working at his convenience store in Mesquite, Texas.92 A store video camera recorded the murder, allowing law enforcement detectives to identify Stroman as the killer. Stroman said during

87 Anti-Muslim hate crimes in the United States increased from twenty-eight during 2000 to 481 during 2001. See "Crime in the United States - 2001," Federal Bureau of Investigation, retrieved on October 30, 2002, from http://www.fbi.gov/ucr/01cius.htm. Anti-Arab and anti-Muslim hate crimes in Los Angeles County increased from twelve during 2000 to 188 during 2001. See "Compounding Tragedy: The Other Victims of September 11," Los Angeles County Commission on Human Relations, p. 12 and 14, retrieved on September 24, 2002, from http://humanrelations.c o.la.ca.us/Our_publications/pdf/2001HCR.pdf. Anti-Arab and anti-Muslim hate crimes in Chicago increased from four during 2000 to sixty during 2001. See "Hate Crimes in Chicago: 2001," Chicago Police Department, p. 13, retrieved on September 24, 2002, from http://www.ci.chi.il.us/ CommunityPolicing/Statistics/Reports/HateCrimes/HateCrimes01.pdf.88 During 2001, Massachusetts had five anti-Arab or anti-Muslim hate crimes before September 11 and eighty-six after. See Marie Szaniszlo, "Study: 9/11 fuels anti-Arab crime," *Boston Herald,* September 25, 2002. During 2001, Phoenix had no anti-Arab or anti-Muslim hate crimes before September 11 and forty-six after. See "Bias Incident Statistics," Phoenix Police Department, retrieved on October 29, 2002, from http://www.ci.phoenix.az.us/POLICE/hatecr2.html.
90 Ibid.
91 Ibid.
92 Michael Tate, "Mesquite seeks clues in killing of gas store owner," Dallas Morning News, October 5, 2001. against those who retaliated against us."
93 In addition to killing Patel, Stroman also shot and killed Waquar Hassan on September 15, 2001 (see below), and also shot Rais Uddin, a gas station attendant, blinding him.
94 Stroman was tried and convicted of capital murder for killing Patel and sentenced to death on April 3, 2002.
94 Ibid.
95 "Death Sentence for Revenge Killing," United Press International, April 4, 2002. While Human Rights Watch believes all bias-motivated crimes should be prosecuted, it does not condone the death sentence in this or any other criminal matter.
96 Alan Cooperman, "Sept.11 Backlash Murders and the State of 'Hate'; Between Families and Police, a Gulf on Victim Count," *Washington Post*, January 20, 2002.
97 Human Rights Watch telephone interview with Zahid Ghani, brother-in-law of Waquar Hassan, August 25, 2002.
98 Ibid.
99 Ibid.
100 The prosecution used Stroman's confession that he killed Hussain during sentencing portion of his trial for the murder of Vasudev Patel. mansoop was in bed with Seever's exgirlfriend.
101 Immediately before killing Almansoop, Seever said that he was angry about the September 11 terrorist attacks. Almansoop pleaded that he did not have anything to do with the attacks.

a television interview that anger over the September 11 attacks caused him to attack any store owner who appeared to be Muslim. He further stated during the interview: "We're at war. I did what I had to do. I did it to retaliate 89 Human Rights Watch interview with Sergeant Mike Goulet of the Mesa, Arizona police department, August 6, 2002. because no perpetrator or perpetrators have been found for whom a motive can be established, police have not classified the murder as a hate crime. California Governor Gray Davis offered a $50,000 reward for information leading to the conviction of Ahmed's killers.109 At the time of this writing, the investigation into Ahmed's murder was stalled because police had run out of leads.110

Adel Karas

---

102 Seever shot Almansoop anyway. Seever acknowledged to police investigators that he killed Almansoop in part because of anger related to September 11. Prosecutors chose to prosecute the matter as a murder, rather than a bias-motivated murder, because they believe Mr. Seever's motivation for murdering Almansoop was motivated in part by jealousy over Almansoop's relationship with is ex-girlfriend. Mr. Seever had been stalking his ex-girlfriend before the murder.
103 *Abdo Ali Ahmed*
On September 29, 2001, Abdo Ali Ahmed,a fifty-one-year-old Yemini Arab and Muslim, and father of eight, was shot and killed while working at his convenience store in Reedley, California.
104 Cash in two registers and rolled coins inside an open safe were left untouched. In addition, Ahmed's gun, which he kept for protection, reportedly remained in its usual spot, indicating that he may not have felt in mortal danger.
105 Two days before his murder, Ahmed had found a note on his car windshield which stated, "We're going to kill all of you [expletive] Arabs."
106 Instead of contacting the police, Ahmed threw the note away.
107 Ahmed's family and local Muslim leaders have told the local press that they believe his killing was a hate crime.
108 However, largely
101 Alan Ccoperman, "Sept. 11 Backlash Murders and the State of 'Hate'; Between Families And Police, a Gulf On Victim Count," *Washington Post*, January 20, 2002.
102 Ibid.
103 Ibid.
104 Evelyn Nieves, "Slain Arab-American May Have Been Hate-Crime Victim," *New York Times*, October 6, 2001
105 Karen de Sa"Local Muslims Convinced Central Calif. Killing was hate crime," *San Jose Mercury News*, December 6, 2001.
106 Karen Breslav, "Hate Crime," *Newsweek,* October 15, 2001.
107 Ibid.
108 Jennifer Fitzenberger, "Family sees hate crime in Reedley homicide Relatives say victim was shot because he was Muslim; officials draw no conclusions," *Fresno Bee*, October 1, 2001.
109 "Police," *Fresno Bee*, November 29, 2001.
110 Human Rights Watch telephone interview, Sergeant Tony Reign, Fresno Police Department, California, September 16, 2002.

On September 15, 2001, Adel Karas, a forty-eight-year-old Arab and Coptic Christian, and father of three, was shot and killed at his convenience store in San Gabriel, California. According to press reports, his wife, Randa Karas, believes he was murdered because he was mistaken for a Muslim. She points out that no money was taken from the cash register and that her husband had a thick wad of bills in his pocket. Local police told Human Rights Watch that they do not believe his murder was bias motivated because there is no evidence to indicate anti-Arab or anti-Muslim bias. The murder remained unsolved at the time of this writing. 111

Ali W. Ali

Ali W. Ali, a sixty-six-year-old Somali Muslim, died nine days after being punched in the head while standing at a bus stop in Minneapolis, Minnesota on October 15, 2002.112 According to press reports, the only known witness to the attack saw the assailant walk up to Ali, punch him, stand over him, and then walk away.113 His son and Somali community members attributed the attack against Ali to anger created against Somalis by a front page local newspaper article that appeared two days before the attack.114 The article said that Somalis in Minneapolis had given money to a Somali terrorist group with links to Osama Bin Laden.115 After originally finding that Ali had died of natural causes, the Hennepin County medical examiner's office on January 8, 2002 ruled Ali's death a homicide.116 Ali's family regards his murder as a hate crime. Both local police and the FBI have been unable to find Ali's assailant.117

Assaults

Violent assaults related to September 11 were numerous and widespread. A review by the South Asian American Leaders of Tomorrow (SAALT) of news articles

111 Human Rights Watch telephone interview, Lieutenant Joe Hartshorne, Los Angeles County Sheriff's Department, September 16, 2002.
112 "Somalis discuss freedom and fear; U.S. flags, worries of backlash abound as community meets," *Star Tribune* (Minneapolis, MN), October 25, 2001.
113 David Chanen, "FBI questions witness in alleged hate assault," *Star Tribune* (Minneapolis, MN), November 16, 2001.
114 Lou Gelfand, "Readers say Sunday article spurred unfair attacks on local Somalis," *Star Tribune* (Minneapolis, MN), October 21, 2002.
115 "Somalis, Muslims denounce paper's story," *Star Tribune* (Minneapolis, MN), October 16, 2001.
116 David Chanen, "Bus stop assault is ruled homicide; Somali victim's family maintains it was hate crime," *Star Tribune* (Minneapolis, MN), January 9, 2002
117 "FBI questions witness in alleged hate assault," *Star Tribune* (Minneapolis, MN), November 16, 2001.

published during the week following September 11 found reports of forty-nine September 11-related assaults.118 CAIR received 289 reports from Muslims of assaults and property damage incidents across the United States from September 11 until the second week of February.119

Issa Qandeel

On the morning of September 13, 2001, Issa Qandeel, a Palestinian Muslim and an Arab, was leaving the Idriss Mosque in Seattle, Washington when he smelled gas near his jeep and saw a man, subsequently identified as Patrick Cunningham, come out from behind his jeep. Cunningham was carrying a can of gasoline and a gun. When Qandeel asked Cunningham what he was doing behind the jeep, Cunningham walked away.

Kulwinder Singh

On September 13, 2001, Raymond Isais Jr. allegedly assaulted Kulwinder Singh, a turbaned Sikh taxi worker, in SeaTac, Washington. After getting into the back seat of Singh's taxi, Isais told Singh, "You have no right to attack our country!" He then started choking Singh. After both men then got out of the taxi, Isais started punching Singh, pulled out tufts of his beard and knocked off his turban. Isais called Singh a terrorist during the assault. Local police were able to apprehend Isais Jr. the same day using a description provided by Singh. He was charged with a hate crime by local country prosecutors. 121

Swaran Kaur Bhullar

118 "American Backlash: Terrorists Bring War Home in More Ways Than One," South Asian American Leaders of Tomorrow, p. 7, retrieved on August 28, 2002, from http://www.saalt.org/ biasreport.pdf. SAALT is a national South Asian advocacy organization
119 "Number of Reported Incidents by Category," Council on American-Islamic Relations, retrieved on August 30, 200, from http://www.cair-net.org/html/bycategory.htm. When Qandeel tried to stop him, Cunningham shot at Qandeel three times, although his gun did not discharge any bullets. Cunningham then started running away and Qandeel chased him. Cunningham shot at Qandeel again and this time a bullet did discharge, although it missed Qandeel. Cunningham was apprehended when he crashed his car trying to get away. Police later discovered that Cunningham planned to burn cars in the mosque driveway because of anger at the September 11 attacks. Federal authorities prosecuted Cunningham for attacking Qandeel and attempting to deface a house of worship. He pled guilty on May 9, 2002 and was scheduled to be sentenced on October 18, 2002. He faces a minimum of five years of incarceration.120
120 Human Rights Watch interview with Issa Qandeel, July 31, 2002.
121 Human Rights Watch telephone interview with Kulwinder Singh, August 3, 2002.

On September 30, 2001, Swaran Kaur Bhullar, a Sikh woman, was attacked by two men who stabbed her in the head twice as her car was idling at a red light in San Diego. The men shouted at her, "This is what you get for what you've done to us!" and "I'm going to slash your throat," before attacking her. As another car approached the traffic light, the men sped off. Bhullar felt that she would have been killed by the men if the other car had not appeared. She was treated at a local hospital for two cuts in her scalp and released later that same day. Local police and federal law enforcement officials have been unable to identify Bhullar's attackers.122

Faiza Ejaz

On September 12, 2001, Faiza Ejaz, a Pakistani woman, was standing outside a mall in Huntington, New York waiting for her husband to pick her up from work. According to press reports, Adam Lang, a seventy-six-year-old man sitting in his car outside the mall, allegedly put his car in drive and started driving towards her. Ejaz was able to avoid the car by jumping out of the way and running into the mall. Lang then jumped out of his car and screamed that he was "doing this for my country" and was "going to kill her." Mall security agents seized Lang. Sergeant Robert Reecks, commander of the Suffolk County Bias Crimes Bureau, told reporters: "if she hadn't jumped out of the way, he would have run right over her."123 Lang was charged with first-degree reckless endangerment, which requires an enhanced penalty if the crime is bias motivated.

FK

On June 18, 2002, FK, an American Muslim woman who wears a hijab, was allegedly assaulted by a woman in a drug store near Houston, Texas. Before assaulting FK, the woman told her that she had learned about "you people" over the last ten months and doesn't trust "a single damn one of you." Before FK could get away from the woman, she slammed FK to the floor and began pulling at her headscarf, which had the effect of choking her. Though FK told the woman she could not breathe, she kept pulling at the headscarf. FK then pulled off her headscarf, in violation of her religious obligations in a desperate effort to alleviate the choking. The woman then dragged FK by her hair to the front of the store. When police arrived, the woman was holding FK by her ponytail on the front sidewalk of the store. She told police that she was making a citizen's arrest. The police 122 Human Rights Watch telephone interview with Swaran Kaur Bhullar, June 27, 2002. 123 Pat Burson, "Terrorist Attacks; Driver Arrested in Hate Crime at Mall," *Newsday*, September 13, 2001. told her to let FK go, at which point FK was able to put her headscarf back on.124

195

Karnail Singh

Karnail Singh is a Sikh man who owns a motel in SeaTac, Washington. In mid-October, 2001, John Bethel, a local vagrant who sometimes came into Singh's motel for coffee and food, told Singh, "You better go back to your country. We're coming to kick your ass." A few days later, on October 19, Bethel entered Singh's motel and shouted, "You still here? Go back to Allah!" before hitting Singh with a metal cane while he stood behind the counter in the motel lobby. Singh, who bled profusely from the blow, spent half a day in the hospital and required ten stitches on his head. Bethel was sentenced to nearly two years in prison for assault with a deadly weapon.125

Satpreet Singh

On September 19, 2001, Satpreet Singh, a turbaned Sikh, was driving in the middle lane of a two-lane highway in Frederick County, Maryland. A pickup truck pulled up close behind Singh and the driver started making profane gestures towards him. The pickup truck then moved alongside Singh's car on his left and the driver took out a rifle. Singh increased his speed to get away from the pickup truck. Seconds later he heard rifle shots. No bullets hit Singh or his car. The pickup truck then turned around and started traveling in the opposite direction. Singh filed a criminal complaint with the local police. At the time of this writing, local authorities have not been able to ascertain the identity of the person who shot at Singh.126

Place of Worship Attacks

Mosques and places of worship perceived to be mosques appeared to be among the most likely places of September 11-related backlash violence. SAALT's survey of bias incidents reported in major news media found 104 bias incidents against places of worship reported during he first week after September 11.127 Of these 104 bias incidents forty five were telephone threats, twenty-four involved harassment of mosque worshippers outside mosques, twenty-two involved

---

124 Human Rights Watch telephone interview with FK, August 21, 2002. FK's name has been changed at her request.
125 Human Rights Watch interview with Karnail Singh, August 2, 2002.
126 Human Rights Watch telephone Interview with Satpreet Singh, August 19, 2002. The Sikh Coalition, a Sikh civil rights organization formed in the wake of the September 11 backlash, received nineteen reports of turbaned Sikhs being harassed by other motorists while driving since September 11. Human Rights Watch telephone interview with Prabhjot Singh, director, Sikh Coalition, August 16, 2002.

property damage from vandalism, arson, or gun shots, and three were assaults on mosque worshipers.128

Arab churches, Sikh *gurdwaras* (houses of worship), and Hindu temples were also objects of backlash violence. The number of worshippers at the attacked mosques decreased for weeks following the attacks, apparently because of fear of additional violence.129 Although September 11 backlash violence against individual Arabs and Muslims decreased markedly by November 2001, attacks continued against mosques or houses of worship perceived to be Arab or Muslim. On November 19, 2001, four teenagers burned down the Gobind Sadan, a multi-faith worship center Oswego, New York, because they believed the worshippers were supporters of Osama Bin Laden.130 On March 25, 2002, a man who stated to police that he hated Muslims crashed his pickup truck into a mosque in Tallahassee, Florida thirty minutes after evening prayers.131 On June 11, 2002, in 127 South Asian American Leaders of Tomorrow, "American Backlash: Terrorists Bring War Home in More Ways Than One," retrieved on August 26, 2002, from http://www.saalt.org/biasreport.pdf.

Guru Gobind Singh Sikh Gurdwara

On the night of September 11, 2001, somebody threw three Molotov cocktails into the Guru Gobind Singh Sikh Gurdwara, a Sikh house of worship in Bedford, Ohio. The Molotov cocktails started a small fire that was quickly extinguished by

128 Ibid. These statistics were compiled after analyzing reports listed in the "American Backlash" report.
129 Human Rights Watch telephone interview with Imam Ayaaz, Iman of Islamic Foundation of Irving, July 17, 2002; Human Rights Watch telephone interview with Dr. Magdy Adbelhady, member of United Muslim Masjid, July 18, 2002.
130 Catie O'Toole, "2 in Temple Case Denied Shock Camp; Joshua Centrone, William Reeves Can't Get Out Early After Admitting Hate Crime," *Post-Standard Syracuse*, June 23, 2002.
131 "Florida Mosque Attack Result of Anti-Muslim Rhetoric, Says CAIR," *U.S. Newswire*, March 26, 2002. Charles D. Franklin was indicted in federal court on April 17, 2002 for the alleged crime. Milipitas, California, vandals broke into a mosque under construction, scrawled derogatory remarks such as, "F …??Arabs" and damaged the interior of a construction trailer near the mosque.
132 On August 24, 2002, federal authorities announced they had discovered a plan by a doctor in Tampa Bay to bomb and destroy approximately 50 mosques and Islamic cultural centers in south Florida.133 The doctor's home contained rocket launchers, sniper rifles and twenty live bombs.134
132 "Vandals Attack California Mosque Under Construction; Derogatory Remarks Written Inside Mosque, Police Suspect Hate Crime," *U.S. Newswire*, June 13, 2002.
133 Stephen Thompson, Paula Christian and Natashia Gregoire, "Agents Say Mosques Target Of Arsenal," *Tampa Tribune*, August 24, 2002.
134 Stephen Thompson, Paula Christian and Natashia Gregoire, "Agents Say Mosques Target Of Arsenal," *Tampa Tribune*, August 24, 2002.

Aladdin Elaasar

the gurdwara's caretakers. Two windows were also broken. A report was filed with local police. No one has been apprehended for the crime.135

Mosque Foundation of Bridgeview

On September 12, 2001, over one hundred police officers were deployed to stop approximately three hundred protestors from marching on the mosque in Bridgeview, Illinois. The mosque is located in a neighborhood of mostly Arab and Muslim American families. Stopped two blocks from the mosque, the protestors then demonstrated for approximately three hours shouting anti-Arab and anti-Muslim insults such as "Arabs go home" and harassing passersby who looked Muslim or Arab. Similar protests, though smaller in size, were held over the next two days. Police from various jurisdictions cordoned off the area around the mosque, only allowing persons into the neighborhood who could prove they lived there. Many of the Muslim and Arab families remained in their homes for the next few days because they feared hostility once outside the police cordon. Scores of police protected the mosque during Friday prayers on September 14, 2001.136

Islamic Center of Irving, Texas

On the night of September 12, 2001, someone fired at the Islamic Center of Irving, leaving thirteen to fourteen bullet holes in the building. The shots were fired after the evening prayer had ended and the building was empty. For the first two or three days after the attack, local police provided security for the mosque. Immediately after the attack, the imam reported a noticeable decline in prayer attendance. He estimated that daily prayer attendance dropped from 150 to thirty or forty persons. Friday prayers dropped from one thousand to five hundred persons. Mosque attendance normalized after a few weeks.137

St. John's Assyrian American Church

On September 23, 2001, the St. John's Assyrian American Church was set on fire in Chicago, Illinois in the early morning, causing approximately $150,000 worth of damage. The fire was caused by someone who put a piece of paper through the church mail slot and then dropped a lit match onto it. Water from fire department fire extinguishers ruined holy pictures, carpeting, and floor tiles. According to the

135 Human Rights Watch telephone interview with Dr. Tara Singh Mangat, President, Guru Gobind Singh Sikh Gurdwara, August 16, 2002.
136 Human Rights Watch interview with Saffiya Shillo, director, Ethnic Affairs, Office of Illinois Lieutenant Governor, June 12, 2002.
137 Human Rights Watch telephone interview with Imam Ayaaz, Iman of Islamic Foundation of Irving, July 17, 2002.

church's pastor, Reverend Charles Klutz, the person whom he believed set the fire had asked a local resident whether the church was a mosque. Reverend Klutz also stated that local police initially asked whether the church was a mosque when they first arrived at the church even though many crosses were located prominently on the church premises. Local police and federal authorities were investigating the cause of the fire at the time of this writing.138

Islamic Foundation of Central Ohio

Sometime during the evening of December 29, 2001, vandals broke into the Islamic Foundation of Central Ohio in Columbus, Ohio. The vandals broke a bathroom pipe and clogged the sink, forcing it to overflow for hours; tore frames encasing religious verses off a wall; destroyed a chandelier in the main prayer hall; flipped over the pulpit; cut the wires of high mounted speakers and amplifiers and threw them to the ground; tore posters off a mosque classroom wall; pulled down curtains and drapes; and tipped over bookcases and file cabinets in a classroom and threw approximately one hundred copies of the Quran onto the floor.139

Water from the stopped-up third-floor sink seeped into the second floor main prayer hall, causing plaster pieces from the main prayer hall ceiling to fall. A torn Quran and a smashed clock from the mosque were found in the mosque parking lot. The damage to the mosque was estimated at $379,000. The mosque was closed after the incident but planned to reopen in October 2002. Both local police and the FBI are conducting investigations.140

United Muslim Masjid

On November 16, 2001, during an evening Ramadan prayer service, rocks were thrown through two windows of the United Muslim Masjid in Waterbury, Connecticut. Approximately thirty-five to forty people were in the mosque at the time. Local police are investigating the incident as a possible hate crime. Dr. Magdy Adbelhady, a member of the mosque, said that local police were responsive to mosque member concerns and seemed to be taking the matter seriously. He said that immediately after the attack on the mosque, mosque attendance had dropped but was now back to normal.141

138 Human Rights Watch telephone interview with Dr. Magdy Adbelhady, member of United Muslim Masjid, July 18, 2002.
139 Many Muslims consider it disrespectful to leave the Quran or any book of knowledge on the floor.
140 Human Rights Watch telephone interview with Siraj Haji, member of the Islamic Foundation of Central Ohio, July 19, 2002.
141 Human Rights Watch telephone interview with Dr. Magdy Adbelhady, member of United

Arson

There have been press reports of more than fifteen arsons and attempted arsons that may be part of the post-September 11 backlash. 142 Local law enforcement agents believe that fires at six houses of worship were September 11- related hate crimes.143 The other press documented cases of arson involved places of business owned or operated by Muslims, Arabs, or those perceived to be Muslim or Arab. There have been three convictions and one indictment thus far for September 11-related arsons.144

Curry in a Hurry Restaurant

On September 15, 2001, James Herrick set fire to the Curry in a Hurry restaurant in Salt Lake City, Utah, causing minimal damage. Herrick admitted to setting the fire because he was angry over the September 11 attacks and knew the restaurant owners were from Pakistan. A federal district court in Utah sentenced him on January 7, 2001 to fifty-one months in jail.145

Prime Tires

On September 16, 2001, someone allegedly set fire to Prime Tires, a Pakistani-owned auto mechanic shop located in an enclave of Pakistani businesses in Houston, Texas. The fire destroyed the store. The store had received threats immediately after September 11. Thus far, police have been unable to ascertain who started the blaze and the motive of the perpetrator.146

Muslim Masjid, July 18, 2002.
142 These reports are from newspaper accounts and Muslim, Arab, Sikh, and South Asian community organization accounts.
143 In particular, the arsons or attempted arsons against houses of worship generally thought to reflect September 11-related animus were against the Gobind Sadan, a multicultural interfaith center in Oswego, New York; St. John's Assyrian American Church in Chicago, Illinois; Guru Gobind Singh Sikh Gurdwara in Bedford, Ohio; Idriss Mosque in Seattle, Washington; Omar al-Farooq Mosque in Mountlake Terrace, Washington; and a Hindu temple in Matawan, New Jersey.
144 Convictions were obtained for the arson of the Gobind Sadan in Oswego, New York; Curry in a Hurry restaurant in Salt Lake City, Utah; and the attempted arson of the Idriss Mosque in Seattle, Washington. A charge of arson has been brought for the attempted arson of the Omar al-Farooq mosque in Mountlake Terrace, Washington.
145 Angie Welling and Anne Jacobs, "Feds hope hate-crime sentence is warning," *Deseret News*, January 8, 2002.
146 "Fire at Pakistani Shop May Be Hate-Fueled Arson," *Houston Chronicle*, September 19, 2001.

VI. FEDERAL, STATE, AND LOCAL HATE CRIME PREVENTION EFFORTS BEFORE AND AFTER SEPTEMBER 11

Government efforts to protect people from bias motivated violence varied from state to state and city to city in the United States. Our research found different practices with regard to critical anti-bias crime measures such as hate crime investigation protocols, prosecution, bias crime tracking, and community outreach. The most successful efforts to combat backlash violence- as in Dearborn, Michigan, where only two violent September 11-related assaults occurred in a city with thirty thousand Arab-Americans-correlated with prior recognition that backlash attacks against Arabs, Muslims, Sikhs, and South Asians are a recurring problem; a high degree of affected community access and input into law enforcement planning and decision making; and combined efforts by local, county, state and federal authorities. Government officials face a complex challenge in seeking to prevent spontaneous, unorganized bias-motivated acts of violence. The experiences discussed below reveal the importance, first of all, of a serious commitment to act decisively before, during, and after outbreaks of such violence. They also reveal the efficacy of specific steps taken in some jurisdictions that may serve as a model for others.

Public Condemnation

Hate crimes are symbolic acts conveying the message that the victim's religious, ethnic, or racial community is unwelcome.147 Animosity against Arabs, Muslims, and those perceived to be Arab or Muslim, reflects a belief that persons from these communities are "foreigners" who are not "loyal" Americans and who are intrinsically linked to an Arab and Muslim terrorist enemy. The man who killed Balbir Singh Sodhi yelled, "I'm an American."148 The person who attempted to run over Faiza Ejaz screamed he was "doing this for my country."149 The protestors at the Bridgeview mosque chanted, "USA!"150 Professor Leti Volpp describes the phenomena in this way: Many of those racially profiled in the sense of being the targets of hate violence or being thrown off airplanes are formally citizens of the United States, through birth or naturalization. But they are not considered citizens

---

147 Human Rights Watch telephone interview with Jack Levin, Professor, Northeastern University, August 18, 2002.
148 Human Rights Watch interview with Sergeant Mike Goulet of the Mesa, Arizona police department, Augut 6, 2002.
149 Owen Moritz, "Local Victims Of Backlash Deny Accusations," *Daily News* (New York), September 14, 2001.
150 Human Rights Watch interview with Saffiya Shillo, director, Ethnic Affairs, Office of Illinois Lieutenant Governor, June 12, 2002.

as a matter of identity....151 Public statements embracing the millions of law-abiding Arabs and Muslims as part of American society and communicating that hate crimes would not be tolerated were among the most effective measures that countered and contained September 11-related violence.152 Arab and Muslim activists believe that anti-backlash "messages" by prominent political and civil society leaders helped stem the number of backlash attacks.

The most notable public figure decrying September 11-related hate crimes was U.S. President George W. Bush. On September 12, 2001, in published remarks to New York Mayor Rudolph Giuliani, President Bush stated: "Our nation should be mindful that there are thousands of Arab-Americans who live in New York City, who love their flag just as much as [we] do, and...that as we seek to win the war, that we treat Arab-Americans and Muslims with the respect they deserve."153 Less than a week after the September 11 attacks, President Bush made a highly visible visit to the Islamic Cultural Center in Washington, D.C., and in a speech there stated:

I've been told that some fear to leave; some don't want to go shopping for their families; some don't want to go about their ordinary daily routines because, by wearing cover, they're afraid they'll be intimidated. That should not and that will not stand in America. Those who feel like they can intimidate our fellow citizens to take out their anger don't represent the best of America, they represent the worst of humankind, and they should be ashamed of that kind of behavior.154

Similar statements were made by U.S. Attorney General John Ashcroft and Assistant Attorney General for Civil Rights Ralph Boyd, and released to the press in public meetings with Arab, Muslim, Sikh, and South Asian community groups.155 Around the country, and in every city researched for this report, governors and mayors appeared publicly with victim communities to condemn

151 Leti Volpp, Critical Race Studies: The Citizen and the Terrorist, 49 UCLA L. Rev. 1575, 1592 (2002).
152 Human Rights Watch interview with Raed Tayeh, director, American Muslims for Global Peace and Justice, February 21, 2002; Human Rights Watch telephone interview, Deepa Iyer, South Asian American Leaders of Tomorrow, February 26, 2002.
153 President George W. Bush, in a telephone conversation with New York Mayor Rudy Giuliani, September 12, 2001, retrieved on September 9, 2002, from ttp://www.aaiusa.org/PDF/healing_the_nation.pdf.
154 Remarks of President George W. Bush at the Islamic Center, September 17, 2001, retrieved on September 9, 2002, fromhttp://www.usdoj.gov/crt/legalinfo/bushremarks.html.
155 Excerpts of remarks by Attorney General John Ashcroft and Assistant Attorney General for Civil Rights Ralph Boyd, retrieved on September 1, 2002, from http://www.usdoj.gov/crt/legalinfo/dojstatements.html.

backlash hate crimes and went on record as saying that perpetrators would be prosecuted.156

Leaders of affected community groups said the willingness of public officials to directly condemn hate crimes made those communities feel more secure during a time of significant fear and imparted an important message to the public that backlash hate crimes were unacceptable and misguided.157

In addition to public statements from individual government officials, legislative bodies also condemned backlash crimes. The United States House of Representatives passed a resolution on September 15, 2001 condemning hate crimes against Arabs, Muslims, and South Asians.158 Similarly, the United States Senate, recognizing the disproportionate number of attacks against turbaned Sikhs, passed a resolution introduced by Senator Richard Durbin condemning hate crimes against Sikhs in the United States and calling for their prevention and prosecution. 159 City entities acted as well. For example, the city of Seattle passed a resolution decrying hate crimes in Seattle. The resolution also called on citizens to report hate crime incidents to government authorities.160

Though the overwhelming majority of public figures in the United States condemned acts of bias after September 11, there were a few who expressed contempt for or bias against Arabs and Muslims. Just a week after September 11, a member of Congress, John Cooksey, told a Louisiana radio station, "If I see someone [who] comes in that's got a diaper on his head and a fan belt wrapped around the diaper on his head, that guy needs to be pulled over."161 Similarly, while speaking to law enforcement officers in Georgia, Representative C. Saxby Chambliss stated: "just turn [the sheriff] loose and have him arrest every Muslim that crosses the state

156 Remarks of Washington Governor Gary Locke, September 4, 2001, retrieved on September 1, 2002, fromhttp://www.governor.wa.gov/press/pressview. sp?pressRelease=977&newsType=1
157 Human Rights Watch telephone interview with Jean Abi Nader, Arab American Institute, February 25, 2002.
158 House Concurrent Resolution 227, "Denouncing Bigotry Against Arabs, Muslims, South Asians," September 15, 2001, retrieved on September 1, 2002, from http://usinfo.state.gov/usa/race/hate/t091801.htm.
159 S. Con. Res. 74, "Condemning bigotry and violence against Sikh-Americans in the wake of terrorist attacks in New York City and Washington, D.C. on September 11, 2001," retrieved on September 1, 2002, from http://www.sikhcoalition.org/LegislativeRes1c.asp.
160 City of Seattle Resolution 30399, retrieved on September 1, 2002, from http://www.cityofseattle.net/civilrights/documents/steinbrueck%20resolution.pdf.
161 Joan McKinney, "Cooksey: Expect Racial Profiling," *Advocate* (Baton Rouge, LA), September 19, 2001.line."
162 Representatives Cooksey and Chambliss both eventually apologized for their remarks.163

In addition, a few significant religious commentators publicly expressed distrust or anger against Muslims. Franklin Graham, son of the well-known Reverend Billy Graham, called Islam: "wicked, violent and not of the same God."164 Televangelist Pat Robertson, also speaking about Islam, said: "I have taken issue with our esteemed President in regard to his stand in saying Islam is a peaceful religion.... It's just not."165 In the same vein, former Southern Baptist President Jerry Vines told conventioneers at the June 2002 annual gathering of the Southern Baptist Convention that the Muslim prophet Muhammad was a "demon-possessed pedophile." Unlike Representatives Cooksey and Chambliss, these religious leaders have stood by their comments.166

Public messages were also used proactively as a tool to prevent future hate crimes. Two weeks before the September 11 one-year anniversary, the San Francisco district attorney's office embarked on a campaign promoting tolerance by placing anti-hate posters on city buses and bus stops.167 The poster includes the faces of four Arab or Muslims persons or persons who may be perceived as Arab or Muslim under the heading, "We Are Not the Enemy."168 The campaign was prompted by concerns the September 11 anniversary might rekindle backlash animosity and anti-Arab and anti-Muslim violence. According to San Francisco District Attorney Terence Hallinan, "With war heating up in the Middle East, we're launching a pre-emptive strike against any backlash against Arab-Americans and Muslims."169 Eight hundred posters were placed on the outside and inside of San Francisco buses. In addition to promoting a message of tolerance, they also encourage citizens to report hate crimes to the San Francisco district attorney's office.

---

162 "Lawmaker Tries to Explain Remark; Rep. Chambliss, a Senate Hopeful, Commented on Muslims," *Washington Post*, November 21, 2001.
163 "Hall of Shame," *Washington Post*, November 22, 2002; Eli Sanders, "Understanding Turbans: Don't Link Them to Terrorism," *Seattle Times*, October 9, 2002.
164 Kevin Eckstrom, "Graham heir keeps stance on Islam talk," *The Times Union* (Albany, NY), November 24, 2001.
165 "Mr. Robertson's Incitement," *Washington Post*, February 24, 2002.
166 Kathy Shaidle, "Full Pews and Empty Gestures," *Toronto Star*, December 23, 2001; Richard N. Ostling, "Falwell labels Muhammad 'terrorist' in TV interview," *Chicago Tribune,* October 4, 2002.
167 "Anti-hate campaign begins in S.F. / Posters urge tolerance as Sept. 11 nears," *San Francisco Chronicle*, August 27, 2002.
168 The title of this report was taken from the title of this poster.
169 Human Rights Watch telephone interview with Terrence Hallinan, San Francisco district attorney, August 28, 2002.

Mixed Messages

While acknowledging the importance of official condemnation of hate crimes and messages supporting tolerance, Arab and Muslim community leaders have expressed concern about federal government "mixed messages."170 Official statements exhorting the public not to view Muslims or Arabs differently than anyone else were countered by measures taken as part of the antiterrorist campaign that cast a cloud of suspicion over all Arabs and Muslims in the United States. Those measures have included, for example, the detention of some 1,200 persons of almost exclusively Arab, Muslim, or South Asian heritage because of "possible" links to terrorism; 171 the FBI requests to interview over eight thousand men of Arab or Muslim heritage; and the decision that visitors to the United States from certain Middle Eastern countries would be fingerprinted.

Activists believe these actions reinforce an image of Arabs and Muslims as potential terrorists or terrorist sympathizers.

The recent practice of government officials after the arrest of six Muslim men in suburban Buffalo, New York, points to ways in which the government may reconcile efforts to combat terrorism with its duty to prevent hate crimes. 173

Soon after the arrests of the six men, who were accused of having attended an al-Qaeda-run training camp in Afghanistan, New York Governor George Pataki met with local Muslim leaders and stated during a press conference that the arrests should not be used as an excuse to commit hate crimes.174 Similarly, Peter Ahearn, special agent in charge of the FBI's Buffalo field office, publicly stated that hate crimes would not be tolerated.175 The practice in Buffalo, where an announcement of an alleged terrorism investigation breakthrough was coupled with messages decrying bias, proved effective.

170 Human Rights Watch interview with Pramila Jaypal, executive director, Hate Free Zone, July 31, 2002; Human Rights Watch interview with Raed Tayeh, director, American Muslims for Global Peace and Justice, February 21, 2002; Human Rights Watch interview with Joshua Salaam, Civil Rights Coordinator, Council on American-Islamic Relations, February 21, 2002.
171 Human Rights Watch, "Presumption of Guilt: Human Rights Abuses of Post-September 11 Detainees," *A Human Rights Watch Report*, vol. 14, no. 4(G), August 2002.bly asking, 'If government doesn't trust these people, why should I?'" 172
172 Human Rights Watch interview with Joshua Salaam, Civil Rights Coordinator, Council on American-Islamic Relations, February 21, 2002.
173 "Pataki Reassures Islamic Community, Announces Terrorist Tip Line," *Buffalo News*, September 17, 2002.
174 Ibid.
175 "Arrests Stir Resentment Against Buffalo Suburb's Yemeni-Americans; Neighborhood Had Seen Little Ethnic Tension Before, Residents Say," *St. Louis Post-Dispatch*, September 16, 2002.

Policing

Given the difficulties of preventing spontaneous, individual acts committed independent of any organization, police were often not as successful in their efforts to contain backlash violence as they had hoped. Every city researched by Human Rights Watch experienced record levels of hate violence against Arabs, Muslims and those perceived to be Arab or Muslim following September 11, 2001.

Perhaps the best police successes were in Dearborn, Michigan, a city with thirty thousand Arab-Americans that only experienced two violent September 11-related hate crimes. In Dearborn, unlike many cities, the police had a prior working relationship with the Arab and Muslim community, which enabled them to mobilize quickly following September 11. Thus long before September 11, officials within the Dearborn police department were familiar with communities and areas vulnerable to backlash violence, conscious of the history of backlash violence and aware of the possibility that it might occur in the future. Police departments in other parts of the United States did not have this level of previous engagement with backlash issues before September 11. Their policing, therefore primarily consisted of responding to backlash crimes after they occurred. The measures discussed below detail some of the strategies police used to contain and investigate September 11-related backlash violence.

Backlash Planning

Given the relative predictability and severity of anti-Arab and anti-Muslim backlash violence prior to September 11, activists and experts called for law enforcement agencies to create and coordinate "emergency plans" to mitigate any possible future backlash.176 Nevertheless, none of the law enforcement or officials in the major cities Human Rights Watch visited during the course of research? Seattle, Phoenix, Chicago, New York or Los Angeles had devised any written emergency plans to prepare for future backlash violence.

In Portland, Maine, by contrast, the Center for the Prevention of Hate Violence is working with city officials to create a "Rapid Response Plan" to mitigate backlash discrimination in case of any future terrorist act blamed on Arabs or Muslims.177

176 Human Rights Watch telephone interview with William Haddad, President, Arab American Bar Association, June 17, 2002; Human Rights Watch telephone interview with Stephen Wessler, executive director, Center for the Prevention of Hate Violence, August 27, 2002.
177 The pursuit for the creation of a "Rapid Response Plan" in Portland, Maine comes from a recommendation contained in a report published by the Center entitled, "After September 11: Under standing the Impact on Muslim Communities in Maine," retrieved on September 24, 2002, from http://www.cphv.usm.maine.edu/report.doc.

Stephen Wessler, executive director of the center and author of a report on September 11-related backlash violence against Muslims in Maine stated his fear that "if there is another terrorist attack, we will see a more intensified reaction towards the affected communities...If there is anything government can do to prepare, that will be a big step." Among the measures the center has discussed for possible incorporation into any rapid response plan are:

1) issuance of immediate public statements from government officials condemning discrimination immediately after an event that may trigger a backlash; 2) development of public service immediately after an event that may trigger a backlash; which may be broadcast immediately in case of an emergency; 3) gathering intelligence on areas of the city especially vulnerable to backlash violence and creating a plan to rapidly deploy law enforcement officers in those areas in case of an emergency; and 4) creating a "buddy program" which would gather volunteers from non-Muslim communities to travel with Muslims, especially women who wear the hijab, who are afraid to travel alone during a backlash period.178

Police Deployment

Among the most helpful measures in preventing anti-Arab and anti-Muslim attacks after September 11 was the immediate deployment of police officers in areas with high concentrations of the vulnerable communities. Cities differed, however, in how quickly police were deployed to patrol vulnerable communities. These differences usually reflected the amount of interaction a police department had with the vulnerable communities prior to September 11.

The Dearborn Police Department was exemplary in its immediate deployment of police officers in sensitive areas of Dearborn immediately after the September 11 terrorist attacks. According to community leaders, police were patrolling Arab neighborhoods and mosques by early afternoon on September 11.179 Police on foot stood in areas that could have been attacked and police cars patrolled Arab neighborhoods on September 11 and in the days afterwards.180 The presence of a specially appointed "Arab community police officer" before September 11 also allowed police to gain important intelligence on areas in Dearborn vulnerable to

178 Human Rights Watch telephone interview with Stephen Wessler, executive director, Center for the Prevention of Hate Violence, August 27, 2002.
179 Human Rights Watch interview with Imad Hamad, Midwest regional director, American Arab-Anti-Discrimination Committee, June 5, 2002.
180 Ibid.
181 Human Rights Watch interview with Imad Hamad, Midwest regional director, American Arab-Anti-Discrimination Committee, June 5, 2002; Human Rights Watch interview with Hassan Jaber,

attack. 181 Arab community leaders stated that during the weeks after September 11 most members of the Arab community "felt safer in Dearborn" than outside it because of the increased and visible police presence in their communities.182

Although police departments in New York, Phoenix, and Los Angeles did not have strong pre-existing relationships with the Arab and Muslim community, after the September 11 attacks, these departments nonetheless dispatched police officers to protect primarily Muslim or Sikh places of worship and areas with high Arab, Muslim, Sikh, or South Asian concentrations.

In Phoenix, the day after September 11, after consulting with concerned members of the Arab and Muslim communities, the police department established twenty-four hour patrols at area mosques.183 The Phoenix Police Department's bias crime unit credited the department's Muslim community liaison for providing the department with information on the Muslim and Arab community in Phoenix gained through prior interaction with those communities before September 11.184 In Los Angeles, the Los Angeles County Commission on Human Relations on September 11 notified the police department of vulnerable "hotspots,", such as mosques and Arab-owned convenience stores. As a result, police were dispatched to protect some of these vulnerable areas.

In New York City, Sikh community leaders reported that after a gurdwara was vandalized on September 11, police officers patrolled the area around the gurdwara by foot during the next week. New York City police also provided protective escorts for busloads of Sikhs traveling from Queens to Manhattan for a Sikh community vigil on September 15, 2001, in

Initial Classification of Crimes

In some instances after September 11, the decisions of police officers not to classify crimes as possible hate crimes meant that no further investigation of possible bias motive was conducted. For example, Kripa Ubadhyay, program coordinator for the Anti-Discrimination and Hate Crimes Program of the South Asian Network

---

executive director, ACCESS, June 4, 2002; Human Rights Watch interview with Daniel Saab, Dearborn community police officer, June 1, 2002.
182 Ibid.
183 Human Rights Watch interview with Sergeant Jerry Hill, Phoenix Police Department, August 8. 2002.
184 Ibid.
185 Human Rights Watch telephone interview with Prabhjot Singh, director, Sikh Coalition, August 16, 2002.

(SAN), cited the case of two Bangladeshi Muslims who were held up at gun point while numerous ethnic epithets were yelled at them. For months, there was no investigation of possible bias motivation for the crime because the responding officers chose to classify the matter as a robbery. Only after SAN directly appealed to the Los Angeles County's bias crime investigator was the matter recorded and investigated as a possible hate crime.186 Police departments in different cities had differing standards on the discretion available to responding police officers to classify a matter as a possible hate crime.

In New York, if a responding police officer believed that a hate crime might have occurred, he or she was to report this to the duty captain in the police precinct. If the duty captain also believed the crime to be bias-motivated, the matter was referred to the police department's Hate Crimes Task Force for investigation as a possible hate crime.187 Linda Wancel, head of the Civil Rights Bureau within the Brooklyn district attorney's office, stated that whether a matter was investigated by police as a possible hate crime was "contingent on the duty captain calling it a hate crime... We disagree sometimes with the duty captain not classifying cases as a possible a hate crime."188

In Seattle, staff at the Office of Civil Rights expressed frustration that complaints they received about bias-motivated criminal acts did not appear in monthly hate crime reports produced by the police department. According to staff, the discretion responding police officers to not classify a crime as a possible hate crime, created the possibility that they would investigate many crimes as possible hate crimes despite evidence that they may have been so motivated. 189

The Phoenix Police Department, on the other hand, required responding officers to indicate on a police report whether either the victim or the responding officer believed bias motivated the crime. Where any such belief that a bias crime may have occurred existed, no matter how seemingly inconsequential to the responding officer, the responding officer police report was forwarded to the Phoenix Bias Crime Detail, where officers specially trained to investigate hate crimes determined whether there was any bias motivation for the crime.

186 Human Rights Watch telephone interview with Kripa Ubadhay, Anti-Discrimination and Hate Crimes Program Coordinator, South Asian Network, August 21, 2002.
187 Human Rights Watch telephone interview with Adil Almontaser, American Muslim Law Enforcement Officers Association, August 27, 2002.
188 Human Rights Watch telephone interview with Linda Wancel, Civil Rights Bureau, Brooklyn district attorney's office, August 26, 2002.
189 Human Rights Watch interview with Julie Pate, Seattle Office of Civil Rights, July 31, 2002.

Aladdin Elaasar

Hate Crime Units and Institutional Support for Hate Crimes Training

Police departments in all of the cities Human Rights Watch researched stated that they trained their officers on the basic elements of a hate crime. With the exception of Dearborn, Michigan, they also all have at least one officer who investigates bias crimes exclusively. In the Seattle, Phoenix, Chicago and New York police departments, a bias crime unit officer is responsible for investigating any incident where evidence exists that a bias motive was present. The utility of this protocol for investigating bias crimes, according to Sergeant Jerry Hill, head of the Phoenix Police Department's Bias Crime Detail, is that it "ensures someone with expertise on hate crimes is investigating the matter.

It takes pressure off the responding officer to make the call on whether this was a hate crime."190

Prosecution

After September 11, 2001, prosecutors across the country acted conscientiously to use their authority to bring hate crime perpetrators to justice. Numerous state attorneys general and county prosecutors issued statements condemning anti-Arab and anti-Muslim hate crimes, visited affected communities, encouraged them to report hate crimes to authorities and vowed to prosecute them vigorously.193 During our research, Human Rights Watch found that prosecutors were proceeding actively on serious hate crimes that had occurred in their jurisdiction. The number

190 Human Rights Watch interview with Sergeant Jerry Hill, Phoenix Police Department, August 8, 2002. Many local police departments, however, did not have the resources or a sufficient bias crime caseload to justify training all officers on how to investigate bias crimes or to appoint a specialized bias crime investigator. In Maine, the attorney general's office attempted to address this problem by asking each law enforcement agency in Maine to appoint a "civil rights officer" to review all crime reports for bias motivation indicia. Any report that contains indications of bias is forwarded to the attorney general's office for further review and guidance. Thomas Harnett, a prosecutor in the attorney general's office, stated that this system allows the office to assist local law enforcement agencies with bias crime investigations and also provides a layer of review for their work.
191 In the aftermath of September 11, this system was used to refer September 11-related bias incidents to the Maine attorney general's office for review and consultation on further action.192
191 Human Rights Watch e-mail correspondence with Thomas Harnett, prosecutor, Maine attorney general's office, August 26, 2002.
192 Ibid.
193 See "Charges Filed in Recent Hate Crimes," Press Release, King County prosecutor's office, September 19, 2001, retrieved on August 30, 2002, from http://www.metrokc.gov/proatty/News/Current/Hatecrim.htm; "Attorney General Napolitano, Maricopa County attorney Romley, Others Band Together To Urge Reporting Of Hate Crimes," Press Release, Arizona attorney general, September 20, 2001, retrieved on August 30, 2002, from http://www.attorney_general.state.az.us/press_releases/sept/092001.html.

of September 11-related hate crimes prosecuted was, not surprisingly, smaller than the number of September 11-related hate crimes reported. But the proportion of September 11-related crimes that have been the subject of indictment and trial does not appear to vary significantly from the usual rates of indictment and trial for other types of crime. Many variables influence prosecution rates including the ability of the police to identify a suspect, the quality of the evidence developed against him or her, the seriousness of the crime, and available prosecutorial resources. While our research did not uncover any instances of prosecutorial reluctance to take hate crimes seriously, some community activists expressed concern to us that prosecutors were placing insufficient priority on hate crime prosecutions.

The Department of Justice prosecuted twelve September 11-related hate crimes and cooperated with local county prosecutors in the prosecution of approximately eighty more. The prosecution of twelve bias crimes in a single year is the highest number of bias crime prosecutions by the Justice Department since the federal hate crimes statute was enacted in 1964. It is more than double the yearly average of hate crime prosecutions conducted by the Department each year.

On the local level, the Cook County state's attorney's office prosecuted six September 11- related hate crimes.194 The Los Angeles County district attorney's office prosecuted three September 11-related crimes. In Maricopa County, containing Phoenix, there were three September 11-related hate crime prosecutions.195 Not all post-September 11 bias crimes were prosecuted as hate crimes under state or federal hate crimes legislation. For example, of the twelve September 11-related crimes prosecuted by the U.S. Justice Department, only half were charged under the federal hate crimes statute.

Prosecuting a crime as a hate crime places an additional evidentiary burden on the prosecutor to prove in court not only the regular elements of the crime, but the existence of bias motivation as well.196 Proof of such bias was difficult to demonstrate unless the defendant confessed his motivation, made statements during the crime demonstrating direct bias, or had otherwise clearly signaled his views. In the absence of strong evidence of bias, prosecutors often preferred to utilize regular criminal statutes to secure a conviction. 197

194 Human Right Watch interview with Neera Walsh, prosecutor, Cook County prosecutor's office Bias Crime Unit, June 18, 2002.
195 Human Rights Watch interview with Bill Fitzgerald, public relations officer, Maricopa County district attorney office, August 3, 2002.
196 Human Rights Watch interview with Genna Gent and Daniel Levy, prosecutors, Michigan Attorney General's
Hate Crimes Prosecution Team, June 3, 2002.
197 Ibid.

Publicizing Prosecutions

September 11-related hate crime prosecutions did not only secure justice for particular victims. They also communicated society's repudiation of the crimes. Prosecution of September 11-related crimes conveyed the message that violent bigotry against Arabs and Muslims was not condoned and that law enforcement took seriously their obligation to protect all members of society and to bring those who committed crimes to justice.

According to Thomas Harnett, a prosecutor in the Maine attorney general's office, hate crime perpetrators "believe that their actions have community support." Publicizing prosecutions communicates the error of this belief to potential hate crime perpetrators as well as to the community at large. Indeed, according to Harnett, "one of the reasons we publicized [September 11-related] cases and successful enforcement actions was to instill in the community the belief that these incidents should be reported and when they are reported, victims are safer not more at risk."198 Deepa Iyer of the South Asian American Leaders of Tomorrow concurred that publicizing prosecutions lets affected community members know that the government is committed to protecting them and encourages victims to report hate crimes against them.199

In Los Angeles and Phoenix, the district attorneys held press conferences and issued press releases announcing prominent September 11- related prosecutions. In Seattle, the Kings County prosecutor's office issued press releases on September 11-related prominent prosecutions. 200 At the federal level, the Civil Rights Division of the U.S. Department of Justice issued press releases on most of its twelve September 11-related prosecutions. The Civil Rights Division, however, did not hold any press conferences to publicize its prosecutions, even though some community groups thought press conferences would secure greater coverage.201

The Civil Rights Division nevertheless spread notice of its prosecutions by directly informing Arab, Muslim, Sikh, and South Asian community leaders and by sending the news to community e-mail lists.202 Although these communications

198 Human Rights Watch e-mail correspondence with Thomas Arnett, August 26, 2002.
199 Human Rights Watch telephone interview with Deepa Iyer, February 26, 2002.
200 "Charges Filed in Recent Hate Crimes," Press Release, King County prosecutor's office, September 19, 2001, retrieved on August 30, 2002, fromhttp://www.metrokc.gov/proatty/News/Current/Hatecrim.htm.
201 Human Rights Watch telephone interview with Prabhjot Singh, director, Sikh Coalition, August 16, 2002.
202 Human Rights Watch telephone interview with Joseph Zogby, special assistant for the Civil

did not reach the broader American public, they at least informed the affected communities that the federal government was working to punish bias crime perpetrators. The Civil Rights Division also publicized most of the prosecutions on its website, although the website was not always up to date.203

Hate Crime Prosecutor Units

In some larger cities, efforts to bring hate crime perpetrators to justice were enhanced by the presence of specially trained hate crime prosecutors. For example, Chicago, Los Angeles, Phoenix, and New York City all have prosecutors who specialize in the prosecution of bias motivated crimes.

According to Neera Walsh, head of the Cook County prosecutor's office Bias Crime Unit, the existence of a bias crimes prosecution unit permitted the development of specialized expertise to handle the unique challenges posed by hate crimes cases.204 Since September 11, the Bias Crimes Unit has been responsible for the prosecution of six September 11-related bias crimes. Phoenix police investigators also stated that working with prosecutors who specialize in bias crime prosecution gave them more confidence that the effort they put into investigating bias crimes would be taken seriously and better understood by prosecutors with training on understanding the nature of bias crimes.205 Community leaders believe specialized units provided them with a central point of contact and thus enabled them to develop a better relationship with country prosecutors.206

Many small counties did not have the resources or large enough vulnerable communities to justify the creation of bias crime prosecution units. Recognizing the difficulty that small counties had undertaking the prosecution of September 11-related hate crimes, Michigan's attorney general created in May 2002 a Hate Crimes Prosecution Team to enhance the capacity of local prosecutors in smaller counties.207 The team trains local prosecutors in the prosecution of hate crimes against Arab-Americans and Muslims as well as members of any other group that may be targets of bias-motivated violence. It also offers to assist with the prosecution of the bias element of a hate crime during trial.208 The Michigan

Rights Division's Backlash Initiative, August 25, 2002.
203 See www.usdoj.gov/crt, retrieved on September 20, 2002.
204 Human Right Watch interview with Neera Walsh, prosecutor, Cook County prosecutor's office Bias Crime Unit, June 18, 2002.
205 Human Rights Watch interview with Sergeant Jerry Hill, August 8. 2002
206 Human Rights Watch interview with Manjari Chawla, staff attorney, Asian Pacific American Legal Center, June 30, 2002.
207 Human Rights Watch interview with Genna Gent and Daniel Levy, June 3, 2002.
208 Ibid. Since its creation, the team has offered its assistance to local prosecutors in two matters,

attorney general's program was unique among the cities and states Human Rights Watch visited because it allowed local prosecutors to have access to expertise in bias crime prosecution without having to develop such expertise within their own agencies.

Crimes with Mixed Motives

Some crimes had multiple motives, including anti-Arab and anti-Muslim bias. For example, the murderer of Ali Almansoop, who found Mr. Almansoop in bed with his ex-girlfriend, appears to have been motivated by both jealousy and post-September 11 biases. In cases that have mixed motives, some departments did not investigate the crime as possibly being bias motivated.

The Seattle police department's bias crime investigator, for example, told Human Rights Watch that the department would not treat violence motivated only in part by anti-Arab or anti-Muslim bias as hate crimes.209

Prosecutors in such cases, including in the Almansoop case, typically chose to proceed under ordinary criminal law.

Even if state law only permits hate crimes prosecution when bias is the sole motive, it is nonetheless important where crimes have multiple motives that police record such crimes as hate crimes to establish a barometer of a given population's vulnerability.210 Illinois amended its hate crimes law so that a crime may be prosecuted as a hate crime when it is motivated "in any part" by bias.211 Though the purpose of the amendment was to facilitate the use of the Illinois hate crime statute in mixed motive cases, one of the benefits of the law is that tracking of mixed motive crimes is no longer precluded.

According to Elizabeth Schulman-Moore of the Lawyer's Committee for Civil Rights in Chicago, as a result of this amendment all crimes with a bias motive "no matter how small" are recognized as such by local government officials. 212

---

one involving the beating of an African-American and the other involving vandalism to the office of U.S. Congressman.

209 Human Rights Watch interview with Detective Christie Lynn-Bonner, Seattle Police Department, August 2, 2002.

210 Human Rights Watch interview with Elizabeth Schulman-Moore, attorney, Lawyer's Committee for Civil Rights, June 17, 2002.

211 Daniel C. Vock, "House passes bill expanding hate crimes," *Chicago Daily Law Bulletin*, February 25, 2002.

212 Human Rights Watch interview with Elizabeth Schulman-Moore, June 17, 2002.

Affected Community Outreach

Prior to the September 11 attacks, many government agencies in the cities researched had scant relationships with Arab and Muslim communities, even in cities with substantial Arab and Muslim populations and despite previous histories of bias-motivated attacks. Nevertheless, outreach efforts after the September 11 backlash were robust. Outreach efforts included meetings at mosques, community forums, printed materials translated into languages spoken in the communities, and the creation of hate crime "hotlines."

Relationship With Affected Communities Before September 11

Nowhere were the benefits of a pre-existing government relationship with potential victim communities more apparent than in Dearborn, Michigan. Community leaders in Dearborn told Human Rights Watch that before September 11 they had regular and consistent meetings with the Dearborn mayor's office, the Dearborn Chief of Police, the Wayne County prosecutor's office, the state attorney general's office and the U.S. attorney for the Eastern District of Michigan on a range of issues affecting Arabs and Muslims in and around Dearborn.213 According to community leaders, these meetings ensured that government agencies "more or less knew our concerns, regardless of whether we were always in agreement." 214

The open channels of communication and high level of interaction between Dearborn officials and members of the Dearborn Arab and Muslim communities enabled community leaders to mobilize officials promptly to address a potential backlash after the September 11 attacks.215 City leaders also had access to information with which to assess the needs of the Arab and Muslim communities following the September 11 attacks. According to Imad Hamad, Midwest Director of the ADC in Dearborn, Michigan:

We were able to call the mayor's office on the morning of September 11 about our concerns that our community members would be attacked. By 11:30 a.m. we were meeting with the Mayor and Chief of Police about a possible backlash against our community. By 1:00 p.m. the Mayor was on the local cable public access channel

213 Human Rights Watch interview with Hassan Jaber, executive director, ACCESS, June 4, 2002; Human Rights
Watch Interview with Daniel Saab, Dearborn community police officer, June 1, 2002.
214 Human Rights Watch interview with Imad Hamad, June 5, 2002.
215 Human Rights Watch interview with Imad Hamad, June 5, 2002; Human Rights Watch
interview with Hassan Jaber, executive director, ACCESS, June 4, 2002; Human Rights Watch
interview with Nasser Beydoun, American Arab Chamber of Commerce, June 5, 2002.

warning people against committing hate crimes against Arabs in Dearborn and the police cars were patrolling our shopping areas and neighborhoods.216

Outreach after September 11: Barriers to Trust

The general fear of government among Arab and Muslim immigrant communities remained one of the more significant challenges posed in creating working relationships with those communities on hate crime issues after September 11. According to Rita Zawaideh of the Arab America Community Coalition, an umbrella group of Arab organizations in western Washington: "In countries where many Arab immigrants are from, the government and the police are repressive, they are not your friend."217 This general fear of government was aggravated by the detention and deportation of Muslims and Arabs by the federal government after September 11 and by fears that reporting hate crimes would draw attention to non-citizens who had violated the terms of their visas.218 Kripa Ubadhyay, hate crimes coordinator for the South Asian Network in Los Angeles related her experience organizing a community forum on September 11-related civil liberties issues: "We invited the FBI and INS. One hundred and fifty people attend a similar past forum, however only sixty attended this one. We later found out from many [who didn't attend] that they were afraid 216 Human Rights Watch interview with Imad Hamad, June 5, 2002. of being detained by the INS."219 Similarly, Stephen Wessler of the Center on the Prevention of Hate Violence in Portland, Maine, stated: "what struck me most was not a fear of hate crimes [in the Muslim community], it was a fear of the federal government. The fear of detention or deportation continued even when the fear of hate crimes ended."220

Cultural Competency

Cultural competency is "a set of behaviors and attitudes integrated into the practices and policies of agencies or professional service providers that enables them to understand and work effectively in cross-cultural situations."221 Because many of the persons affected by the September 11 backlash are foreign-born, cultural competency training was important for police officers and other government

217 Human Rights Watch interview with Rita Zawaideh, Spokesperson, Arab American Community Coalition, August 5, 2002.
218 Human Rights Watch telephone interview with Stephen Wessler, August 27, 2002. *See also*, "Fear Of Detention Haunts South Florida Muslims; Dozens Held By U.S. Agencies In Terror Inquiries," *South Florida Sun-Sentinel,* July 9, 2002.
219 Human Rights Watch telephone interview with Kripa Ubadhay, Anti-Discrimination and Hate Crimes Program Coordinator, South Asian Network, August 21, 2002.
220 Human Rights Watch telephone interview with Stephen Wessler, August 27, 2002.
221 "Cultural Competency," retrieved on September 21, 2002, from http://www.aoa.gov/may2001/factsheets/CulturalCompetency.html.

officials who regularly interacted with Muslim, Arabs, Sikhs or South Asians after September 11.222 The importance of such training was underscored by Sheila Bell, Communications Director for the Muslim Law Enforcement Officers Association of New York City. As an example, Bell cited the practice in Middle Eastern culture of not looking authority figures in the eye during discussions because doing so is a sign of disrespect.

Bell stated that officers in the New York City police department have mistaken this habit as an effort to be deceitful.223 Similarly, Guru Roop Kaur Khalsa, a gurdwara official in Phoenix, narrated a discussion she had with a police officer who along with other officers were assigned to protect the gurdwara shortly after Balbir Singh Sodhi's murder, discussed in section III above.224 The police officer reported to Khalsa that the members of the officers' families were "very nervous" about them protecting the gurdwara because they thought Sikhs might be terrorists affiliated with Osama Bin Laden because of their turbans and beards. 225 After gaining exposure to Sikhs while protecting the gurdwara, the officer told Ms. Khalsa that they felt much more comfortable performing their duties to protect them. 226 On the federal level, the Community Relations Service of the Department of Justice (CRS) organized and sponsored numerous cultural competency training sessions nationwide after September 11 for a wide range of federal employees, including congressional staffers, FBI agents, and federal civil rights officials.227

These forums usually involved presentations by members of the Muslim and Sikh faiths on aspects of their faiths and cultures that may impact the work of federal officials. The sessions typically ended with a question and answer period. On the local level, cultural competency training often was done "on the fly" with government officials and police officers learning about relevant cultural traits of the various communities as they worked with them after September 11.228 In Seattle for example, the police force did not have any training on Muslim practices

222 Human Rights Watch interview, Pramilla Jaypal, executive director with Hate Free Zone of Washington, July 31, 2002.
223 Human Rights Watch telephone interview with Sheila Bell, communications director, Muslim Law Enforcement Officers Association, August 27, 2002.
224 Human Rights Watch interview with Guru Roop Kaur Khalsa, Phoenix Gurdwara, August 9, 2002.
225 Ibid.
226 Ibid.
227 Human Rights Watch interview with Sharee Freeman, executive director, Community Relations Service, Department of Justice, May 5, 2002.
228 Human Rights Watch interview with Sergeant Jerry Hill, August 8. 2002; Human Rights Watch telephone interview with Robin Toma, executive director, Los Angeles Human Relations Commission, August 27, 2002,

for police officers. Instead, officers who worked with these communities learned about basic Muslim beliefs as they visited city mosques after September11. 229

Language Barriers

Because many of the September 11 backlash victims were foreign-born, the inability to speak or comprehend English was a barrier to effective interaction with government officials. Sheila Bell of the Muslim Law Enforcement Officers Association of New York City pointed out that language has also been a barrier to effective communication with the New York City Police Department because crime victims calling the Department in an emergency were sometimes not been able to speak English well enough to be understood completely.230 Language was also a barrier for community groups organizing outreach events with government agencies. For example, Rita Zawaideh of the Arab America Community Coalition noted that even though police officers in the Seattle Police Department initiated and participated in outreach meetings at every mosque in Seattle after September 11: "They weren't always understood because not everyone speaks English."231

In the Dearborn Police Department, language barriers have been overcome by the appointment of an Arab community police officer who speaks Arabic.232 At the national level, the Civil Rights Division has made a concerted effort to publish brochures explaining civil rights protections in the languages of the backlash affected communities. The brochures, written in languages such as Arabic, Farsi, and Punjabi, have been distributed in the Arab, Muslim, Sikh, and South Asian communities by mailing them to community organizations and places of worship.

The Civil Rights Division states that it has mailed thousands of these brochures to affected community groups since September 11.233 They are also available on the Civil Rights Division website.

229 Human Rights Watch interview with Detective Christie Lynn-Bonner, Seattle Police Department, August 2, 2002.
230 Human Rights Watch telephone interview with Sheila Bell, August 27, 2002.
231 Human Rights Watch interview with Rita Zawaideh, August 5, 2002.
232 Human Rights Watch interview with Officer Daniel Saab, Dearborn Police Department, May 31, 2002.
233 Human Rights Watch interview with Joseph Zogby, special assistant for the Assistant Attorney General's 9/11 Backlash Initiative, U.S. Department of Justice, March 29, 2002. See http://www.usdoj.gov/crt/legalinfo/nordwg_brochure.html, retrieved on September 23, 2002.
234 In the Sikh and South Asian communities the CRS was in many cases the first federal government agency to ever contact them.235 The Civil Rights Division appointed specific persons to undertake outreach with each of the affected communities. These persons took calls from community leaders, e-mailed news of progress in backlash-related matters to community e-mail listserves, and spoke at eight community forums organized by the Civil Rights Division nationwide on September 11-related civil rights issues.

Community Liaisons

The creation of community liaisons, whether they be individuals or committees, was an effective tool utilized by some governments to work with vulnerable groups. After September 11, the Department of Justice Community Relations Service (CRS) was especially helpful in identifying civil rights leaders and organizations in the Sikh and South Asian community with whom the Civil Rights Division could work once it was clear that those communities were vulnerable to backlash violence.

Community organizations in New York, especially in the Muslim, South Asian, and Sikh community expressed frustration in their level of interaction with the New York City Police Department and other city officials who might have been of assistance on hate crime issues. Especially in the Sikh and South Asian communities, civil rights activists stated that there was only one community police officer in the whole police department assigned to interact with members of the huge Sikh and South Asian communities.240 Furthermore, Sikh and South Asian community leaders stated that in general government agencies had not organized any forums for the community members to educate them on police protections from hate crimes and that community members did not know who to contact if they were a victim of a hate crime.241

236 Leaders of community organizations reported a very high level of satisfaction with their access to liaisons and ability to discuss urgent matters with them.

237 The Civil Rights Division was generally known for having an "open door policy" in which "a meeting with division heads can be arranged anytime there is an issue of pressing concern."

238 In Seattle, the Mayor created an Arab advisory council after September 11. The Seattle Police Department also made presentations on hate crime issues in each of the eleven mosques in Seattle, providing names and numbers of persons that community members could contact in 234 Human Rights Watch interview with Sharee Freeman, executive director, May 5, 2002.

235 Human Rights Watch interview with Sharee Freeman, executive director, Community Relations Service, Department of Justice, May 5, 2002.

236 Human Rights Watch interview with Joseph Zogby, special assistant for the Assistant Attorney General's 9/11 Backlash Initiative, U.S. Department of Justice, March 29, 2002. See, http://www.usdoj.gov/crt/legalinfo/nordwg_brochure.html, accessed on September 23, 2002.

237 Human Rights Watch interview with Nawar Shora, attorney, Arab American Anti-Discrimination Committee, February 28, 2002.

238 Human Rights Watch telephone interview with Prabhjot Singh, August 16, 2002. case they were a victim of a hate crime.

239 In Chicago, the creation eight years ago of an Arab Community Advisory Council in the mayor's office greatly facilitated interaction between the mayor's office, the chief of police, and the Arab community both before and after September 11.

239 Human Rights Watch interview with Rita Zarweih, August 3, 2002.

240 Human Rights Watch telephone interview with Sin Yen Ling, attorney, Asian-American Legal Defense Fund, August 26, 2002. Human Rights Watch interview with Pritpal Singh, Sikh Youth of America, August 25, 2002.

241 Human Rights Watch interview with Pritpal Singh, August 25, 2002.

Creation of Hotlines on Hate Crimes

Some cities and states as well as the federal government created specific hate crime hotlines to give affected community members a point of contact in government when backlash hate crimes occurred. Seattle, Arizona, California, and, at the federal level, the U.S. Commission on Civil Rights, all created and advertised the creation of September 11-related hate crimes hotlines. Community organizations generally reported satisfaction with the hotlines, stating that they were important in letting victim communities know that they could easily contact government. The creation of a federal September 11 hate crimes hotline encountered serious difficulties.

On September 14, 2001, the U.S. Commission on Civil Rights announced the creation of a "National Complaint Line… to solicit and catalogue discrimination complaints from Arab and Muslim Americans."242 The number was publicized by numerous Arab, Muslim, and South Asian organizations as a means to complain about hate crimes to the federal government. The number listed on the press release, however, was incorrect, forwarding callers to a dating service.243 Once the correct number was released by the commission three days later, the commission received approximately 140 calls from September 17 to October 2 that it considered possible hate crimes.244

Nevertheless, many persons who called the line did not understand that their complaints would not be forwarded to federal law enforcement authorities. The commission, when requested by Civil Rights Division to forward reports of hate crimes to it or the FBI, refused to do so. The commission maintained that it needed to protect the callers' anonymity so that they would not be discouraged from calling the commission. It also insisted it was an information gathering service rather than a complaint referral service.245

Bias Crime Tracking

Federal, state, and city governments made varied efforts to track bias crimes after September 11. Many city governments created separate classifications for

242 "U.S. Commission On Civil Rights Announces Complaint Line To Protect Rights Of Arab, Islamic Communities; Urges Tolerance In The Face Of Tragedy," United States Commission on Civil Rights, September 14, 2001.
243 "Rights panel keeps hot line data from Justice; Claims of bias directed at Arabs, Muslims at issue," *Washington Times*, October 13, 2001.
244 Ibid.
245 Ibid.

September 11-related crimes in an effort to track the course of investigations and better inform the public on such efforts. Reliable national statistics on September 11 hate crimes did not exist at the time of this writing, however, because the federal Department of Justice had not yet published its annual hate crimes report for the year 2001.

Federal Hate Crime Statistics

In the United States, the Hate Crime Statistics Act of 1990 requires the Department of Justice to collect statistics on hate crimes using the Uniform Crime Reporting System (UCR).246 According to Michael Lieberman, a long time activist on hate crime issues for the Anti-Defamation League: "The [federal] hate crime reporting statute is the most important hate crime law. It has pushed law enforcement to train police officers to detect bias-motivations for crimes in communities... It has revolutionized awareness of hate crime issues by creating a measure of accountability in communities."247

Under UCR, law enforcement authorities around the United States are asked to aggregate the number of hate crime incidents by offense type and the racial, religious, national origin or sexual orientation of the victim every quarter and report these totals to the FBI. These local reports are compiled by the FBI and published yearly by the Bureau of Justice Statistics, in the form of simple data on the number of hate crimes committed each year in a particular jurisdiction and the number of hate crimes committed against a particular victim type in each jurisdiction. The Bureau of Justice Statistics report is the only government-produced national snapshots on hate crimes each year.

Over the past eight years, the FBI has encouraged local jurisdictions to report incidents of crime, including hate crime, using the National Incident Based Reporting System (NIBRS). The NIBRS reporting system provides more than a simple summary count of the number of hate crimes committed in each jurisdiction and the victim type. Under incident based reporting, local law enforcement agencies provide an individual record for each crime reported to the FBI. Details about each incident include detailed information on the type of offender, victim, offense, weapon used, and location of the offense.

246 Bureau of Justice Statistics website, http://www.ojp.usdoj.gov/bjs/nibrs.htm, retrieved on September 3, 2002.
247 Human Rights Watch telephone interview with Michael Lieberman, Washington Counsel, Anti-Defamation League, August 15, 2002.

Participation in both the reporting systems is voluntary. Though most police agencies in the United States report hate crimes to the FBI, not all do so. Furthermore, among the agencies that do report hate crimes, many significantly underreport the occurrence of hate crimes in their jurisdiction. A study funded by the Department of Justice found that 83 percent of the law enforcement agencies who participate in either the UCR or the NIBRS report that they had no hate crimes each year.248

Nevertheless, the study found that many of those jurisdictions had hate crimes that were not reported to the FBI. 249 This "false-zero" reporting to the FBI is so severe that the study estimated six thousand hate crimes, almost 75 percent again as much as the total number of hate crimes reported nationwide each year to the FBI, are not included in reports to the FBI.250 Further complicating matters with regard to tracking anti-Arab violence is that the FBI does not track specific ethnic community hate crimes, instead generically classifying any anti-ethnic violence into a single ethnic crime category.

City and State Hate Crime Tracking

In addition to federal efforts to collect hate crime data, a handful of city and state agencies in the United States also collect and publish their own hate crime statistics. Most notable among these are California, Illinois, Chicago, and Los Angeles County, which all publish detailed statistics each year on hate crimes. The law enforcement agencies in the cities researched for this report Dearborn, Chicago, Seattle, Los Angeles, Phoenix, and New York all participate in the UCR system at the federal level. Some cities and states, like California and Chicago, also have specially tracked and published statistics on September 11-related bias crimes, while others, like Seattle and New York, did not. The Office of the Attorney General for California was the most aggressive in collecting data on September 11-related hate crimes and widely publishing it.

The California attorney general's office issued two "Interim Reports" listing the number of September 11- related bias on hate crimes against Arab and Muslims and those perceived to be Arab or Muslim in six large California cities. The attorney general published the data because he believed the information was

248 "Improving The Quality And Accuracy Of Bias Crime Statistics Nationally: An Assessment Of The First Ten Years Of Bias Crime Data Collection," The Center for Criminal Justice Policy Research College of Criminal Justice Northeastern University and Justice Research and Statistics Association, September 2000.
249 Ibid.
250 Ibid.

"central to developing effective measures to combat these despicable acts."251 The first report was issued on October 11, 2001 once it was clear that a widespread backlash, numbering ten incidents per day, was occurring in California; the second was issued on December 11, 2001, after the backlash had significantly decreased to one incident per day.252 To our knowledge, the California attorney general's office was the only state or local government agency to publish data on the September 11 backlash while it was occurring.

In addition to making a special effort to track and publish September 11-related crimes, California also publishes a yearly hate crimes report containing detailed statistical data on the type of hate crimes occurring, the victims, the offenders, location of attacks, and prosecution rates. The yearly report for the year 2001 was published on September 18, 2002. The report found that: "the overall number of hate crimes reported last year actually would have decreased five percent from a year earlier if not for the bias-motivated assaults against Californians victimized because they are Muslim or appeared to be of Middle Eastern descent."253

The Los Angeles County Commission on Human Relations also publishes a comprehensive annual hate crimes report with detailed statistics on hate crimes in Los Angeles County. According to the commission's executive director, the report is the oldest yearly hate crimes report of any jurisdiction in the United States, having been published since 1980.254 Like the California attorney general's report, it includes detailed statistical data on hate crimes each year, including information on the type of the victims, the offenders, location of attacks, prosecution rates, and type of hate crimes occurring. On September 9, 2002, the commission published its annual report for the year 2001.255

The Chicago Police Department has published a comprehensive annual hate crimes report since 1995. On June 27, 2002, it issued its annual "Hate Crimes in Chicago

251 "Attorney General Releases Interim Report on Anti-Arab Hate Crimes," Office of the Attorney General State of California, October 11, 2001.
252 "Attorney General Releases Interim Report on Anti-Arab Hate Crimes," Office of the Attorney General State of California, October 11, 2001; "Attorney General Releases Interim Report on Anti-Arab Hate Crimes," Office of the Attorney General State of California, December 11, 2001.
253 "Attorney General Lockyer Releases Annual Hate Crime Report Showing Spike From Post 9/11 Anti-Arab Attacks," Press Release, Office of the California Attorney General, September 18, 2002, retrieved on September 18, 2002, from http://caag.state.ca.us/newsalerts/2002/02-106.htm.
254 Human Rights Watch telephone interview with Robin Toma, August 27, 2002.
255 See http://humanrelations.co.la.ca.us/Our_publications/pdf/2001HCR.pdf, retrieved on September 10, 2002.

Report."256 The report stated that Chicago police separately tracked September 11-related hate crimes and listed the number of September 11-related hate crimes in Chicago. Like the Los Angeles County Commission on Human Relations and the California attorney general's annual hate crime reports, the Chicago Police Department report includes information on the type of victims, the offenders, location of attacks, and types of hate crimes occurring, but it does not contain data on prosecution rates.

The Chicago Police Department's annual report is unique in that it also lists the number of "hate incidents," a category which includes bias motivated conduct that may fall short of violating criminal laws.257 The collection of hate incident statistics gives law enforcement officers clues on areas of the city where racial or ethnic tensions exist that could escalate into hate crimes.258

The Phoenix Police Department simply published on its website the number of anti-Arab and anti-Muslim hate crimes that occurred in Phoenix for the year 2001, noting with an asterisk that all anti-Arab hate crimes in Phoenix occurred after September 11.259 The published numbers also made the error of separately listing "anti-Muslim" and "anti-Islamic" hate crimes even though the terms are synonymous.

The Dearborn Police Department separately categorized September 11-related hate crimes and logged them for internal investigatory purposes. The Department, however, has not published hate crimes statistics in the past.260 Information on hate crimes in Dearborn is published each year as part of the Michigan State Police department's submission of data to the FBI's Uniform Reporting System program.261

Neither New York nor Seattle publishes yearly data on hate crimes. The Bias Crimes Unit of the New York City Police Department did, however, track the number of September 11-related hate crimes in the three months after September 11 for internal investigatory purposes.

---

256 See http://w4.ci.chi.il.us./caps/Statistics/Reports/HateCrimes/index.html, retrieved on September 10, 2002.
257 Ibid.
258 Ibid.
259 See http://www.ci.phoenix.az.us/POLICE/hatecr2.html, retrieved on September 10, 2002.
260 Human Rights Watch Interview with Sergeant Timothy Harper, Dearborn Police Department, June 3, 2002.
261 See http://www.state.mi.us/msp/crd/ucr98/ucr_h07.htm, retrieved on September 10, 2002.

Seattle did not track such data, and indeed, unlike any city researched for this report, did not track September 11-related hate crimes at all.262 The only published data on hate crimes in New York and Seattle is the data published yearly by the FBI in its annual hate crimes report. This data, as described above, is cursory in nature, providing only the number of hate crimes committed each year and the types of victims attacked. Information on hate crime perpetrators, the location of attacks, the type of crimes committed, or prosecution rates is not included in the Uniform Crime Reporting system used by New York City and Seattle.

262 Human Rights Watch interview with Julie Pate, Seattle Office of Civil Rights, July 31, 2002; Human Rights Watch interview with Detective Christie Lynn-Bonner, Seattle Police Department, August 2, 2002.

APPENDIX

Backlash Preparation
Center for the Prevention of Hate Violence
Stephen L. Wessler
(207) 780-4756
e-mail: CPHV@usm.maine.edu
website: http://www.cphv@usm.maine.edu

Hate Crimes Prosecution
Michigan Attorney General's Taskforce on Hate Crimes
Michigan Attorney General Hate Crimes Prosecution Team
(517) 335-0804

Hate Crime Tracking
Los Angeles County Commission on Human Relations
Marshall Wong
Hate Crimes Coordinator
(213) 974-7617
www.LAHumanRelations.org

Affected Community Outreach
Special Counsel to the Assistant Attorney General on Backlash Discrimination
Joseph Zogby
(202) 514-6534
e-mail: Joseph.Zogby@usdoj.gov
website: www.usdoj.gov/crt/nordwg.html

Corporal Daniel Saab
Community Policing Officer
Dearborn Police Department
(313) 943-2800

Hate Crimes Investigation Support
Office of the Maine Attorney General
Civil Rights Team Project
Attorney General Thomas Harnett
(207) 626-8800
website: www.maine.gov/ag/civilrights.html

ACKNOWLEDGMENTS

This report was written by Amardeep Singh, U.S. Program researcher at Human Rights Watch, based on research he undertook in Washington, D.C. and five other cities across the United States. It was edited by Jamie Fellner, director of the U.S. Program, and Joe Saunders, interim program director, with legal review provided by Dinah Pokempner, general counsel. Jonathan Horowitz, program coordinator, provided significant research and production assistance.

Human Rights Watch would like to thank the many public officials and community activists who provided us with information, documentation, and insights about backlash crimes and government responses to it following September 11.

Human Rights Watch is grateful to the William and Flora Hewlett Foundation and to Atlantic Philanthropies for providing the funding that made this report possible. Human Rights Watch is dedicated to protecting the human rights of people around the world.

We stand with victims and activists to prevent discrimination, to uphold political freedom, to protect people from inhumane conduct in wartime, and to bring offenders to justice. We investigate and expose human rights violations and hold abusers accountable. We challenge governments and those who hold power to end abusive practices and respect international human rights law. We enlist the public and the international community to support the cause of human rights for all.

Human Rights Watch
350 Fifth Avenue 34th Floor
New York, N.Y. 10118-3299
http://www.hrw.org

THE AUTHOR'S CONCLUSION:

Time to Heal: Time to Reconcile

By
Aladdin Elaasar

" Education is not the filling of a pail, but the lighting of a fire." W.B. Yeats, Irish Poet and dramatist (1865-1939).
From James Waller's *Prejudice Across America (1)*

" The purpose of education, finally, is to create in a person the ability to look at the world for himself, to make his own decisions, to say to himself this is black, or this is white, to decide for himself..."
James Baldwin, American novelist.

More than two years have passed after the 9/11 terrorist attacks on our nation, yet we are still recuperating from the shock that this sad and tragic event has caused us, as a society. The American people are still trying to make sense out of what happened.

Almost three years later, the terrorist attacks of September 11, 2001 are still at the forefront of the nation's mind as we continue to overcome grief, remember those who were lost, and fight to ensure the safety and well-being of the nation.

September 11, 2001 will forever be remembered as the day the American spirit was tested to a greater degree than at any time since World War II. For Arab Americans, the deep shock and anger over this national trauma and grief over lost relatives and friends were compounded by a rush by some to blame Arabs collectively for the attacks. Arabs and Muslims in this country were suddenly confronted with the double pain of mourning an attack on their country and simultaneously having to defend themselves, their families, and their stature as Americans.

The first anniversary of the attacks is an appropriate time to document the Arab American experience in the days, weeks, and months following the terrorist attacks and to tell some of the stories of the past year that have yet to be told: the Arab American firefighters and doctors who rushed to Ground Zero to help in the recovery efforts. The hundreds of thousands of dollars raised by Arab and Muslim groups to aid victims. The Americans across the nation who lent assistance and support when their Arab and Muslim neighbors were threatened. Blood drives, interfaith prayer vigils, and fundraisers that brought together Americans from all backgrounds and faiths.

From "Healing the Nation", a report compiled on the first annual anniversary of 9/11 by the Arab American Institute, AAI.

"After the attacks law enforcement and public officials were unified and clear in cautioning Americans to refrain from taking vengeance against their fellow citizens who may be Muslims or of Arabic Ancestry. President Bush cautioned Americans to refrain from reprisals against innocent Arab/Muslim-Americans. Indeed, all of our former Presidents, Ford, Carter, Bush, Sr., and Clinton, have urged restraint and promoted the rule of law. The Governor of New York and the Mayor of New York City have urged their citizens to refrain from using violence, and Chicago's Mayor Richard Daley very passionately appealed to Chicagoans to obey the law, stating that Arab-Americans are among Chicago's most prominent and loyal citizens. Members of Congress and religious leaders have also spoken out. Local law enforcement have publicly announced criminal complaints against individuals accused of hate crimes in an effort to deter more of these attacks", explained William Haddad, President of the Arab-American Bar Association, who had been instrumental in documenting the plight of Arab and Muslim Americans in the aftermath of 9/11.

"We are in the midst of a national nightmare of unimaginable proportions. Arab Americans, like all Americans, are transfixed by this tragedy. We have family and friends who worked in the World Trade Center. We mourn for those who lost their lives and those who were injured. We mourn, as well, for our country in this time of national trauma, *from an Arab American Institute press release, Sept. 11, 2001*

"Will hate bring it all back?

Fear of reprisals against Arab and Muslim Americans in the USA motivated the Brokaw Inc./Ad Council/Arab American Institute anti-hate poster "Twin Towers."

The ad read: "Will hate bring it all back? Will it bring back the innocence? The sense of security? Will it bring back the husbands and wives and sons and daughters? Will hate make us better than those who hate us? Or merely bring us closer to them? Will hate help us destroy our enemies? Or will it laugh as we destroy ourselves? There are those who say we don't know who our enemy is.

"But we do. Our enemy is a neighborhood mosque defaced by vandals. An Arab-American storekeeper in fear of reprisal. A scared Muslim child bullied because she is different. Hate is our enemy. And when we start to hate other Americans, we have lost everything. Hate has taken enough from us already. Don't let it take you."

"I am an American"

Some of the widest-reaching efforts to stem the tide of hate violence and intolerance after September 11 came from some dedicated media professionals. Taking a leading role, the New York-based Ad Council launched a powerful series of print, radio, and television public service announcements against hate, their largest single advertising campaign since World War II.

The campaign against hate began with a series of "I am an American" television spots that featured faces representing the diversity of America's racial and ethnic backgrounds, including Middle Eastern, South Asian and other groups most victimized by the backlash.

"I know that you are suffering with all America "

While 9/11 caused some reprisals and hate crimes against Arab and Muslim Americans, nevertheless, outpouring support came from many directions. It was best represented in an email to the Arab American Institute by an American citizen. "I know that you are suffering with all America because of the events of the past few days, and are being forced by some to endure even more sorrow because of your ethnicity. Please know that your pain is not going unnoticed and that the whole country is not against you."

- Joe Borghi

"My heart and thoughts are with you and all Arab and Muslim Americans. I am sickened at the misdirected anger of our fellow citizens."

- Alison Locke

Yet, in another touching letter, ordinary Americans expressed their support to fellow Arab and Muslim Americans. It is the best expression of the American spirit of kindness, generosity, and tolerance. This letter speaks volumes. "What is done to any American, regardless of their background, is done to all of us, and those who persist in expressing their ignorance and hatred only help those that mean to do us harm. We are deeply sorry that you have to have such burdens added to an already overwhelming sense of violation."

- Gregg Ferencz and Barbara Taylor

"Maybe we need to sing louder !"

Naomi Shihab Nye, the acclaimed Arab American author and poet, heard from a man who said that he was afraid for his daughter to admit that she is half-Arab. Her response was: "never deny it. Maybe Arab Americans are twice as sad as other people. But we are still proud of everything peaceful and beautiful that endures. Then speak beauty if we can - the beauty of culture, poetry, tradition, memory, family, daily life. "Because men with hard faces do violent things, because fanaticism seizes and shrinks minds, is no reason for the rest of us to abandon our songs. Maybe we need to sing louder."

Media interest in the Arab American viewpoint was obviously at its peak after 9/1. An editorial in *The Economist* remarked that "Rather than railing against the Islamic world, most Americans are desperate to understand it. The best-seller lists are full of books on Islam, the Taliban and the Middle East. University students are crowding into courses that touch on the current crisis. Washington's Middle East Institute reports that applications for Arabic courses have doubled." *"America the Sensible: The Country is More Rock-Ribbed than Outsiders Think," the Economist, October27, 2001.*

Arab and Muslim Americans rallied to reach out to aid and educate other fellow Americans on issues of their ethnic background that seemed misunderstood. New Yorker Debbie Almontaser, an American citizen who came to the US from Yemen at the age of three, was deeply struck by the Sept. 11 tragedy. A teacher with the NYC Board of Education, she was overwhelmed with requests by community groups to help foster interfaith dialogue after the attacks, and has discussed her faith and heritage in countless classrooms and panels. Debbie co-founded Brooklyn Bridges, a program in which volunteers escorted students of Arab and South Asian origin who feared for their safety. With the help of the Christian Children's Fund, she established the Sept. 11 Curriculum Project, a group of educators who developed materials and workshops to educate other teachers about Arab and Muslim culture. And in February, she put together a multicultural festival and fundraiser with Arab, Jewish, and South Asian performers

Still, to the average citizen, there is a great deal of ignorance and confusion about the Arab World, the Middle East, and the Islamic world. The general public does

not really know yet the difference between an Arab, a Moslem, a Persian, an Indian, where they came from? What do they worship? What are their issues and backgrounds?

Who's Next?

Historically, violence against minorities in a America is not a new trend. Arabs, Muslims or people of Mid Eastern ancestry were not the only ethnic groups that have received its share of bigotry, homegrown violence and urban terrorism. " We have been through all of this before. During the controversy of the Alien and Sedition Acts in 1798, the enemy took the form of the French ethnicity and ideology, and Americans associated with that ideology. The 1850s saw the vilification of the Irish "savages" whom, for the first time had migrated in substantial numbers to the USA. In the years during and after the World War I yielded intense hatred of the Germans and German Americans among us. During World War II, the hatred of the Japanese enemy and of loyal Americans of Japanese ancestry, who looked like the enemy, resulted in the forced incarceration of seventy thousand Japanese American citizens, and between thirty and forty thousand Japanese aliens in domestic internment camps. During the 1950s, fear of the communist enemy was played out in the frequent interrogations of immigrants from Southern eastern European Countries, in suspicions regarding their ethnicity, and in the blacklisting of the Jews."

In general, 9/11 has negatively impacted the lives of Arab and Muslim Americans, other minority groups perceived to be of Middle Eastern origins, like Assyrians, Persians, Indians, and even Hispanics. Fear is looming, as we get closer to the 9/11 anniversary. Fear, not as much of the potential terrorist attacks against us, but fear from the enemy within. Fear of xenophobes, bigots; hate crime perpetrators, traditional hate groups, and the zealot next door. Fear of government legislations that can limit, or hinder our civil rights, or even our basic human rights, that might not after all make us feel safer.

The National Asian Pacific American Legal Consortium (NAPALC) has pointed out that the "solidarity between communities identified as the enemy' has in some cases forged a new alliance between Japanese Americans and Arab Americans and Muslims." In the words of NAPALC President Karen Naranski, "Let us take to heart the lessons of WWII when … Japanese-American families were herded behind barbed wire simply because they looked like the enemy...No one should be presumed to be any less loyal to our country just because of the color of their skin, their national origin, their immigration status or the religion that they follow." repeat historical mistakes of the Japanese internment camps or of the McCarthy era. Wade Henderson, executive director of the Leadership Conference on Civil Rights, warned that "History has shown us that, in past times of national calamity, civil rights and civil liberties fall victim to the crisis just as surely as the human victims whose loss we all grieve. Working with the ACLU and other civil rights advocacy groups, Arab Americans are closely monitoring the activities of the federal government regarding the welfare of the several hundred individuals still being held.

Many actions taken since September 11 have far-reaching implications not just for those of Arab or Muslim descent, but also for all Americans.

Asian-American fears

In an article titled *"Next Time -- Patriot Act Threatens Asian Americans"*, attorneys Victor M. Hwang and Ivy Lee of the Pacific News Service interviewed Asian American Wen Ho Lee, marking the anniversary of 9/11. *September 12, 2001**

"Early last year in a meeting with civil rights leaders, Sen. Dianne Feinstein singled out the Asian American community as the one that would face the greatest threat to civil liberties in the foreseeable future. Because of the rise of China as a global threat, Feinstein explained, Chinese Americans and Asian Americans would be the target of increasing hate violence and government targeting similar to that experienced by Los Alamos scientist Dr. Wen Ho Lee. Charged with violating atomic energy and espionage acts and suspected of passing secrets to China, Lee spent nine months in solitary confinement. Charges were dismissed on Sept. 13, 2000. "

"Nine days after the terrible tragedy of Sept. 11, 2001, the Department of Justice was already circulating a proposal to drastically expand its ability to investigate and prosecute those suspected of "domestic terrorism." It was quickly passed by a panicked Congress with little scrutiny or debate, even though there was little evidence that any of the new provisions under the so-called Patriot Act would have prevented the 9-11 attacks. Few dared to question the wisdom of yielding civil rights in the aftermath of the terrorist attacks. Many thought this "Patriot Act" would apply only to others: foreign terrorists or Arab Americans."

"But in fact, many of the new federal powers had been on the Justice Dept. wish list before 9-11 and some of them likely were a response to the department's inability to fully effectuate their witch hunt of Lee. As a community that has been historically branded as perpetual and un-assimilable foreigners, we Asian

Americans need to critically question the motivation, necessity and reach of hastily passed legislation designed to target those suspected of "domestic terrorism."

"Among the host of new powers, the Patriot Act broadened the reach of the Foreign Intelligence Surveillance Act (FISA) to include the right to physically search and spy on U.S. citizens without first obtaining a warrant. By allowing law enforcement to search or wire-tap citizens whenever they claim that national security is "a significant purpose" of the surveillance, the act cuts against long-standing constitutional guarantees of personal privacy and freedom from arbitrary searches."

"In the case of Wen Ho Lee, the FBI had applied for and was denied a warrant under FISA because they had engaged in selective investigation and prosecution. If the Patriot Act had been in effect at the time, there would have been no independent review of the FBI's desire to tap Lee's phone or search his home. Without these procedural safeguards in effect, we can expect many more unwarranted invasions of our privacy and selective prosecutions."

"Provisions of the act allow the government to search our homes without prior notice, broaden the government's ability to monitor our Internet and telephone communications, and expand the right of the federal government to detain, deport and deny fundamental due process rights to lawful immigrants, including the right to legal counsel and public hearings. Under the Patriot Act, Lee would not have had the right to a trial or to a lawyer, or the ability to confront the evidence or accusers against him. As in many fascist police states, Lee and other Asian Americans suspected of aiding foreign nations might simply be "disappeared," at the discretion of Attorney General John Ashcroft, never to be heard of again".

"Are we Asian Americans next? According to one report, more than 30 percent of the Justice Department's pending espionage investigations are against individuals with Asian surnames. We need to speak up as patriots against the erosion of our civil rights."

*(PNS contributors Victor M. Hwang and Ivy Lee are attorneys for API Legal Outreach, a nonprofit that provides legal services for Asian and Pacific Islander people.) Published on Alternet.org

Hispanic Americans share a similar fear

A November 2001, a report by the North American Congress on Latin America (NACLA) expressed fear that in the wake of the 9-11 attacks progress on the status of undocumented workers would be reversed due to an increased association between immigration and security threats resulting from the attacks. The report points out that restrictive immigration provisions have been included in new anti-terrorism measures, leaving the immigrant rights community with new sets of civil liberties and civil rights concerns. On the other hand, the war on terrorism has forced the administration to adopt more of a global and regional perspective than it previously had, to secure future collaboration with its partners in other countries and to think about meeting future threats from a multinational position.

The specific impact on immigrant communities is summarized in the NACLA as follows:

> Many foreign nationals, immigrants, and first-generation U.S. citizens are included among the numerous victims and heroes of the attacks. Family members of some immigrant workers, however, have been hesitant to report missing loved ones out of fear of the INS; further, many of these immigrants and their family members, due to severe restrictions on eligibility for public services, have been unable to access certain public programs such as disaster relief programs and unemployment insurance. Many more immigrant workers found themselves among the unemployed as a result of cutbacks in travel and other affected industries. And despite strong statements from U.S. officials urging racial and ethnic tolerance, reports of violence, harassment, and hate crimes against Arab Americans, Muslim Americans, and others simply mistaken for "terrorists" have been distressingly common. In the wake of the attacks, some people immediately called for even more severe restrictions on immigrant admissions and a further curtailment of the rights of immigrants already in the country. Issues that previously had low priority such as national ID cards, increased border enforcement and INS restructuring have re-appeared in light of recent events.

Yet, immigrants from the Arab and Muslim worlds are *"the weakest link in the civil rights chain,"* and that places them squarely on the front line in the defense of civil liberties.

African-Americans share the common fear

The Congressional Black Associates organized a panel discussion on November 16, 2001, hosting representatives of the Hispanic, Sikh and African-American communities in challenging the effectiveness and legality of profiling as a law enforcement tool. Several of the panel participants noted that although profiling is now being directed primarily at Muslims and people who look "Middle Eastern," experience shows that it will also be used against other minorities. Many African Americans oppose profiling Arab and Muslim Americans since the practice has been deployed against blacks.

America has been known to be home of the brave, land of the free, and a nation of immigrants. Americans can always trace their ancestry to an immigrant or a refugee who came from one of the four corners of the earth. Sure 9/11 has negatively impacted the lives of immigrants in the USA and even the lives of tens of thousands of potential immigrants and refugees who have been on waiting lists to come to America. They have suffered due to the post 9/11 legislations and attitudes.

"If only we would learn to " *care*"

In the process of writing his book *Prejudice Across America*, James Waller, professor of psychology at Whiteworth College in Washington State, took twenty-one students on a journey across America.... "to study the corrosive legacy of racism in the United States, at the end of the second millennium. They saw that although the face of hatred might change from generation to generation, the inheritance remains the same- forbidden opportunities, unfilled dreams, inner guilt, tension, fear, societal strife, and diminished productivity." (2)

" Waller is a champion of diversity, an avatar of the " Salad Bowl" metaphor who truly believes that a better America is just around the bend if only we would learn to " *care*". (3)

" The truth is that until we can understand the pain we inflict on each other because of hatred and exclusion, we will never fully understand why racial reconciliation is so essential to the future of America. The pain is not meant to be a destination in and of itself. Recognizing that pain, however, is a crucial step in the healing of America."

" How do we become aware of our own prejudicial attitudes and discriminatory behavior? Unless we are brutally honest with ourselves, most of us protect our self-esteem by excluding our personal stereotypes, prejudices, and discriminatory behaviors from conscious self-awareness. It is only when we actually engage in contact with members of different groups that we become aware of our deepest biases. (5)

In her 1883 poem " The New Colossus' dedicated to the Statute of Liberty, the great American poet Emma Lazarus, wrote her eternal words, exemplifying the American spirit at its best, as a haven for the oppressed and a nation of immigrants:

A mighty woman with a torch, whose flame
Is the imprisoned lightning, and her name
Mother of Exiles. From the beacon-hand
Glows world-wide welcome; her mild eyes command
The air-bridged harbor that twin cities frame
" Keep ancient lands, your steroid pump!" cries she
With silent lips." Give me your tired, your poor,
Your huddled masses yearning to breathe free,
The wretched refuse of your teeming shore.
Send these, the homeless, tempest-tost to me,
I lift my lamp beside the golden door!" (6)

List of Abbreviations

AAAEA	Arab American Association of Engineers & Architects
AABA	Arab American Bar Association
ACLU	American Civil Liberties Union
ADC	American-Arab Anti-Discrimination Committee
AAI	Arab American Institute
CAAO	Congress of Arab American Organizations
CAIR	Council on American Islamic Relations
ISNA	Islamic Society of North America
MPAC	Muslim Public Affairs Council
NAAJA	National Arab American Journalists Association
SAAJ	Society of Arab American Journalists, SAAJ
UMAA	United Muslim Americans Association

List of Arab & Muslim American Media Sources

The Arab American View
Hajjar Mohammed-Herbert,
Managing Editor
PO Box 2127
Orland Park, IL 60462
708-403-3380 Voice & FAX
"mailto:rayhanania@aol.com"

The Jerusalem Times
Hanna Siniora,
Publisher
PO Box 20185,
19 Nablus Road,
East Jerusalem
Telephone: 972-2-6273293
"http://www.jerusalem.times.com/" "mailto:tjt@palnet.com"

The Palestine Times Newspaper
Editor-in-Chief,
Mahmoud al Khatib
PO Box 10355,
London NW2 3WH, UK
"mailto:paltimes@ptimes.com"
"http://www.ptimes.com/"

The Beirut Times Newspaper
Publisher: Michel Bou Abssi
PO Box 93475, Los Angeles,
CA., 90093-0475 USA
"mailto:info@beiruttimes.com"
"http://beiruttimes.com/"

The Arab World Newspaper
720 N. Valley St. #E
Anaheim, CA 92801
714-758-3507
FAX: 714-758-3605
"mailto:lanamanale@aol.com"

"http://www.thearabworld.net"

Al-Jadid Magazine
Arab Culture and the Arts
Editor, Elie Chalala
PO Box 24DD2,
Los Angeles, CA.,
90024-0208
818/782-8462,
FAX: 818/782-8535
"mailto:aljadid@jovanet.com"
The Middle East Research
& Information Project
"http://www.merip.org/"

Arab American Mirror
Electronic Newspaper
Adham Rashidi, Editor
"http://www.alif.com/mirror"
"mailto:mirror@alif.com"

Al-Nashra
Hikmat Beaini, Editor
1510 H. Street NW #975
Washington DC 20005
202/898-8053
FAX: 703/551-2086
"http://www.arabmedia.com/"
"mailto:info@arabmedia.com"

Middle East Times, Cairo
"http://www.metimes.com/"
"mailto:johnfalc@link.com.eg"

Al-Bayan Newspaper
"http://www.albayan.co.ae/"
Khaled Moh'd Ahmed,
General Manager
Dubai, Arab Emirates
"mailto:hani@albayan.co.ae"

The Minaret
America's Source on Islam
"http://islam.org/"
Dr. Aslam Abdullah,
Editor-in-Chief
434 S. Vermont Ave
Los Angeles CA., 90020
213/384-4570
FAX 213/383-9674

Washington Report on ME Affairs
Andrew Kilgore, Publisher
Richard H. Curtiss, Exec. Editor
Janet McMahon, Managing Editor
Shawn Twing, News Editor
Michael S. Lee, Book Club
"mailto:wrmea@aol.com"
"http://www.washington-report.org/"

Phoenicia Newspaper
PO Box 924717
Princeton, Florida 33033
Abed el Jalil Alwan, New York
718/937-1073 718/797-0780 Fax
Ali K. Ballout, Florida
305/247-8179 305/247-9861 FAX
"mailto:m3147@aol.com"

Islamic Horizons Magazine
Omer bin Abdullah, Editor
PO Box 38, Plainfield, IN 46168-0038
317/839-8157 317/839-1840 FAX
"mailto:isna@surf-ici.com"

Arab American Journal
Nouhad el-Hajj, Publisher
Mohamad Ozeir, Editor-in-Chief
663 S. Bernardo Ave, Suite 206
Sunnyvale, CA 94087
TEl 650/969-4333
FAX 415/681-9042 FAX

"mailto:alarabi97@aol.com"

Al-Offok Al Arabi
Kawathar Othman, Publisher
PO Box 1085, Bedford Park, IL 60499
708/544-5461 Voice/Fax

AL-MARAYA NEWSPAPER
P.O.BOX 720474
HOUSTON-TX 77272
713 266 5355
EDITOR-IN-CHIEF
NIDAL ZAYID
TEL: 832 309 9457
FAX: 713 572 4994
"mailto:Almarayanews@aol.com"

Al-Itidal
Samir Tahhan, Editor-in-Chief
PO Box 2186,
Clifton NJ 07015
973/472-3633
FAX: 973/472-5978
"mailto:Alitidal@aol.com
"http://www.al-Itidal.com/"

Al-Horeya
Nader Guirguis,
Editor-in-Chief
(Egyptian Coptic Newspaper)
Andrew Berneshawi,
Editor, English Section
PO Box 339 Middletown, NJ., 08850
973/728-7585
Fax: 973/728-3830
Email: "mailto:andy70367@aol.com"
"http://www.al-Itidal.com/"

The News Circle Publishing House
Joseph Haiek,
Publisher

THE NEWS CIRCLE
PUBLISHING HOUSE
PO Box 3684, Glendale,
CA 91221, USA
Phone: (818) 507-0333,
Fax: (818) 245-1936
"http://home.pacbell.net/newscirc"

Al Manassah
Dr. Mohrez El-Hussini
Publisher & Editor-in-Chief
10 King Street, Hillside,
NJ 07205
"mailto:almanassah@aol.com"
Tel: 908/352-4966
Fax: 908/352-3917

The Arab Voice Newspaper
Publisher: Walid Rabah
973-523-7815
"mailto:wrabah@arabvoice.com"
"http://www.arabvoice.com/"

MIZNA Journal
PO Box 14294
Minneapolis, MN., 55414
Editors: Saleh Abudayyeh
and Kathryn Haddad
612-377-5366
"mailto:miznainc@hotmail.com"

The Arab Star
Dallas, Texas
Editor, Aziz Shihab
Editor/journalist
Monthly, Circulation, 50,000
"mailto:staraziz@aol.com"
"http://www.arab-star.com/"
214-683-6462
Fax 214-348-1681

Via Dolorosa Newspaper
Eddy Calis, Editor
8039 Eastern Ave, Suite 102
Silver Spring, MD 20910
301-587-6037
FAX: 301-608-2167
"mailto:eddycalis@earthlink.net"

Palestine Chronicle
Ramzy Baroud, Editor
"mailto:ramzy5@worldnet.att.net" "mailto:palestinechronicle

Voice of Jordan Newspaper
Ihsan Sweis,
Co-Publisher
Ziad Zureikat,
Co-Publisher
PO Box 671,
Oak Lawn, IL 60453
708-599-1300
FAX: 708-599-2121
email: "mailto:vojnews@aol.com"
"http://www.voj.homepage.com/"

The Muslim Magazine
Published by
American Muslim Assistance
Dilshad Fakroddin,
Managing Editor
PO Box 1065, Fenton, MI 48430
810-714-2296
FAX: 810-222-2885
www.naqshbandi.org
"mailto:staffmuslimmag.net"

American Muslim Magazine
Dr. Souheil Ghannouchi,
Editor
PO Box 43841,
Brooklyn Park, MN 55443
612-250-0847

FAX: 612-549-2649
"mailto:editor@americanmuslim.org"

A1 Arab Newspaper
PO Box 720474, Houston, TX 77272
713 266 5355 FAX: 713-914-9946
"mailto:a1news@aol.com"

Zaitonah Newspaper
Publication of the Islamic Assn for Palestine
PO Box 743533
Dallas, Texas, 75374
"http://www.arabies.com/"
"mailto:pr@arabies.com"

Pharaohs Business Magazine
1825 Eye Street NW
Suite 400
Washington DC 20006
202-572-9974

Arab American Business Magazine
PO Box 753
Huntington Beach, CA 92648
714-893-0121
Fax :714-893-0073
Nidal Ibrahim, Publisher
www.arabamericanbusiness.com
"mailto:Ibrahim@ArabAmericanBusiness.com"

The Orient Newspaper
PO Box, 7560,
Ann Arbor, MI., 48107
734-481-1930
FAX: 734-481-1931
"mailto:editor@the-orient.net"
"http://www.the-orient.net"

Arab Community News newspaper
9973 Bustleton Ave
Philadelphia, PA 19115

215-715-1801 FAX: 215-464-9404
Editor/Publisher: Aziz Al Taee

Falesteen Newspaper, Chicago
708-237-1400
FAX: 708-237-1408
Publisher: Khawla Abdel Razeq

Arab Radio
AM700 Washington DC
Fadel Lamen, Host
"mailto:fadellamen@yahoo.com"
6166 Leesburg Pike, A 204
Falls Church, VA 22046

Arab American Journal
Dearborn Michigan
Last Updated: May 16, 2001
Nouhad El-Hajj,
Publisher
Mohamad Ozeir,
Editor-in-Chief
"mailto:maysoon13@aol.com",
Managing Editor
14628 W. Warren Ave
Dearborn MI 48126
313-846-0250
FAX: 312-846-0115
"mailto:aramjo@aol.com"

Arab American News
Dearborn Michigan
"mailto:osiblani@aol.com",
Publisher
5706 Chase Rd
Dearborn, Michigan 48126
(313) 582-4888
(313) 582-7870
"mailto:aramjo@aol.com"

Islamic Broadcasting

Network Radio
WWTL 700 AM Radio
Washington DC
Fadeel Al-Amin,
News Director
PO Box 4893
Falls Church, VA 22044
(703) 241-9659
(703) 241-9658
877-TALK IBN
The "Roundtable"
Friday's 4:30 Eastern

Azizah Magazine
WOW INC.
PO Box 43410
Atlanta, GA 30336
Tayyibah Taylor,
 Publisher, Editor-in-Chief
678-945-5800
FAX: 678-945-1986
"mailto:letters@azizahmagazine.com"
"http://www.azizahmagazine.com"

Houston Arab Radio Program
Host: Said Fattouh
KPFT Houston 90.1 FM
Wed. 10 PM - 11 PM
Live Cal-in: 713-526-5738
You can also listen live via the Internet http://www.PalestineAffairsCouncil.org"

Palestine Radio Program
Montreal, Canada
Last Updated: August 24, 2002
1280 AM Montreal
Monday's 11:30 AM
for info: Mohamed S. Kamel
"mailto:sherif@unforgettable.com"

The Bridge
PO Box 307112

Columbus, Ohio 43230-7112
614-470-2784
"mailto:aaco-subscribe@yahoogroups.com"

Muslim Advocate Newsletter
Muslim Americans for Civil
 Rights & Legal Defense
7667 W. 95th Street
Suite 2W
Hickory Hills, IL 60457
Tel/Fax: 708-598-6640
"mailto:info@muslimcivilrights.com"
"http://www.MuslimCivilRights.com"

ADC Times
American Arab Anti-Discrimination
 Committee
4201 Connecticut Ave NW,
Suite 300
Washington DC., 20008
202-244-2990
Fax: 202-244-3196
"http://www.adc.org"
"mailto:adc@adc.org"

Northwest Ethnic Voice
Bi-monthly review of ethnic and cultural trends
PO Box 2766
Salem, Oregon 97308
"mailto:mistep@teleport.com"
"mailto:rjrossi@navicom.com"
Includes information on all ethnic groups, including Arab Americans. Food, religion, traditions, music, literature and culture are discussed regularly. Welcomes submissions.

RAWI Newsletter
PO Box 220
Prince St. Station
New York, NY 10012
Newsletter of the Radius of Arab Writers Inc.,

based in New York , a cooperative of Arab American literary writers and authors from around the country

Profile News Newspaper
2041 Centre Street
West Roxbury, MA 02132
617-363-0503

Inta Fil Howwa
(You're On the Air) Radio Program
Yusef Shibley, on air Host
Live call in program
On Air Direct Line:
708-524-9762
FAX: 708-848-9220
708-749-0686
Studio Line: 708-524-9762
Broadcast on WPNA 1490 AM
Sat. 5-7 pm on Saturdays, live.

Voice of Jordan Newspaper
Ihsan Sweiss, co-Publisher
Ziad Zureikat, co-Publisher
PO Box 671
Oak Lawn, IL 60454
708-599-1300
FAX: 708-599-2121
email: "mailto:vojnews@aol.com";
"http://www.voj.homepage.com/"

Al Salbeel
The Universal School, Publisher
Khawla Rezaq, Editor
7350 W. 93rd Street
Bridgeview, IL 60455
708/599-4100

Arab Community Voice TV
Cable Channel 23 TV
Monday, Tuesday in Arabic 5 - 5:30
Wednesday in English

Osama Abu-Irshid, manager
Voice/FAX: 773-588-9821

Arab Voice of Chicago
Community Radio
WCEV 1450 Radio
Saturday 4 - 6 pm
Yousif Marei, Manager & Host
Ashraf Abu Khalf, Host
Ribhi Awad, Host
Tel: 773-202-0448
Studio Line: 773-777-1450
P. O. Box: 300544
Chicago, IL. 60630

Muslim Journal
PO Box 2164
Bridgeview IL 60455
708-974-1278
Leila Diab,
Correspondent/Photographer
email: "mailto:Ldiab@aol.com"
Ayesha Mohammad, Editor
Office: 929 W. 171st St
Hazel Crest, IL 60429-0754
708-647-9600
Fax: 708-647-0754
Email: "mailto:Muslimjrnl@aol.com"

Freelance Muslim Journalist
"mailto:dinarashed@home.com"

Al Shaab Newspaper
Hassan Dawed, Publisher
Souheri Al-Halaby, Editor
"http://www.slshaab.net"
PO Box 936
Postage Indiana 46368
219-752-1986
FAX: 810-277-0776

Chicago Muslim Newsletter
Council of Islamic Organizations
of Greater Chicago
PO Box 181
Orland Park, IL 60462
Last Updated: June 20, 2001
"mailto:arkpub@hotmail.com"

Arab American View Newspaper
Haj Mohammed Herbert,
Managing Editor
PO Box 2127
Orland Park, IL 60462
Last Updated: July 29, 2002
708-403-3380 Voice & FAX
"mailto:rayhanania@aol.com"

Arab Services Online
"http://www.Arabservices.com"
Yusef Riadi, Publisher
866-YES-Arab

**Media Monitors Network
(MMN)**
 P.O. Box 9785 Brea,
CA 92822
(1 866 633 42 63)
Fax Toll-free: 1 877 375 90 36
E-fax: (810) 454 04 84
 www.MediaMonitors.net"
www.MediaMonitors.org"
"http://216.71.207.129/mmn/"
 "http://www.MMN.inc"
"mailto:ContactUs@MediaMonitors.net"
 Editor: "mailto:Editor@MediaMonitors.net"

Middle East News OnLine
"http://www.Middleeastwire.com"
Editorial Board:
Fadi Chahine,
Executive Editor & Chief Executive FChahine@MiddleEastWire.com"

Max Mukelabai, Chief Financial Officer
":Max@MiddleEastWire.com"
Ramzy Baroud, Managing Editor
"NewsEditor@MiddleEastWire.com"
Amer Farid,
Director of Business Development
AFarid@MiddlEastWire.com"
Warren Herndon, Public Relations
WHerndon@MiddleEastWire.com"
Tanya Shaheene, News Content Specialist
Tanya@MiddleEastWire.com"
Patience Mucha, News Coordinator
Patience@MiddleEastWire.com"

Arab View Web Page
"http://www.Arabview.com"
"http://www.Arab.net"

Islam Online
"http://www.Islamonline.net"

Palestine Chronicle Online
"http://www.PalestineChronicle.com"
Ramzy Baroud,
Palestinian writer
"mailto:Ramzy5@aol.com"

List of Arab & Muslim American Organizations

Arab American Bar Association
PO Box 81325
Chicago IL 60681
312/946-0110
President: William Haddad

Arab American Institute
1600 K St., Suite 601
Washington, DC 20006
(202) 429-9210
(202) 429-9214 (fax)

Council on American-Islamic Relations, CAIR
Research Center
Dr. Mohamed Nimer,
Director of Research
453 New Jersey Ave., SE
Washington, D.C. 20003
Tel: 202-488-8787
Fax: 202-488-0833
E-mail: cair@cair-net.org
http://www.cair-net.org

Islamic Supreme Council of America
1400 Sixteenth Street NW, #B112
Washington, DC 20036
Phone: (202) 939-3400
Fax: (202) 939-3410
Web site: http://www.islamicsupremecouncil.org
E-mail: staff@islamicsupremecouncil.org

Council of Islamic Organizations of Greater Chicago
330 East Roosevelt Road, Suite G5
Lombard, Illinois 60148
Tel: (630) 629.7490
Fax: (630) 629.7492

Email: Council@ciogc.org

Islamic Society of North America, ISNA
P O Box 38
Plainfield, IN 46168,
(317) 839 - 8157 Fax:
(317) 839-1840
Ahmed ElHattab,
Director General,
aelhattab@isna.net
Mohamed Elsanousi
 International Relation &
Media Coordinator
 melsanousi@isna.net
(317) 839-1821
Mukhtar Ahmad ,
Community Development
& Training
 mahmad@isna.net 231
Omer Bin Abdullah Editor,
Islamic Horizon
horizons@isna.net
(703) 742-8108

Muslim Public Affairs Council
MPAC Los Angeles
Executive Director
Salam Al-Marayati
Mailing Address:
3010 Wilshire Boulevard, # 217
Los Angeles, California 90010
Phone (213) 383-3443
Fax (213) 383-9674
"mailto:salam@mpac.org"
Community Relations Director,
Kamal Abu-Shamsieh
Mailing Address:
3010 Wilshire Blvd, # 217
Los Angeles, California 90010
"mailto:kamal@mpac.org"

MPAC Washington D.C.
Communications Director:
Sarah Eltantawi
Mailing Address:
994 National Press Building
529 14th Sreet NW
Washington, D.C. 20045
Phone (202) 879-6726
Fax   (202) 879-6728
"mailto:sarah@mpac.org"
MPAC Los Angeles
MPAC Chapters Coordinator:
Nagwa Ibrahim
"mailto:nagwa@mpac.org"
MPAC Los Angeles
Hate Crimes Prevention Coordinator:
Susan Attar
Mailing Address:
3010 Wilshire Blvd, # 217
Los Angeles, California 90010
e-mail: "mailto:sattar@mpac.org"
MPAC Houston
Hannah Hawk, Coordinator
Mailing Address:
6601 Kirby Drive, # 660
Houston, Texas 77005
Phone: 713-797-MPAC (6722)
Fax: 713-799-9098
"mailto:hannah@mpac.org"

United Muslim Americans
Association (UMAA)
President: Dr. Sabri Samirah
Executive Director,
Ms. Manal El-Hrissie
10661 S. Roberts Rd. #202,
Palos Hills, IL. 60465
Tel. (708) 974-4472
Fax (708) 974-4479
"http://www.theumaa.org"

**Society of Arab American
Journalists, SAAJ**
Ali Alarabi, director
PO Box 1224
LaGrange Park, IL 60526
"http://www.saaj.org"

**Arab American Chicagoland
Census Organization**
7905 S. Cicero Ave
Suite 200
Chicago IL 60652
773-735-7755
Fax: 773-735-8466

United Holy Land Fund
6000 W. 79th Street
Lower Level
Burbank, IL 60543
708-430-9731

Lifta Association for Charity
P.O. Box 528247
Chicago, IL 60652
Mofeed Bages, President
773-418-1564
Club House Location:
6000 W. 79th Street
Burbank, IL
708-599-3300

**Palestine American
Community Center**
AbdelGhafer Al-Arouri,
President
708-233-6623
6000 W. 79th Street
Burbank, IL 60453

**Arab American Association
of Engineers & Architects, AAAEA**

P.O. Box 2160
Bridgeview, IL 60455
708-802-1148
Dr. Soliman Khudeira P.E., President
Dr. Ahmad Hammad P.E., Chairman
E-mail: "mailto:aaaea@aaaea.org"
"http://www.aaaea.org/"

**Jordanian Arab American
Business Association, JAABA**
Ihsan Sweiss
PO Box 671
Oak Lawn, IL 60453
708-599-1300
FAX: 708-599-2121
"mailto:vojnews@aol.com"

The Ramallah Club of Chicago
Sam Salamy, President
2700 N. Central Ave
Chicago IL 60639
FAX 773-237-0214

Turmusiya Palestine Club
1257 N. Milwaukee Ave, 3rd Floor
Chicago, IL 60613

Chicago Islamic Cultural Center
3357 W. 63rd Street
Chicago IL 60629
773-436-8083
773-436-8785 fax

**Fuheis American Association
of Chicago**
Samih Ayed Sweis, President
7905 S. Cicero Ave, Ste 206
Chicago, IL 60652
773-284-0201
fax:773-284-0210.
"http://fuheisclub.org/"

**Arab American
Educational Council**
Frank Bustany
708-243-7523

**Committee for a Democratic
 Palestine**
Younis Al-Jazaran
773-672-1290

Beitunia American Club
Kayyad Hassan, President
708-923-6312
708-923-7301 FAX

**Advisory Commission
on Arab Affairs
Chicago Commission
on Human Relations**
740 N. Sedgwick St, Suite 300
Chicago IL 60610
312-744-4115
312-744-1081

**Muslim Americans for Civil Rights
and Legal Defense**
7667 W. 95th St, Suite 2 W
Hickory Hills, IL 60457
708-598-6640

Aqsa School
7361 W. 92nd Place
Bridgeview, Illinois

**Midwest Federation of
Syrian & Lebanese Clubs**
PO Box 6835
Villa Park, IL 60181-6835
Emil Haddad, coordinator
Jackie Haddad, Chairman

"http://www.midwestfederation.org/"

**Arab American Republican
Federation**
12231 W. Lady Bar Lane
Orland Park, IL 60462-1085
708-301-4269
Shibli Sawalha, Ph.D.

**Islamic Community Center
of Illinois, MCC**
4003 W. Montrose Ave
Chicago IL 60641
773-725-5020
773-725-4103

**American Islamic
College of Chicago**
640 W. Irving Park Rd
Chicago IL 60613
773-281-4700
Dr. Assad Busool

**American Friends
Service Committee**
637 S. Dearborn, 3rd Floor,
Chicago, IL 60605.
Tele: 312-427-2533.
Jennifer Bing-Canar,
Middle East program Director

**Arab American Medical
Association**
Lilly Hussein, MD, President
11025 Terrace Lane
Hillside, IL 60102
312-633-7117

Arab American Family Services
Itedal Shalabi
Nareman Taha

6441 S. Pulaski Rd
Suite 214
Chicago, IL 60629
773-767-3025
773-767-3027 FAX

**Arab Business & Professional
Association, ABPA**
Talat Othman, President
3432 Monitor Lane
Long Grove, IL 60047

**Institute for International
& Cultural Studies
North Park University**
3225 W. Foster Ave
Chicago IL 60625
773-244-5592
FAX: 773-583-0858
Robert Hostetter
773-244-5666

Chicago Lebanese Club
P.O Box 235
Gurnee, Illinois 60031
President Mark Bendok
Vice-President Daisy Malek
847-549-9417
"http://www.leb.net/clc"

**Jordan Arab American
 Association**
3206 W. Lawrence Ave
Chicago IL 60625
773-588-1098
FAX: 773-267-6844

List of Arab, Muslim, and Christian Religious Institutions In the Greater Chicagoland Area

St. George Antiochian Orthodox Church
"The Miraculous Lady of Cicero, Illinois"
1220 S. 60th Court
Cicero, IL 60804
708-656-2927
FAX: 708-656-1166
Archpriest Nicholas Dahdal
"http://www.stgeorgecicero.org"

ALAMEH
Association of Lutherans of Arab
and Middle East Heritage of the
Evangelical Lutheran Church
in America
6705 Hohman Ave.
Hammond, Indiana 46324
312-380-2840
219-932-9070
Yusuf Husary, Treasurer
396 Haas Avenue
San Leandro, CA 94577
Grace el Yateem, President

St. John the Baptist Church
200 E. North Avenue
Northlake, IL 60164
847-279-1407
FAX: 847-437-3162

Al Salam Mosque Foundation
3247 W. 63rd Street
Chicago, IL 60629
Imam Abdelrahman Manasra
773-925-0677

The Mosque Foundation
7360 W. 93rd Street

Bridgeview, Illinois
708-430-5666
Fax: 708-430-5235
Sheikh Jamal Said, Imam
"mailto:themosque@aol.com"

The Islamic Cultural Center, ICC
& Northbrook Mosque
1810 Pfingsten Rd
Northbrook, IL 60062
Imam Senad Agic
847-272-0319

Our Lady of Lebanon
Phoenician Club
Father Victor Kayrouz
425 N. Hillside
Hillside, Illinois, 60162

The Universal School
Bridgeview, Illinois
708-599-4100
773-925-0677

Chicago Islamic Cultural Center
3357 W. 63rd Street
Chicago IL 60629
773-436-8083
773-436-8785 fax

St. Elias Arabic Lutheran Church
1500 West Elmdale Ave
Chicago IL 60660
773-274-8828

Arabic Baptist Church of Chicago
7654 W. Berwyn Ave.
Chicago, IL. 60656
Phone: (773) 594-9130
Pastor Winston Mazakis
"mailto:cabc7@yahoo.com"

St. Mark Coptic Orthodox Church
15 West 455 79th Street
Burr Ridge, IL 60521
630-655-3468
FAX: 630-323-5986
Rev. Samuel

St. Mary's Coptic Orthodox Church
2100 NW Frontage Road
Palatine, IL 60078
847-776-9698
Rev. Ishaq Tanious

Orthodox Christian SYNERGY
7313 Waukegan Rd
Niles, IL 60714-4321
847-647-8398
Rev. Samuel Sherry, President

Islamic Community Center
of Illinois, MCC
4003 W. Montrose Ave
Chicago IL 60641
773-725-5020
773-725-4103

American Islamic College
of Chicago
640 W. Irving Park Rd
Chicago IL 60613
773-281-4700
Dr. Assad Busool

Islamic Foundation
of Villa Park
300 W. Highridge Road
Villa Park IL

St. John's Assyrian Church
1421 W. Lawrence

Chicago IL 60640
Rev. Charles H. Klutz
312-271-1116
312-465-4777
FAX: 312-465-0076

List of Arab, Muslim, and Christian Community Organizers, Activists, and Speakers in the Greater Chicagoland Area

Aladdin Elaasar,
773-279-8525
773- 350-8 604
omaraladin@aol.com
Journalist, translator,
bilingual teacher, public speaker,
Cross-cultural & media consultant
Arab & Muslim Americans Issues
/Middle East/Current events

Father Nicholas Dahdal, Pastor,
708-656-2927
St. George Antiochian Orthodox
Church in Cicero, Illinois
Chicago's Christian Arab community

Father Victor Kairooz, Pastor,
708-449-5558
Our Lady of Lebanon Catholic Maronite
Church, Hillside, Illinois
Chicago's Christian Arab community

Kareem Irfan, President,
847-925-3455
Council of Islamic Organizations
of Greater Chicago
Chicagoland's Muslim Arab community

Assad Busool, Professor,
847-675-1204
American Islamic College, Chicago
A Muslim and religious scholar

Arab Firefighters
Frank Isa, 708-460-0100 or
UHLF Ofc. 708-430-9731

POLITICS/MEDIA/
CHRISTIAN ARABS
Ray Hanania,
708-403-1203,
or 312-755-3568
Columnist,

PALESTINIAN ARAB COMMUNITY
Abdel Ghafar Al-Arouri, President,
708-233-6623
Palestinian American Community Center

SOCIAL SERVICES
Nareman Taha, Itedal Shalabi,
 Co-Owners,
773-767-3025
Arab American Family Services

BIGOTRY & DISCRIMINATION,
IMMIGRATION
Rouhy Shalabi, attorney,
708-636-1015
Board member, Chicago Commission
on Human Relations, Arab American
Bar Association President: Issues of bigotry
and discrimination, local community.

BIGOTRY & DISCRIMINATION,
IMMIGRATION
William Haddad, Executive Director,
312-856-1114
Arab American Bar Association

ISLAMIC COMMUNITY/
CIVIL RIGHTS
708-598-6640
Muslim Americans for Civil Rights
and Legal Defense,
Chicagoland's Muslim American
community, Islamic issues, discrimination

and current status of INS and
Justice Department prosecutions.

ARAB JOURNALISM/
GENERAL CONTACTS
Aladdin Elaasar,
773-8661358
773-583-9191x256
aelaasar@wr.org
omaraladin@aol.com
Journalist, translator,
bilingual teacher, public speaker,
Cross-cultural & media consultant,
and NAAJA spokesman

Ali Alarabi, journalist,
708-442-8622,

Omar Karmi, journalist,
773-755-4156

JORDANIAN ARABS
Samih Sweis, President,
773-284-0201
Fuheis American Association
Jordanian American community
Ihsan Sweis, Consul General of Jordan,
708-599-1300
Bridegview, Illinois

PALESTINIAN AMERICAN
VETERANS
Kayyad Hassan, President,
708-923-6312
Palestinian American Veterans Assn
Zyad Hasan, Chicago Director
Association of Patriotic
Arab Americans in Military
213-204-2830

EDUCATION & SCHOOLS

Miriam Zayed, teacher,
708-349-4828
Chicago elementary school
teacher, former candidate
for Suburban High school board.

ISLAMIC STUDIES
Assad Busool, Professor, 773-281-4700
American Islamic College, Chicago
Academic understanding of Islam
and its impact on society.

LEBANESE AMERICANS
Maha Noujeme, President,
847-549-9417
American Lebanese Clubs of Chicago
Mark Bendok, Chicago Lebanese Clubs,
312-969-0369

POLITICS/REPUBLICAN ARABS
Shibli Sawalha, coordinator, 708-301-4269
Arab American Republican Federation
Samir Khalil, coordinator 773-767-3333
Chicago Democratic Club

CHICAGO'S ARAB COMMUNITY
DR. Marwan Amarin, Chairman, 773-316-4466
Arab Advisory Commission,
Chicago Commission on Human Relations

INTERNATIONAL LAW
DR. Cherif Bassiouni,
DePaul University,
312-362-8332
Professor of Law, President,
International
Human Rights Law Institute

ARAB AMERICAN DEMOGRAPHICS
Jack Mansour,
708-857-1500

Realtor and businessman
Ned Malley,
708-857-1510
Realtor and businessman

Glossary

Ablution (Wudu)

The ritual of washing one's body in preparation for prayer.

Adhan,

The call to prayer by muezzin.

Allah

The Arabic word for God is Allah, whether the Arabic speaker is referring to the Christian or the Muslim God. Some Muslims believe that the word Allah cannot be translated into other languages and maintain its identification with the one true God. Allah has ninety-nine other sacred names. Allah is simply the Arabic world for God, related to the Hebrew Elohim; it can be seen as analogous to the German word Gott, the French Dieu, or the Spanish Dios. It's not the personal name of a deity within a pantheon, like Thor, Aphrodite or Siva.

Arab

One who speaks Arabic and shares the heritage of Arabic culture is an Arab. An estimated 95% of Arabs are Muslim; the remainder is primarily Christian. However only 20% of Muslims worldwide are Arabs (the largest Muslim country is Indonesia).

As-salaam alaikum

This is the usual English transliteration of the traditional Arabic greeting, which is translated "peace be upon you." The one being greeted reverses the blessing in response with "and upon you, peace," or wah alaikum as-salaam.

'Asr

In Arabic, this word meaning "afternoon" is also the name of the afternoon prayer that is among the five obligatory daily prayers for Muslims.

Barakat

Blessings

Bismillah

This is the usual English transliteration of the first word of the first line of the Koran. Translated as "in the name of God," it is used frequently as an invocation at the start of an action no matter how trivial.

Fajr

The Arabic word for dawn, fajr is the first of the five obligatory daily prayers for Muslims; it is performed before the rising of the sun. The others are dhuhr, asr, maghreb, and 'isha.

Fardh

Obligatory deeds to be observed by a Muslim, like Salat, Fasting, and other duties

Fasting, siyam

Abstaining from eating, drinking, smoking, sexual encounters from sunrise to sunset during the holy month of Ramadan

Hafez

The person capable of memorizing the whole Quran

Hajj

Hajj is performing the pilgrimage to Makkah and Medinah by those who are capable of doing it physically and financially once in a lifetime. It is the fifth pillar of Islam.

Halal

The English transliteration of the Arabic term referring to something that is permitted. For example, halal meat has been slaughtered and prepared according to Muslim standards.

Haram

The English transliteration of the Arabic term with two core meanings. One means a sacred precinct or area set aside from the world (for example, Mecca). In English, it became harem and referred only to the Ottoman custom of sequestering women of nobility in separate living quarters. The second refers to that which is proscribed by Muslim law and tradition and forbidden to the faithful, such as the eating of pork.

Hijra

The Arabic word for the migration of Muhammad from Mecca to Medina in 622 A.D. The Muslim calendar dates from this year.

'Id al-Fitr

One English transliteration of the Arabic name for the feast that celebrates the end of the month-long Ramadan daylight fast (also called Eid al-Fitr).

Imam

This term has different meanings for the Sunni and Shi'a branches of Islam. For the Sunni, the term refers to the prayer leader at a mosque. As there is no priesthood in Islam, this person is not equivalent to priest or pastor. He is merely conversant in the Koran and chosen by consensus. For the Shi'a, the term is reserved for the successors to the sons of 'Ali (Muhammad's son-in-law) and their spiritual and political leaders.

'Isha

The Arabic word for evening, this is the closing prayer of the day (about 1-1/2 hours after sunset), one of five obligatory prayers for Muslims.

Islam

Literally, the Arabic word Islam means submission. For a Muslim (one who submits), Islam is peace through submission to the will of Allah

Masjid

Mosque, the place for prayer.

Isma'ilis

A sectarian offshoot of Shi'a Islam. The leader of the Nizari branch holds the title Aga Khan. The current one is 49th in an unbroken line of descent. There are perhaps 2 million Isma'ilis worldwide.

Jihad

The English transliteration of the Arabic word for "struggle." When used to mean a fight in defense of Islam, it has taken the connotation of "Holy War."

Jum'ah

One English transliteration of the Arabic term for the mid-day Friday congregational prayer service, usually in a mosque (others are juma and jumu'a).

Koran

The traditional English spelling for the book containing Allah's revelations in Arabic to Muhammad through the angel Gabriel is Koran. It also is transliterated from the Arabic as Qur'an, or Quran. The language of the Koran, as the spoken world of God, became the basis of formal or classical Arabic.

Maghrib, or maghreb

The Arabic word for sunset, maghrib is one of five obligatory daily prayers for Muslims. The term also denotes, collectively, the Muslim countries of North Africa, the "land of the setting sun" west of Arabia.

Mahdi

Part of a collection of words meaning variously messiah, prophet, anointed one. Mahdism is the belief that a divinely guided restorer of Islam will establish a prophetic kingdom at the end of history. The best-known person claiming the title of Mahdi was the Muslim warrior who fought the British in the Sudan in the 1880s, defeating Gen. Gordon at Khartoum.

Medinah

The second holy city in Islam, where prophet Muhammad and his successors were buried, and were he migrated to and lived in till the end of his life.

Mihrab

The niche in the center of the front wall inside a mosque noting the direction of the Ka'aba in Mecca, the direction Muslims face for prayer.

Muslim

One who practices Islam is Muslim (the now out-of-favor English transliteration is Moslem).

Omrah

The journey to Mekkah at any time of year to perform a ritual similar to Hajj. Some people prefer to it as " smaller Hajj".

Peace Be Upon Him

Sometimes abbreviated in print as PBUH, this exclamation often is used by Muslims after mentioning the name of one of the prophets, especially Muhammad. Native speakers of Arabic sometimes use the English transliteration of the Arabic text, "sala Allah alayhi wa salaam", (which also can be translated "God's blessings and peace be upon him"). Some Muslims also add "subanna watallah" (or "Glory be upon him") following mention of the name Allah.

Pillars of Islam

The five essentials of Islam are the profession of faith (shahadah), performing the prayers (salat), the giving of 2.5% of one's net income to charity (zakat), pilgrimage to Mecca (hajj) and fasting during Ramadan (saum).

Ramadan

The ninth month of the Islamic year is spent fasting from sunrise to sunset.

Shahadah (or shahada)

The public confession whereby one becomes a Muslim, hence one of the pillars of Islam. One English translation is, "There is no God but Allah and Muhammad is the Prophet of Allah."

Shari'ah, or shari'a

The English transliteration of the Arabic term referring to Islamic law, which is based on the Koran and the hadith. There are four main schools of shari'a which disagree with each other on a variety of interpretations (named for their founders, they are Hanafi, Hanbali, Maliki and Shafi'i).

Shi'ia Islam

About 10% of practicing Muslims are Shi'ite. The name derives from Shi'a, meaning partisans or followers, and refers to those who believe that the successors to Muhammad should come only from descendants of his family. The first Shi'ites were partisans of Ali ibn Abi Talib, Muhammad's son-in-law and husband of his favorite daughter, Fatima.

Sunnah, or sunna

The English transliteration of the Arabic term for the "true path" or example set by Muhammad, the way he behaved and acted during his life. Sunnah Acts and deeds observed by the prophet Muhammad, pbuh, but not considered Fardh (obligatory), more of a volunteer nature.

Sunni Islam

About 90% of practicing Muslims are Sunni, a term derived from sunna and meaning people who follow the "true path".

Ulema

The English transliteration of the plural for the Arabic 'alim, which means a learned person. Ulema usually refers to "orthodox" Islamic theologians, scholars and teachers.

Ummah, or umma

The English transliteration of the Arabic word denoting at one level the religious community in which a Muslim participates and at another, the entire community of believers in Islam.

Qazi, kazi

Judge

Umrah

Paying a visit to Ka'bah, performing Tawaf around it, and walking between the mounts of Safa and Marwah seven times in the prescribed rituals.

Zakat ul-Fitr

Zakat ul-fitr is the charity or almsgiving, which must be paid by every Muslim, young and old, male and female, at the end of the month of fasting (Ramadan).

Bibliography

- Eli Kedourie, *Nationalism*, New York: Prager, 1960.

- Juan Perea, *Immigrants. Out!, The New Nativism and the Anti-Immigrant Impulses in the United States*, New York University Press, 1997.

- Gary Leupp, *Challenging Ignorance on Islam: a Ten-Point Primer for Americans*

- Ernest McCarus, *The Development of Arab American Identity,* The University of Michigan Press, 1997.

- Nabeel Ibrahim, *Anti-Arab Racism and Violence in the United States*, included in *The Development of Arab American Identity*, The University of Michigan Press, 1997, p 161.

- *Washington Times*, interview of FBI Assistant director, Oliver B. Revel in January 1986 in which he dismissed the allegations that Gaddafi sent suicide terrorists as " a complete fabrication.

- Nabeel Ibrahim, *Anti-Arab Racism and Violence in the United States*, included in *The Development of Arab American Identity*, The University of Michigan Press, 1997.

- *Harassment and violent Log Sheet*, US Congress, 1988, 67-69.

- John Higham, Strangers in the Land, (2nd ed.; New Brunswick, N. J.: Rutgers University Press, 1988).

- James Aho, *This Thing of Darkness: A Sociology of the Enemy* (Seattle: University of Washington Press, 1994).

- James Morton Smith, Freedom's Fetters12, 20-21 (Ithaca, N.Y.: Cornell University Press, 1956)

- Joe R. Feagin, " Old Poison in New Bottles: The Deep Roots of Modern Nativism, chapter two.

- Ronald Takaki, A different Mirror 378-85(Boston: Little Brown, 1993); Allan R. Bosworth, America's Concentration Camps 18 (New York: W. N. Norton, 1967).

- Juan F. Perea, " Demography and Distrust: An Essay on American Languages, Cultural Pluralism, and Official English," 77 Minnesota Law Review 269, 337-40(1992).

- Wayne Cornelius, "Perspective on Immigration; Neo-Nativism Feed on Myopic Fears; No Industerial Country Is Able to Keep Foreign Workers From Settling In, They become "Our Own", Los Angeles Times, July 12, 1993, Metro.

- Abraham, Nabeel and Andrew Shryock (eds.). *Arab Detroit: From Margin to Mainstream.* Detroit: Wayne State University Press, 2000.

- Abraham, Sameer and Nabeel Abraham (eds.). *Arabs in the New World: Studies on Arab-American Communities.* Detroit: Wayne State University Press, 1983.

- Abu-Laban, Baha and Faith T. Zeady (eds.). *Arabs in America: Myths and Realities.* Wilmette, Illinois: Medina University Press International, 1975.

- Abu-Laban, Baha and Michael W. Suleiman (eds.). *Arab-Americans: Continuity and Change.* Belmont: Association of Arab-American University Graduates, 1989.

- Ameri, Anan and Dawn Ramey (eds.). *Arab American Encyclopedia.* Detroit: Arab Community Center for Economic and Social Service (ACCESS), 2000.

- Ashabranner, Brent. *An Ancient Heritage: The Arab-American Minority.* New York: Harper Collins, 1991.

- Aswad, Barbara C. (ed.). *Arabic Speaking Communities in American Cities.* New York: Center for Migration Studies, 1974.

- Aswad, Barbara, and Barbara Bilgé. *Family and Gender Among American Muslims: Issues Facing Middle Eastern Immigrants and Their Descendants.* Philadelphia: Temple University Press, 1996.

- Castronova, Frank V. *Reference Library of Arab America.* Four volumes. Farmington Hills, MI: Gale Group, Inc., 1999.

- El Guindi, Fadwa. *Veil: Modesty, Privacy and Resistance*. Oxford: Berg Publications, 1999.

Hagopian, Elaine C. and Ann Paden. *The Arab Americans: Studies in Assimilation*. Wilmette, IL: Medina University Press International, 1969.

- Hooglund, Eric. J. (ed.). *Crossing the Waters, Arabic-Speaking Immigrants to the United States before 1940*. Washington: Smithsonian Institution Press, 1987.

- Kadi, Joanna (ed.). *Food for our grandmothers. Writings by Arab-Americans & Arab-Canadian Feminists*. Boston: South End Press, 1994

- Kayal, Philip M. and Joseph M. Kayal. *The Syrian-Lebanese in America: A Study in Religion and Assimilation*. Boston: Twayne, 1975.

- McCarus, Ernest. *The Development of Arab-American Identity*. Ann Arbor: University of Michigan Press, 1994.

- Naff, Alixa, *The Arab Americans*. New York: Chelsea House Publishers, 1988.

- Naff, Alixa, *Becoming American: The Early Arab Immigrant Experience*. Carbondale: Southern Illinois University Press, 1985.

- Orfalea, Gregory, *Before the Flames: A Quest for the History of Arab Americans*. Austin: University of Texas Press, 1988.

- Samhan, Helen. *Arab Americans*. Article in *Grolier's Multimedia Encyclopedia*. www.grolier.com.

- Samhan, Helen. *Arab American Organizations and Political Activism*. In *Arab American Encyclopedia*. Detroit: Arab Community Center for Economic and Social Service (ACCESS), 2000.

- Samhan, Helen. *Not Quite White: Race Classification and the Arab American Experience*. In *Arabs in America: Building a New Future*, Michael Suleiman, ed. Philadelphia: Temple University Press, 1999.

- Samhan, Helen. *Notes on Anti-Arab Racism*. President's Initiative on Race, February 1998.

Sawaie, Mohammed (ed.). *Arabic-Speaking Immigrants in the United States and Canada: A Bibliographical Guide with Annotation*. Lexington, KY: Mazda, 1985.

- Shakir, Evelyn. *Bint Arab: Arab and Arab American women in the United States.* Westport, CT: Praeger, 1997.

- Suleiman, Michael W. editor. *Arabs in America: Building a New Future.* Philadelphia: Temple University Press, 1999.

- Waugh, Earle H., Baha Abu-Laban, and Regula B. Qureshi (eds.). *The Muslim Community in North America.* Edmonton: University of Alberta Press, 1983. Wormser, Richard. *American Islam; Growing up Muslim in America.* New York: Walker and Comapny, 1994

- Younis, Adele L., *The Coming of Arabic-Speaking People to the U.S.* New York: Center For Migration Studies, 1995

- Zoghby, James (ed.). *Taking Root, Bearing Fruit: The Arab-American Experience.* Washington, DC: American-Arab Anti-Discrimination Committee, 1984.

- Zoghby, John. *Arab America Today: A Demographic Profile of Arab Americans.* Washington: Arab American Institute, 1990.

- Inea Bushnaq, Arab Folktales (New York: Pantheon, 1986). John Esposito, Islam: the Straight Path (New York: Oxford University Press, 1988). A concise and clear presentation of the main features of Islam historically and in contemporary contexts. Fernea, Elizabth Warnock and Robert A. Fernea, The Arab World: Forty years of Change (New York: Doubleday, 1997).

- John Hayes, ed., The Genius of Arab Civilization: Source of Renaissance (Cambridge, MA: MIT Press, 1983). Chapters on historic Arab contributions to the arts and sciences.

- Albert Hourani, A History of the Arab Peoples (Cambridge, MA: Harvard University Press, 1991). Thorough discussion of Arab history from pre-Islamic times to the mid-1980s. Includes detailed bibliography.

- Bernard Lewis, The Arabs in History (Oxford: Oxford University Press, 1993). Concise treatment of Arab history with emphasis on Arabs and Islam.

- Shaheen, Jack, *The TV Arab*, Bowling Green State university Popular Press, Ohio, 1984.

- Shaheen, Jack, *Reel Bad Arabs*, How Hollywood Vilifies a People, Olive Branch Press, 2001.

- Naff, Alixa, The Arab Americans (New York: Chelsea House Publishers, 1998). Lars Rodseth et al., Arab World Mosaic: A Curriculum Supplement for Elementary Teachers (Detroit, 1994).

- Audrey Shabbas, ed., Arab World Studies Notebook (Berkeley, CA: Arab World and Islamic Resources, and Washington, DC: Middle East Policy Council, 1998). Irfan Shahid, "Pre-Islamic Arabia," The Cambridge History of Islam, P.M. Holt et. al., eds., (Cambridge: Cambridge University Press, 1970), I: 3-29.

About the Author

Aladdin Elaasar is a journalist, educator, poet, short-story writer, public speaker, cross-cultural and media consultant whose writings have been published in several newspapers in the USA and overseas, in both English and Arabic. He has contributed articles for on-line portals on the Middle East like; Estart.com,Plane tarabia.com (CA, USA). He had produced several programs and documentaries and taught media studies, translation and creative writing.He has also been a frequent guest as a commentator on Middle Eastern affairs on several local American TV and Radio networks.

Printed in the United States
29663LVS00003B/49-84